Parables of Coercion

Parables of Coercion

Conversion and Knowledge at the End of Islamic Spain

SETH KIMMEL

The University of Chicago Press

CHICAGO AND LONDON

SETH KIMMEL is assistant professor of Latin American and Iberian cultures at Columbia University. He lives in New York.

The University of Chicago Press, Chicago 60637
The University of Chicago Press, Ltd., London

Printed in the United States of America

24 23 22 21 20 19 18 17 16 15   1 2 3 4 5

ISBN-13: 978-0-226-27828-5 (cloth)
ISBN-13: 978-0-226-27831-5 (e-book)
DOI: 10.7208/chicago/9780226278315.001.0001

The University of Chicago Press expresses appreciation to the Schoff Fund at the University Seminars at Columbia University for their help in publication. Material in this work was presented to the University Seminars: The Renaissance.

Library of Congress Cataloging-in-Publication Data

Kimmel, Seth, author.
Parables of coercion : conversion and knowledge at the end of Islamic Spain / Seth Kimmel
pages cm
Includes bibliographical references and index.
ISBN 978-0-226-27828-5 (cloth : alk. paper)—ISBN 978-0-226-27831-5 (e-book)
1. Moriscos. 2. Muslims—Spain. 3. Jews—Conversion to Christianity—Spain. 4. Catholic Church—Spain—History. 5. Spain—Intellectual life—1516–1700. 6. Spanish literature—Classical period, 1500–1700. I. Title.
DP104.K56 2015
282'.4609031—dc23
2014050177

♾ This paper meets the requirements of ANSI/NISO Z39.48-1992 (Permanence of Paper).

Contents

INTRODUCTION

To Join the Banquet

"Whatever they may declare and deny, we shall never be able to verify their faith."[1] This was how the Spanish historian Pedro de Valencia described the pastoral conundrum posed by sixteenth-century converts from Islam to Christianity, known along with their descendants as Moriscos. Valencia's distrust may sound like a concession to his adversaries, who at this moment in the early seventeenth century were championing the Moriscos' expulsion from the Crowns of Castile and Aragon. But embedded in his claim was the polemical suggestion that the Moriscos' faith was as difficult to discredit as it was to confirm. Without proof of willful heresy, Valencia insisted, plans for expulsion should be deferred if not abandoned. Instead of punishing the Moriscos as heretics, he recommended embracing them as devoted but imperfect Christians. In his view, only Old Christian charity and civic inclusiveness could successfully integrate this minority population. It was necessary to transform the social conditions of faith rather than directly to police it. Heresy inquisitors should cede some of their authority to royal advisors and civil judges, who, Valencia argued, possessed the necessary discretion to be more lenient than their inquisitorial counterparts. By participating in this debate about the Moriscos, in other words, Valencia did not only reimagine the relationship between Church and Crown. He also defended his own intellectual community's shared humanistic training and interpretive methods.

From the perspective of expulsion advocates like Archbishop of Valencia Juan de Ribera, Valencia's coupling of Morisco assimilation with social reform was misguided. By the end of the sixteenth century, more than seventy-five years after the forced conversion of Spain's last remaining Muslims, Ribera had come to see the Moriscos as stubborn apostates. Previous dispensations negotiated between the converts and the Crown had obstructed rather than facilitated integration. For Ribera and his allies, the time for discussion about strategies of conversion and catechism was over. The spiritual health of the empire and the legitimacy of its inquisitors and evangelizers now hinged upon exclusion rather than assimilation. Analogous to Valencia's opposition, Ribera's advocacy for expulsion was a defense both of the Church's authority to promote orthodoxy and of the scholastic training of canon lawyers.

Disagreement about Morisco expulsion was the newest iteration of a century-long struggle over how to eliminate Islam and its traces from a Christian-ruled Iberian Peninsula. The central claim of this book is that through this struggle, peninsular intellectuals revolutionized canon law, philology, and history writing. In the sixteenth and early seventeenth centuries, the overlapping groups of university theologians, preachers and inquisitors, classicists and Hebraists, and court advisors and recent converts who participated in debate about the Moriscos defended their political relevance and interpretive methods to audiences beyond the confines of their particular communities. Each presented his expertise as uniquely suited to determining the legitimacy and limits of religious coercion, which emerged as one of the fundamental dilemmas raised by Christian conquest and evangelization. To trace the history of these disputes is to study how the figure of the Morisco became a tool of disciplinary change. As the interrelatedness of the Morisco question with anxiety about Jewish apostasy and New World conversion suggests, however, there was more at stake in debates about the Moriscos than the legality of local baptisms or the academic bragging rights of the moment. For Valencia, Ribera, and their interlocutors, the pressing but often implicit questions running through these debates concerned the very definition of religion: Is religion a law or collection of doctrines? Or is it a set of practices and beliefs? Where are the boundaries between the religious and the civic spheres? What, if anything, do all religions share? And, finally, how and by whom should such questions be answered?

In response to these questions about the nature of religious experience and the uses of coercion, some early modern scholars dismissed the Moriscos and their texts as heretical. Others enlisted them as pedagogical or political weapons. Both camps sought to expand the scope of their scholarly authority by participating in this conversation, which toggled between major theological issues and the regional details of Morisco policy. In an array of treatises and personal correspondence, they considered demographic and economic matters related to imperial management; they composed chronicles, historical fiction, and epic poetry recounting pastoral successes and minority uprisings; and they penned Bible commentaries and legal opinions in efforts to render exemplary episodes from the early history of Christianity, such as Jesus's parables in Luke and Matthew and Paul's anecdotes in Corinthians and Galatians, newly relevant to contemporary affairs. I read this corpus of manuscripts and early printed books alongside archival evidence that specialists in Spanish history and culture will find familiar, but I pay particular attention to my sources' narrative conventions and conditions of production and reception. By studying how early modern scholars selected, interpreted, and circulated these varied texts on coercion and conversion, I explore the relationship between debates about religion, on the one hand, and the shifting conditions of knowledge production, on the other hand. Dispute over the conversion and assimilation of peninsular Muslims became a staging ground for the early modern reevaluation of Christian orthodoxy and the renovation of scholarly practice.

Although these disputes later served parallel uses in the Italian, French, and English contexts, I focus on sixteenth-century peninsular scholars because their language and methods uniquely unsettle the relationship between early and late modern religion. Neither Christians nor Spaniards were by any means the only purveyors of religious violence in the early modern period, but the Spanish inquisition has come to be regarded as a test case for the role of coercion in the formation of community. It stands as an example of discipline gone off the tracks laid by scripture and its exegetes. Yet inquisitorial Spain was also remarkably, if dialectically, humanistic. Some inquisitors persecuted not in spite of their ethical commitments but because of them, and writers with diverse agendas joined Valencia in arguing that compulsion could produce social change and political engagement as well as religious orthodoxy.[2] In retrospect, even reformers like Valencia sound vaguely inquisitorial themselves, but, as historians of religion have argued, this is chiefly because we have been conditioned by Protestant reform and the varieties of secularism and religion that it helped to produce.[3] It is beyond the scope of this book to recount Enlightenment and Romantic era histories of how and why peninsular churchmen came to appear too trusting in the transformative power of physical and social coercion or too willing to use religious language and authority to take advantage of pious believers. I aim rather to show that these paired accusations of superstition and cynicism have erroneously rendered some Spanish forms and narratives of religious discipline comprehensible only as religious intolerance. Such accusations obscure the history and consequences of tolerance and intolerance alike.

Organized along a timeline that takes King Fernando II and Queen Isabel I's conquest of Granada and expulsion of the Jews in 1492 as a crucial turning point, peninsular history is rife with flawed paradigms of such tolerance and intolerance. According to one familiar model, occasional outbreaks of popular violence interrupted a cheerfully tolerant medieval Iberia, whose modes of cultural and political exchange across ecumenical boundaries had been shaped by centuries of Muslim rule and interrupted by Christian expansion.[4] In contrast to this Muslim-inspired *convivencia*, as this picture of coexistence has become known, was a Christian social and political insecurity that would in the sixteenth century mature into the outright prejudice of inquisition. The reality was less tidy. We now know that the threat as well as the actual exchange of violence was a structural feature of Christians, Muslims, and Jews living together in the medieval period.[5] Something similar is true of the early modern period, during which disciplinary processes of conversion, assimilation, and expulsion produced flexible new methods of reading and teaching. No less than medieval *convivencia*, early modern persecution hides a more complex intellectual and cultural history in which Islamic Spain seemed to end again and again. With two chapters each on canon law, philology, and history writing, *Parables of Coercion* traces these multiple false endings in a chronological arc. The story begins with the forced conversion of Spain's last Muslims at the beginning of the sixteenth century and ends with the expulsion of the Moriscos in the early seventeenth century.

The authors who defended the conversions that inaugurated the Morisco period sought to protect the validity of institutionally sanctioned religious ritual and social practices while expanding their own power to regulate orthodoxy. Because only Christians were subject to heresy inquisition, the mass baptisms that followed the fall of Granada served an important legal function: they placed the conquered Muslim population under the authority of the Church as well as the Crown. The Hieronymite first archbishop of Granada, Hernando de Talavera, emphasized prayer and meditation rather than compulsion, but he remained in his post for less than a decade. His replacement, the Franciscan statesman, inquisitor, and cardinal Francisco Jiménez de Cisneros, along with the royal confessor and later bishop Antonio de Guevara, took a harder line. They defended the legality of these baptisms, regardless of participants' intentions. Here they drew on Augustine's reading of the parable of the banquet, a passage from Luke in which

Jesus recounts the story of a rich man who "compels" (*compelle*) reluctant invitees to join his private feast. But in making a balanced case for compulsory participation in the metaphorical banquet of Christ, Cisneros and Guevara also invoked Jerome, Augustine's adversary and a defender of dissimulation as well as discipline, particularly in tricky pastoral situations.[6] Like other Spanish inquisitors and evangelizers who read these biblical and patristic sources, Cisneros and Guevara pointed out that if the visible signs of Christian practice could shape rather than merely reflect the beliefs of a newly expansive flock of practitioners, there was good reason to police and manipulate the lives of recent converts. Jesus himself had insisted that his disciples accept a program of discipline, renounce their families, and suffer other social and corporal hardships as the cost of inclusion in his community. So why should sixteenth-century New Christians not acquiesce as well? A royal and ecclesiastical policy of coercion toward converts from Islam and Judaism took shape through an effort to engineer the social infrastructure of faith.

To sideline the question of personal religious sincerity was a way both to address the dilemma of recent converts' apostasy and to guard Rome's monopoly on effective ritual. Insisting that the sacraments were mere signs of God's grace rather than instruments for its advent, Luther had by the middle of the sixteenth century spurred theologians at the Council of Trent to double down on an old notion of ritual efficacy. The technical doctrinal name for such ritual efficacy was *ex opere operato*, or "from the work done."[7] As the literal translation of the Latin suggests, the idea was that the eschatological consequences of the sacraments followed from the performance. Ritual was a condition of salvation. Cisneros, Guevara, and others had for political and pastoral reasons previously cast the net of Augustinian compulsion wider even than Luther had feared or Augustine himself had proposed.[8] But other contemporary scholars with similar concerns about the borders of Christianity, such as the evangelizer Bartolomé de Las Casas and the Salamanca theologian Francisco de Vitoria, subsequently turned the discourses of ritual efficacy and religious coercion to new and different ends. They demonstrated that to determine orthodoxy by glossing New Christian faith was to extend rather than limit the political uses of natural and canon law. To mount this argument against the objections of the humanist Juan Ginés de Sepúlveda and Jesuit missionary José de Acosta, Las Casas and Vitoria linked their criticisms of conquistador violence to a defense of scholastic inquiry's imperial relevance. Interweaving discussions about conversion and heresy in the New and Old Worlds, these scholars and their interlocutors offered a self-interested defense of scholastic pedagogy, but it was a defense that enlarged their colleagues' sense of religious coercion's critical potential.

My goal in the book's first two chapters on canon law is to show that this language of religious coercion and the logic of ritual efficacy provided an intellectual commons where scholars with diverse agendas and affiliations could cultivate their respective arguments. The puzzling but crucial point is that apologists and opponents of both Church- and Crown-sanctioned violence formulated their contrasting projects in the shared philosophical skepticism expressed so well by Valencia in his writings about the Moriscos and by Vitoria in his Thomist glosses. Given the difficulty of excavating buried beliefs, they agreed that it was prudent to focus on the observable indicators of orthodoxy. An obsession with religious interiority paradoxically led to the increasing regulation of observable ritual and culture, even as the link between public signs and private referents began to fray. From this perspective, a Catholic Reformation concern with religious ritual and narrative form begins to look like a judicious response, however imperfect, both to the political challenges posed by a growing empire's diversity and to the epistemological double bind described by Valencia. Sacramental formalism was not simply a reactionary answer to the democratizing and secularizing force at work to the north. "It is difficult to find out what Spaniards believed," a renowned historian of early modern Spain has recently argued, "and more convincing to see how they behaved."[9] This contemporary historical and anthropological puzzle was in the early modern period a theological one.

The third and fourth chapters demonstrate that the cacophonous debate about how to read Christian ritual was also a contest over how to translate and interpret biblical and liturgical texts. As the polymath and editor Benito Arias Montano, the poet and theologian Fray Luis de León, and other contemporary Bible scholars well knew, the material and linguistic features of manuscript and early print culture helped to produce rather than simply reflect a sense of sacredness. An elegant edition of the Bible, printed on vellum with high-quality ink and carefully annotated with glosses on the original Hebrew and Greek texts, looked and felt authoritative. Rome struggled so mightily, if unsuccessfully, over the course of the sixteenth century to safeguard its monopoly on the celebration of effective ritual and the production of sacred scripture and artifacts because even the most provincial of Catholic theologians understood the contingent, material quality of holy authority.[10] As the Latin Vulgate became just one in a series of available biblical texts, which included the Protestant reformers' many vernacular translations, fresh editions and translations of the Greek New Testament, and polyglot editions of the Latin, Greek, Hebrew, and Aramaic versions of the Old and New Testaments, biblical scholars labored to distinguish the dangerous heresies of the Jews and schismatic early Christians from their useful Hebrew and Greek manuscripts. Here emerged a new challenge: employ the texts of nonbelievers to edit and annotate Christian scripture without falling prey to those nonbelievers' mistaken beliefs and practices. Rising to the task, the Hebrew specialists trained by the generation of Jewish converts to Christianity who worked on the Complutense Polyglot Bible began to integrate Aramaic and Arabic into Hebrew education. These scholars followed the comparative philological models fashioned by Roman and Florentine humanists of previous decades, but their effort to shift the peninsular conventions of biblical Hebraism represented a new and important step in the development of Oriental studies in Europe.

The risks facing editorial teams in Alcalá de Henares, Basel, and Antwerp, and troubling doctrinarians in Rome and Trent, paralleled the interpretive and pedagogical hazards awaiting Christian evangelizers in the far-flung reaches of the Spanish empire. As Franciscan and Jesuit missionaries worked to expand their linguistic breadth to match Christianity's new global presence, they attempted to differentiate among the Arabic, Berber, Nahuatl, and Mandarin phonemes ringing in their ears and the myriad local religious traditions that they hoped language fluency would help eliminate. Insulating communication and evangelization against the indigenous draft of unbelief, these practically minded comparative philologists separated linguistic usage from semantic meaning, just as the Church fathers and Catholic Reformation canon lawyers had distinguished between ritual practice and belief, and just as early modern biblical scholars had discriminated between their multilingual codices and the heterodox views of the communities that had for centuries preserved them. Reasoning that language fluency no less than Christian faith was a result of habit, teachers and students focused first on linguistic form and only later turned to the troublesome question of content. This was how Jesuit pedagogues—masters of multilingualism—taught Latin and Hebrew to generations of fledgling peninsular humanists. But the premise, to which some polyglot medieval pedagogues had also subscribed, worked further afield and among other religious orders.[11] Memorizing a translated Ave Maria or Paternoster, uncertain though the meanings may have been to Muslim students of Hernando de Talavera in Granada or indigenous pupils of Archbishop Juan de Zumárraga in Mexico, was perceived to be a pragmatic first step toward belief. Language pedagogy served to inoculate against heresy even as it opened a contested new space for religious experimentation and adaptation, a space that New Christians in Granada and Mexico did not hesitate to claim as their own.

Like baptisms performed by those heretical priests that had concerned Augustine, comparative philological inquiry threatened to blur the boundaries between Christianity and other religions. Multilingualism sometimes facilitated communication between Christians and non-Christians, but it also intensified discord among different groups of Christians. Taking advantage of this anxiety, a small group of well-educated Moriscos from Granada sought to control the plot of their communities' fragile story by going so far as to forge Christian gospels. Bernardo de Aldrete, Gregorio López de Madera, and other contemporary classicists and philologists revisited the history of peninsular Arabic and Spanish as they presented their apologies for and attacks upon these texts, twenty-two Arabic etchings, known as the Sacromonte lead books and discovered in the 1590s in the hills outside of Granada. In so doing, these authors joined the Morisco Arabists Miguel de Luna and Alonso de Castillo in a frank debate about the material and linguistic conventions of orthodoxy. They asked, for instance, whether Christian holy texts must exist in book form and whether such texts could be written in Arabic rather than Hebrew, Greek, or Latin. In a Spanish milieu where we have least come to expect it, these discussions demonstrate an early modern conviction that textual authenticity and linguistic history were the creations of expert readers.

Looking back on nearly a century of debate about the Moriscos, the late sixteenth- and early seventeenth-century historians examined in the book's final two chapters argued over the relative successes and failures of their predecessors' approaches to integration. Were the Moriscos actually Christians? Were they and other New Christians loyal or treasonous subjects? Christianity in the Old and New Worlds was porous, dynamic, and multilingual enough to integrate ancestral practices, creeds, and turns of phrase, so if not by Augustine or Jerome's standard, then by whose should Christianity be defined? Answers to these queries would not only shape legal and linguistic inquiry, but also transform history writing. To formulate a historical narrative of the religious and demographic turmoil of the sixteenth century, it was necessary to evaluate the legitimacy of past coercion, the hidden motivations of minority rebels, and the unsettling prospect of future violence. Whereas fourteenth- and fifteenth-century chroniclers had sought to celebrate their powerful patrons by adding royal deeds to a relatively stable corpus of imperial history, later generations of scholars, embittered by wars on the ecumenical frontiers of the peninsula or hardened by the experience of Mediterranean and Atlantic conquest, penned rebukes to and apologies for power.

Drawing on manuscript evidence, Morisco prophecy, and first-person experience, soldier-historians Luis de Mármol Carvajal, Diego Hurtado de Mendoza, and Ginés Pérez de Hita all published their accounts of the Second Alpujarras War, a Granadan Morisco rebellion that lasted from 1568 to 1571. The war stories woven together by these historians appeared in print only several decades after the events, when debate about the Sacromonte lead books had begun and disagreement over Morisco expulsion had intensified. Authors and editors of the Alpujarras material thus helped shape those later conversations. And unlike previous imperial chroniclers, these authors wrote for a popular as well as a learned audience, and they leveled severe criticisms at King Felipe II's handling of the conflict. By combining documentary accounts with authorial invention, their new forms of critical narrative employed the Moriscos and their history to reimagine the craft of history. This was the moment when a debate over how to write the history of failed integration finally replaced the conversation about strategies for assimilation.

While practices of historical inquiry were in flux at the moment of the Morisco expulsions, two contradictory narratives about Spain's rise and fall as an early modern imperial power were already becoming fixed. Along with Juan de Ribera, the Valencian Jesuit Francisco de Escrivà and the Franciscan historian Marco de Guadalajara y Xavier compiled an archive of anecdotes, treatises, letters, and sermons related to the failure of Morisco assimilation. Pedro de Valencia and his ally, the Morisco Jesuit Ignacio de Las Casas, were shrewd interpreters of scripture and current events, but they were not as print savvy as their opponents, who swiftly published their triumphalist accounts of the expulsion. Pedro Fernández de Navarrete, Martín González de Cellorigo, and other *arbitristas*, as economic theorists of the period were called, subsequently transformed the writing of imperial and economic history in the process of calculating the costs and negotiating the meaning of this decisive resolution to the Morisco question. The choices of the early seventeenth-century present—not only whether and when to expel the Moriscos, but also how to stimulate a sputtering economy and where to seek counsel on these issues—shaped competing interpretations of the past along with the conventions of history writing and archival collection.

This scholarship of the early seventeenth century is the foundation upon which the edifice of early modern Hispanic studies stands today, and perhaps the most contentious of all issues in this field remains the history of inquisition. The chronological parameters of the Holy Office are deceptively clear: beginning in 1478, Pope Sixtus IV granted the *reyes católicos* Fernando and Isabel the authority to name inquisitors, and peninsular heresy inquisition continued to function until 1834, when the institution was finally dissolved. Yet there is marked disagreement about the actual geographic reach and physical violence of inquisition at different points in this period. Despite this uncertainty, neither the Protestant detractors nor the Catholic apologists who fashioned the popular, contradictory images of religion and society in early modern Spain were interested in putting too fine a point on inquisitorial matters.[12] To the Catholic apologists and their nationalist successors, sixteenth-century peninsular intellectuals were confronted on all sides by dissembling heretics who were intent upon sowing discord; Crown and Church officials acted decisively and devoutly to protect a vulnerable Christian community. The noble ends, these scholars argued, justified the harsh discipline. On the contrary, to the Protestant detractors and their secular heirs, those same early modern intellectuals were either such fervent purveyors of castigation that they tended toward bigotry, or such disingenuous exploiters of ecclesiastical language and authority that they could scarcely be considered religious at all. The most pugnacious of contemporary atheists have fashioned a universal rule from the inquisitorial exception.[13] Inquisition has given both early modern Spain and religion itself a bad name.

A skeptical reader might point toward a familiar catalogue of violence to argue that the popular perception of an intolerant early modern Spain is fundamentally accurate: after expelling the Jews from the Kingdoms of Castile and Aragon in 1492, Fernando and Isabel approved the active policing of the beliefs, rituals, eating habits, and work schedules of Jewish converts to Christianity, called *conversos*. And they pressured their neighbor, King Manuel I, to take a similarly firm position concerning the Jews of Portugal. The *reyes católicos* also halted Archbishop Talavera's pastoral work with Granada's Muslims, authorizing his replacement, Francisco Jiménez de Cisneros, to baptize forcibly the population of the conquered city. Antonio de Guevara, meanwhile, was allowed to do the same to the Muslim community of Valencia. Fernando and Isabel's grandson, who ruled the expanded Holy Roman Empire from 1516 to 1556 as Carlos V, continued the process of New Christian integration by levying burdensome taxes on the Moriscos, discouraging their use of Arabic, and attempting to regulate their dress, food, and music, just as his grandparents had with the *conversos*. Carlos V also oversaw decades of horrific violence in the Americas, as the *encomendero* tributary labor system killed thousands of indigenous workers. Carlos V's son, Felipe II, who reigned from the abdication of his father until his own death in 1598, took an increasingly antagonistic approach to the Moriscos, appointing his half brother Juan de Austria to quash the above-mentioned Morisco rebellion before forcibly resettling the rebel survivors throughout the kingdom. His son and successor, Felipe III, whose rule was shaped by the crafty duke of Lerma, Francisco Gómez de Sandoval, expelled the Moriscos, who at the beginning of the seventeenth century numbered two or three hundred thousand.

There are two main alternatives to this account of recurrent intolerance, which modern specialists have come to see as a straw man constructed over several centuries by Spain's critics. The first emerges from the myriad New Christianities created by the two-century eradication of peninsular Jewish and Muslim communities and the conversion of the majority of indigenous subjects in the Americas. The converts organized themselves according to specific laws, doctrines, and scripts. They fostered social networks and juggled multiple belief systems and affiliations. To some scholars of New Christian history and culture, this heterodoxy looks in hindsight something like underground political resistance.[14] If we have for so long overlooked or misread the evidence of this opposition, these scholars argue, it is because previous readers excluded minority sources. They failed to recognize that although heresy inquisition may have anticipated the modern art of management, the goals of inquisition were nonetheless incompatible with a nascent modernity.[15] Conversely, those New Christians who managed to separate their private, heterodox faiths from their public, Catholic obligations were, like Protestant reformers and moderate Catholics north of the Pyrenees, harbingers of religion's retreat to the private sphere. From this perspective, inquisitorial Spain's religious modernity is conjoined with its minorities' fight for existence.

The second alternative to this story of intolerance comes into view by reading familiar printed sources and new archival materials against the triumphalist grain. As early as the 1480s, for example, Fernando and Isabel's royal chronicler, Hernando de Pulgar, considered inquisition to be an illegitimate pastoral and penal method. He insisted that clerics should correct heretics with "sweet reasons and tender reprimands" rather than "that cruel punishment of the fire."[16] Pulgar's allies, the *converso* humanist and royal ambassador Juan de Lucena and Archbishop Hernando de Talavera, developed this defense of pastoral forbearance by pointing to scripture. They invoked Matthew 11:30 and 13:24–30, in which Jesus first offered his interlocutors an "easy yoke" and then recounted the famously irenic parable of the wheat and the tares, a passage that a century later played a crucial role in the debate between Valencia and Ribera over Morisco expulsion.[17] Spanish students of Erasmus, popular mystical groups known as *alumbrados,* and varied post-Tridentine reformers likewise tried to foster Christian piety and personal discipline through education rather than through coercion.[18] Humanist education was not a necessary precondition of opposition to religious and imperial violence, however. Inquisition archives document plenty of ordinary imperial subjects who expressed their own, informal disapproval of royal and ecclesiastical policy. Held to a rigid standard of Christian orthodoxy despite the diversity of religious beliefs in the Spanish empire, some individuals under inquisitorial investigation casually defended the ecumenical possibility that Jews and Muslims might achieve salvation through the mercy of their Gods just as a Christian can through his.[19] From this perspective, accounts of elite and popular tolerance function as rejoinders both to the Spanish apologetic tradition and to anti-Spanish propaganda from beyond the peninsula.

In recounting the histories of individuals and arguments that seem to measure up, in whatever partial way, to the moral and political standards of liberal modernity, these two alternative accounts seek to draw inquisitorial Spain in from the medieval margins.[20] They imply that if some ordinary Christians occasionally found ways to safeguard their own idiosyncratic religious lives, perhaps many others did as well. Correspondingly, if Erasmus's insistence on the power of humanist education to help any poor sinner become a more charitable and knowledgeable Christian found proponents on the peninsula, perhaps sixteenth-century peninsular scholarship was not totally mired in the outdated scholasticism of the inquisitors. It is true, as critics of the medievalist Robert I. Moore have cogently argued, that persecution sometimes toughened its victims. Some communities also ignored or circumvented the rigid creeds of the powerful.[21] But in the Spanish case, neither New Christian apostates nor Old Christian critics were effective in peacefully resolving the religious and political tensions of the day. Scattered accounts of resistance and dissent complicate but do not topple a dominant narrative of injustice.

My objective is different. By reconstructing the interpretive methods of those rival peninsular scholars who negotiated the boundaries of orthodoxy and sought to eradicate heresy, I study the intellectual rather than the political or human consequences of coercion. I neither narrate Morisco community life in Granada nor weave a history of dissent. My concern is less with lived violence per se than with the apologies and polemics that make violence possible and comprehensible.[22] Precisely because inquisitorial Spain is widely recognizable to both specialist and general readers as a portable metaphor for intolerance, telling a more nuanced story about the relationship between religious coercion and scholarly innovation can upend celebratory accounts of "modern" religion and expose some discourses of tolerance as forms of oppression. The entry for *tolerantia* in the *Repertorivm inqvisitorvm*, a lexicon for inquisitors printed in multiple sixteenth-century editions, bluntly displays this point: "we tolerate some, those whom we cannot correct" (*nonnullos toleramus, quos corrigere non possumus*).[23] For early modern Spanish inquisitors and their critics, if not for us as well, tolerance was a local and contingent phenomenon. It was a last resort. The late medieval and early modern Church's strategies of control are so discomfiting today because they seem to have suppressed the sort of agency that makes both dissent and consent possible in the realms of religion and politics. Free acceptance or refusal of a set of creeds, along with free participation in or abstention from shared practices, is the modern gauge of religious sincerity. Needless to say, the long shadow of the Protestant Reformation is visible in this humanistic conception of agency. In response to such a view of agency, generations of Marxist critics have rightly pointed out that the free subject is in some sense a chimera. There are powerful material and institutional forces that limit the freedom to believe and to act. Moreover, many people remain blind even to their own interests as they pursue agendas that compound this structural lack of autonomy. From these two perspectives, cynical authorities coopt discourses of tolerance for their own intolerant ends, while endemic naiveté undermines revolutionary change.

The Spanish approach that I study in this book was to overcome this impasse by rejecting the sort of agency and knowledge now presupposed by both liberal and radical social theorists. Late medieval Bible commentators, such as the *converso* archbishop of Burgos Pablo de Santa María, reconfirmed this rejection by joining Augustine in his invocation of the parable of the banquet from Luke.[24] Later scholars as dissimilar as Pedro de Valencia and Juan de Ribera, in turn, employed Santa María's defense of Augustinian coercion to their own opposing ends. My point is that medieval glosses and the early modern coercive practices they buttressed did not serve inescapably antihumanistic or antirevolutionary ends. The perplexing truth, as anthropologists of religion Talal Asad and Saba Mahmood have argued for the medieval and contemporary periods, respectively, is that participation in longstanding patterns of disciplined dress, sex, and prayer, along with engagement in conventional forms of theological debate, philological inquiry, and historical research, can be a strategy of transformation as well as a feature of subjugation. While Michel Foucault, Pierre

Bourdieu, and Michel de Certeau have in different ways drawn into the secular sphere Christian humanist concepts of self-definition through practice, Asad and Mahmood, along with others interested in the secularism debates of recent years, have returned to theology's central role in theorizing the vocabulary and practices of discipline.[25] Although Asad and his interlocutors have mistakenly reduced the sixteenth century to an age of tactical self-fashioning and allowed peninsular discussions about pastoral practice to fall in the cracks between a history of medieval discipline and an anthropology of the present, they have nonetheless reminded us that like the writing exercises of the student or the daily commutes of the urban dweller, the coercive practices of religious disciples helped to cultivate habits of body and mind. In so doing, they recall the language not only of Augustine, but also of the humanist Juan Luis Vives and the Jesuit educators Juan de Polanco and Jerónimo Nadal, who employed the word "discipline" as I do in this book: to designate a branch of knowledge as well as the practices that demarcate and duplicate the scholarly, religious, and political communities that produce such knowledge.[26] This slippage among the pedagogical, the pastoral, and the penal points toward how and why the negotiation of New Christian discipline entailed reimaging the disciplines themselves.

It may now seem like a contortion of Olympic proportions to see languages and practices of collective religious coercion as tools for mitigating violence or theorizing a common civic identity. But this was the maneuver that some of the most renowned peninsular intellectuals of the early modern period attempted. They failed to shape the course of Spanish imperial history, but in putting the pliability of religious hermeneutics to work, they transformed the rules of scholarship. The story of this transformation offers both a sketch for how to theorize religion in the contemporary world and a parable about the danger of severing religion from its social and political contexts. In recounting the transformative effects of peninsular coercion on canon law, philology, and history writing, this book thus has aims that are more than historical: it challenges the presuppositions that give tolerance and intolerance their analytical power. Despite the discontinuities between Renaissance and post-Romantic humanism, we humanists of the present are nevertheless products of the early modern period. Twenty-first century modes of argumentation and standards of evidence, the attention to linguistic change and textual transmission, and the very claim to disinterested scientific thought are legacies of the sixteenth century. Having critically turned these interpretive tools upon the individuals and institutions that produced them, however, the humanities no longer shine so brightly.

Secular discourses of reason, equality, and tolerance were, like the religious discourses out of which they emerged and which they subsequently transformed, instruments of exclusion and violence in addition to inclusion and reconciliation. What it has been more difficult to acknowledge, though, is that religious discourses of inequality and intolerance also served both exclusive and inclusive agendas. The Spanish intellectual history of New Christian assimilation can guide us toward that acknowledgment. It compels us, like so many unwilling guests at the banquet portrayed in Luke, to participate anew in that factious but dynamic debate about what religion is and should be.

CHAPTER ONE

Legible Conversions

In December 1499, Francisco Jiménez de Cisneros wrote to Pope Alexander VI to report baptizing three thousand Muslims from Granada and the surrounding region in an enormous public ceremony. Wearing his habit and sporting the customary tonsure of a Franciscan friar, Cisneros cast holy water from the baptismal cup upon the Muslim throng.[1] These *mudéjares,* as peninsular Muslims living under Christian political authority were called, had little choice but to attend the mass conversion. Since his return to Granada with the court of King Fernando and Queen Isabel several months prior, Cisneros had taken an increasingly provocative stance toward the city's Muslim residents. With tacit consent of the *reyes católicos,* Cisneros had begun patrolling the Albaicín, Granada's sprawling Muslim neighborhood, in order to interrogate women and children about their beliefs and practices. He unsettled the local population with his imposing personal guard of two hundred men. And in a direct affront to Archbishop Hernando de Talavera's dedication to language study, he had begun publicly burning thousands of Arabic books. Some potential converts undoubtedly were intrigued by the patient example set by Talavera during his seven-year tenure as Granada's first archbishop, and others may have been keen on the economic advantages that conversion afforded, but the majority attended the mass baptism ceremony because of Cisneros's program of intimidation.[2]

Cisneros's return to Granada at the dawn of the sixteenth century signaled a shift in peninsular approaches to evangelization. Signed in late 1491 and ostensibly marking the conclusion of the centuries long *reconquista,* as Christian rulers' expansion into peninsular territory controlled by Islamic sovereigns has become known, the Capitulations of Granada guaranteed the vanquished population the right to practice Islam freely. Nevertheless, King Fernando and Queen Isabel quickly appointed Talavera, then confessor to the queen, as archbishop of the newly conquered city. Charged with transforming Granada from an Islamic capital to a Christian "frontier city," to borrow the historian David Coleman's phrase, Talavera began an intensive missionary campaign.[3] As his early modern biographer José de Sigüenza recalled in a history of the Hieronymite order, first published in 1600, Talavera encouraged the participation of the conquered population in the life of the Church by allowing Arabic language and traditional Moorish music during Christian prayer. He also tried to incorporate the local population into the Christian community by regularly inviting influential Muslims to dine at his Granadan residence. And according to the Morisco negotiator Francisco Núñez Muley, whose late sixteenth-century treatise I examine in more detail below, he traveled to recondite villages in the region's Alpujarras Mountains to perform mass.[4] This economy of hospitality and persuasion had practical as well as symbolic aims. Canon law might not prohibit the Arab and Berber custom of feasting on rug-covered floors rather than seated at tables, for instance, but encouraging Muslims to pick up the eating habits of Old Christians, Talavera reasoned, would facilitate both religious education and social assimilation. Talavera treated *accommodatio* as a two-way street, urging Christians and Muslims to adapt to each other's modes of eating, bathing, working, and speaking. For Talavera and his fellow clergy, this flexibility constituted the essence of pastoral charity, and for the defeated Muslims it was a sign of political and religious goodwill. Talavera was willing to allow the pedagogical process of conversion to run its circuitous course.

Talavera's forbearance, however, did not yield results. Accommodation had worked for Paul, the most famous and effective of early Christian missionaries and a model for Talavera and his crew of evangelizers, but the new archbishop of Granada was not successful at luring the conquered Muslim population to Christianity during the crucial first seven years of his tenure. Granada's Muslims may very well have admired the archbishop's perseverance and integrity, as Sigüenza and other late sixteenth-century hagiographers maintained, but the majority did not convert to Christianity. When King Fernando and Queen Isabel returned to Granada in 1499, they found the still unassimilated Muslim population that they had conquered more than a half decade earlier. As a result, upon departing the city that same year, they left Cisneros to help jump-start the evangelization effort. Recognizing Talavera's pastoral failure and his own royal mandate, Cisneros sought the formal victory of swift, mass conversions. At least in the short term, that is, Cisneros and the *reyes católicos* were less concerned with encouraging the indigenous Muslim population to embrace the Christian faith than with establishing the Muslims' legal status as Christian subjects bound by canon law. Provoked by this new approach, Muslims from Granada and the surrounding Alpujarras Mountains revolted. After this First Alpujarras War in 1501, the Crown insisted that the uprising had voided any previous guarantee of religious freedom. The entire Granadan Muslim population was compelled either to embrace Christianity as the price of royal pardon or to leave the peninsula altogether. A year later, Muslims throughout the Kingdom of Castile faced the same grim choice of conversion or emigration.[5]

Other major centers of peninsular Islam eventually went the way of Castile. Stung by the sarcastic barbs of his French rival King Francis I, Carlos V decided to apply the Castilian mandate to Valencian and Aragonese Muslims in December 1525 and January 1526, respectively. Having been captured in the Battle of Pavia in February 1525 by imperial troops and imprisoned in the Valencian Castillo de Benisano, Francis I had wryly wondered aloud why men dressed like Muslims were working the land outside his cell window on a Christian day of rest. This was not exactly what one would have expected in territory ruled by the Holy Roman Emperor, quipped the jailed *rex Francorum christianissimus,* the most Christian King of the Franks.[6] Despite the efforts of the churchman and humanist Antonio de Guevara, who boasted of baptizing no less than twenty-seven thousand Muslim households in Valencia alone during the 1520s, Valencian and Aragonese *mudéjares,* as well as their already-converted Morisco countrymen, continued to enjoy a great deal of local cultural and religious autonomy well into the sixteenth century.[7] *Mudéjares* and Moriscos lived in shared neighborhoods, dressed and spoke similarly, and remained connected by myriad blood and social bonds. In both Granada and Valencia, two cities frequented by foreign tourists and diplomats, this confusion of demographic boundaries belied the crusader rhetoric employed for centuries to inspire and justify Christian occupation of Islamic lands. Although there had existed large communities of *mudéjares* since the thirteenth century, when Christian expansion began to gather steam—King Jaume I of Aragon conquered Valencia in 1238 and King Fernando III of Castile and Leon took Cordoba in 1236 and Seville in 1248—after the surrender of Granada in 1492, religious diversity in traditional centers of peninsular Islam became a geopolitical embarrassment first to Fernando and Isabel and then to Carlos V. The coerced conversions of the end of the fifteenth and beginning of the sixteenth century were in part an effort to protect the image of peninsular piety.

Yet these conversions were not immediately enforced. Under pressure from regional nobility seeking to safeguard the rents paid to them by Morisco tenant farmers, the Crown granted New Christians from Granada, Valencia, and Aragon temporary or partial reprieves from inquisition, along with delayed implementation of prohibitions on Arabic language, traditional garb, and other markers of Morisco distinctiveness. Subsequent lobbying and bribes by Morisco negotiators and their noble allies resulted in the postponement of at least six successive edicts whose goals were to regulate the minority community more rigidly.[8] This policy of dispensation, which lasted well into the 1560s, prompts the fundamental question: What did the mass conversions like those celebrated by Cisneros and Guevara accomplish?

The inability to nurture Christian orthodoxy among the Moriscos after their conversion may have been a pastoral failure, but it was an unmitigated professional victory. For specialized legal disputes about the efficacy of the sacraments and the orthodoxy of dissimulation, examined over the first half of this chapter, influenced the terminology of imperial apologetics. By insisting upon the binding nature of the dubious Muslim baptisms, the churchmen who served in the Holy Office and advised the Crown presented the case for their own role in political affairs. In this way, I argue, Augustinian discourses of coercion and ritual efficacy became a lingua franca. This was true not only among Old Christian scholars with or without formal scholastic training and writing in Spanish as well as Latin, but also, as we will see in the second half of the chapter, among Moriscos too. From the forced conversions of the early sixteenth century to the Morisco expulsions of the early seventeenth century, these juridical disputes shaped peninsular paradigms of spiritual discipline and religious reform. However logical as a point of departure, to examine the legacy of Cisneros and Guevara's juridical sleight of hand is nevertheless not only to study the professional motivations of peninsular churchmen. It is also to trace the medieval precedents for such pragmatism and to reconstruct the available critical responses to it. These learned disputes about the acceptability of coercion and the feasibility or desirability of assimilation entailed a renewed consideration of the relationship between belief and ritual, the meaning of conversion, and the power of the law in a transatlantic empire.

COMPULSION IN HINDSIGHT

By muddling the clarity of conventional categories of religious difference, the mass conversions of the late fifteenth and early sixteenth century confused an already complicated taxonomy of legal authority. Were these converts, many of whom continued to participate in Islamic rituals and subscribe to their old beliefs, actually Christians? If so, what measure of compulsory participation in the Christian community and obligatory adherence to canon law was licit, and how should resistance to such compulsion be measured? Alternatively, had this population been baptized illegally? Were these apparent converts to Christianity in fact still Muslims who merely lived under Christian rule? If so, to what extent were these *mudéjares* obliged to listen to peaceful preachers of the gospels but free to believe and practice as they pleased? These were the questions before King Carlos V and recently named inquisitor-general Cardinal Alonso Manrique in late 1524 and early 1525. After Manrique requested a series of inquiries into the recent Valencian baptisms, he and the Crown organized a meeting of leading peninsular theologians and political advisors to consider both the newly collected Valencian evidence and established Church precedent relevant to the previous three decades' suspect baptisms. As Henry Charles Lea demonstrated, the objective of the resulting Council of Madrid, which met for twenty-two days in the Franciscan convent of Madrid in the spring of 1525, was to provide a sense of closure and legitimacy to the recent Muslim conversions. Carlos V had already applied to Pope Clement VII to release him from his oath not to compel Muslims to accept Christianity, and Manrique, an erstwhile *erasmista* who sought to consolidate his new peninsular-wide authority and reputation, could scarcely abide limitations on the Holy Office's jurisdiction.[9] In hindsight, the council's decision was overdetermined from the outset.

This decision drew on ample medieval precedent. Collecting arguments that prohibited the compulsory conversion of nonbelievers was, of course, no great challenge. In a discussion of coercion and baptism in his encyclopedic thirteenth-century commentary the *Summa theologica*, Thomas Aquinas argued, for example, that nonbelievers "by no means should be compelled to the faith [*ad fidem compellendi*] in order that they may believe."[10] Aquinas did not, however, offer a comprehensive ban on religious coercion. The Church may justifiably submit Christians to "bodily compulsion" (*corporaliter compellendi*) so that, in Aquinas's allusion to the baptism ceremony, "they may fulfill what they have promised and hold what they at one time received."[11] Both Aquinas and the delegates at the Council of Madrid three centuries later drew on the arguments approved by the Council IV of Toledo, convened in 633 and probably headed by the famous grammarian and theologian Isidore of Seville. In Isidore's seventh-century Visigothic Spain, Christian clerics were concerned about apostatizing converts to Christianity from

Judaism rather than Islam, whose first followers had only recently begun to cohere around the Prophet Muhammad, but the core question of how to foster the integration of new converts while still clearly defining Christian orthodoxy paralleled the concerns of the Madrid delegates. The scholars at Toledo hewed a middle way, agreeing to discipline New Christian apostates while separating Jews and Christians in the cultural sphere.[12] Although this latter, anti-Jewish aspect of the Toledo opinion was part of a decades-long trend toward peninsular balkanization, Isidore and his interlocutors nevertheless did seem, at least at first glance, to prohibit the forced baptism of Jews: "Therefore not by violence but by the free faculty of persuasion they may be converted," declared article 57 of the council's tractate. "They may not be impelled."[13] In this reading, the medieval sources prohibited the coercion of nonbelievers and permitted the coercion of Christians.

The challenge in the seventh and sixteenth centuries alike was to determine the course of pastoral action when the line between nonbelievers and Christians was blurry. Acknowledging this dilemma, the Toledo delegates qualified their prohibition on the coercion of nonbelievers. Although "long ago" baptized Jews were "forced to Christianity," the fact remained that they "were anointed with the cross, and received the body and blood of our Lord."[14] There could be no undoing of such sacramental efficacy, however dubious or remote. The delegates argued that the ban on compulsory conversions applied only to future baptisms: "No one shall *hereafter* force them to belief" (*nemini deinceps ad credendum vim inferre*) (emphasis mine), reads a passage shortly following the apparently comprehensive prohibition mentioned above. Technically a ban on future violence, the crucial "hereafter" also validated prior violence. Echoing Augustine's fifth-century assessment that even baptisms performed by heretical priests were binding, the delegates at the Council IV of Toledo thus underscored both the temporal dilemma of the theologian's ex post facto analysis and the physical nature of the baptism ritual. Neither priestly nor New Christian insincerity, Augustine and the seventh- and sixteenth-century delegates all insisted, could nullify a properly performed sacrament. Given their presupposition that the coerced baptisms of the past were binding, it is no surprise that the Toledo representatives, like their Madrid counterparts nearly a millennium later, contended that it was the solemn responsibility of the baptized not to disrespect their new co-religionists. If the converts' legitimate complaint of coercion did not negate the juridical force of past baptisms, it went without saying that the failure to fulfill the ensuing Christian responsibilities was just cause for punishment. Emphasizing the efficacy of ritual in order to widen the ramparts of the Church, Augustine had employed Luke's parable of the banquet to defend coercive inclusion.

One of the major stumbling blocks to answering this Augustinian line of reasoning was the legally contentious issue of rebaptism. The sacrament of baptism was effective, but rebaptism risked appearing as farce. That is, by pretending to accomplish previously completed work, a second baptism called into question the legitimacy of the first. Medieval canon lawyers fretted about this issue, devising ritual workarounds that in retrospect may seem comical but were deadly serious at the time. For example, this was the formula suggested by the early thirteenth-century pope Gregory IX to clergy celebrating a baptism but uncertain about the status of the baptized: "If you are baptized, then I do not baptize you," the celebrant was supposed to say upon pouring the holy water, "but if you are not baptized, I baptize you, & etc."[15] Bishop of Guadix Martín Pérez de Ayala and his fellow participants in the 1554 Synod of Guadix, which addressed the continuing failure of Morisco assimilation two decades after the Council of Madrid, reiterated this sort of dramaturgical legalese.[16] Here was an attempt to protect the integrity of the sacraments while forestalling the accusation of institutional inconsistency or indifference. Forced baptism and rebaptism were parallel in this sense. On the one hand, the Church was eager to avoid the needless loss of souls. On the other hand, more flexible baptismal practice risked undercutting the Church's claim to efficacy. It is no coincidence that Gregory titled his commentary on baptism "On Baptism and Its Effects," for these debates about baptism were proxies for the display of canon law's power and reach. Despite the protests of some attendees, including the prominent canon lawyer Jaime Benet, the sixteenth-century Council of Madrid presented all nonbelievers of the past as potential apostates of the future. In so doing, they followed their predecessors at the Council IV of Toledo in seeking to justify conversion, like reconciliation, as a punitive ordeal, even as they also attempted to guarantee the freedom of faith and cogency of judicial reason. In sum, to historicize the relationship between compulsion and ritual was theological pragmatism with eminent orthodox precedent.

In addition to distinguishing between past and future baptisms, the delegates at the Council of Madrid attempted to formulate a working definition of coercion and a measure of resistance. In a letter to the vice-royal of Valencia, Carlos V explained that the Madrid delegates had determined that there had been no "precise or absolute force or violence" involved in the recent baptism ceremonies, even if there had occurred some degree of coercion.[17] Carlos V's account echoed the conventional scholastic distinction between absolute and conditional compulsion, a distinction previously formulated by Aquinas and Bonaventure.[18] These medieval commentators had maintained that absolute coercion rendered a baptism invalid, but conditional coercion did not. Or in the Aristotelian terms of Duns Scotus, cited and criticized by Francisco de Vitoria in his commentary on Aquinas's *Summa theologica*, some conversions may be "formally" (*formaliter*) compulsory but "effectively" (*virtualiter*) voluntary.[19] In Vitoria's gloss, a Muslim's apparently compulsory conversion was not actually so, because he would have accepted Christianity freely if only he had understood its superiority. Although these medieval and early modern scholastic commentators also suggested that one possible way to identify the presence of absolute or conditional coercion was to examine the nature of potential converts' resistance, which they hypothesized would be more strident in cases of absolute coercion, such qualifications were formulated at great distance from the violent episodes themselves. And as Carlos V's letter demonstrates, the scholastic impulse to divide and subdivide the meanings of important terms in a storm of distinctions, a process that I examine in a more detail in the next chapter, often served as a retroactive justification for violence rather than as a preemptive brake upon it. Despite Vitoria's assertions to the contrary, in the confusion of pastoral practice, as Cisneros and Guevara's tactics underscore, distinctions among various kinds of coercion and resistance receded into a disappearing horizon of mitigating circumstances.

Even so, this taxonomy of coercion and resistance became key for historians like Alonso de Santa Cruz, who drew extensively on Antonio de Guevara's firsthand accounts and historical research in the section of his *Crónica del Emperador Carlos V* devoted to the Council of Madrid's decision. Writing as a cartographer-historian but sounding at times like Guevara the theologian-historian, Santa Cruz acknowledged that Valencian Muslims were baptized by force at the tail end of the *germanía* uprising, a popular guild revolt against local nobility. But the absence of conclusive evidence of Muslim resistance rendered this admitted force immaterial to the question of the baptisms' efficacy: "The Moors of that kingdom mounted no resistance when they baptized them by force," Santa Cruz maintained, "so that whether they want to or not they must keep the faith that by force they made them accept."[20] In Santa Cruz's telling, the delegates at Madrid decided to declare the mass baptisms of previous decades valid not only because it was impossible to undo the efficacy of the ritual, but also because the absence of resistance undercut the allegation of illegal coercion. Subsequent royal chroniclers, such as Prudencio de Sandoval, repeated Guevara and Santa Cruz's explanation of the

Madrid decision, which came to cement the importance of these scholastic distinctions among varieties of compulsion and resistance for a wider swath of nonspecialist readers.[21]

During the Council of Madrid's debates about Muslim conversions, the rising waters of canon law overflowed their institutional and linguistic levies, saturating the vernacular flood plains of imperial history and regional policy. To define an effective baptism was to expand the jurisdiction of canon law. In dominating the Council of Madrid and shaping the early history of the Morisco period, inquisitors like Manrique staked their claim to a public sphere in transition. This claim may have drawn its ethical energy from a universalizing evangelical impulse, but it nevertheless functioned in practice as a parapet against the recent popularization of legal expertise and a hedge against the Crown's power to name bishops and inquisitors. Despite this *patronato real*, as such power was known in Castile, Aragon, and the various viceroyalties of the Americas, the canon lawyers' counteroffensive was successful to the extent that even the historians, humanists, and court advisors interested in circumscribing ecclesiastical power eventually found it necessary to employ the key terms and arguments of the Holy Office's most zealous apologists.[22] The Council of Madrid's conclusions did not simply lay the groundwork for the definitive expulsion-or-conversion edicts of late 1525 and early 1526. They also signaled that learned debate about New Christian social and political integration was to take place on ecclesiastical terrain. To consider the limits of Christian empire required addressing the intricacies of sacramental theology. It also required learning to dissimulate like an inquisitor.

TO CATCH A HERETIC

The tension between the respective jurisdictions of civil and canon law to define and regulate heresy was not new in the sixteenth century. According to the thirteenth-century legal code the *Siete partidas*, heresy was a type of "insanity" identifiable both by an effort to undermine the word of God and by the desire to remain detached from the Christian community. By the time the workshop of Alfonso X "the wise" began to compose the *Siete partidas* in the mid-1250s, the Crown perceived heresy as a danger to social and political order as well as a challenge to Church authority. Spiritual separation from this community of Christians was undoubtedly a liability for the soul, but the organization of the *Siete partidas* presented this separation as a threat to the *res publica* as well. The title addressing heresy appeared, for example, in the *Siete partidas*' seventh and final section, which outlined the laws for trials and punishments related to prosaic illicit activity ranging from stealing in the marketplace to adultery, in addition to treating issues related to Jews and Muslims under Christian rule. Alfonso X and his team of jurists, scribes, and advisors characterized heresy as a class of civil disobedience even while acknowledging the authority of clerics to police and prosecute it as an ecclesiastical offense.

In his 1555 edition and gloss of the *Siete partidas*, the jurist Gregorio López de Madera underscored that ecclesiastical rather than civil authorities had jurisdiction over questions of heresy. Although there were social and political consequences to defining heresy, and although secular judges carried out the punishments and *autos de fe* stipulated by their inquisitorial counterparts, López de Madera insisted that the Holy Office had jurisdiction over all questions related to heresy. The Alfonsine text itself stressed that heretics should be accused before representatives of the Church, a point that López de Madera reiterated by highlighting the chain of inquisitorial authority from the Holy See to local inquisitors.[23] Alfonso X and López de Madera both argued that civil law had to provide a clearly demarcated public space for religious authority to function.

It was within this ecclesiastical judicial space, clearly demarcated in theory though porous in practice, that Rome had long attempted to define heresy as a word and crime. In the late twelfth and early thirteenth century, Church authorities had become uneasy about Latin Christendom's diversity of local religion and tradition of itinerant preachers. At the conclusion of the Albigensian Crusade in 1229, nearly fifteen years after the Fourth Lateran Council of 1215, the same Pope Gregory IX mentioned above began to commission papal legates to investigate the Cathar and Waldensian heresies, which previous *inquisitiones* by local bishops had not been able to eradicate. By the early fourteenth century, inquisition had become a method of targeting factions of the clerical elite. And beginning in the late fifteenth century, newly established Iberian inquisitions, authorized by Pope Sixtus VI but largely controlled by the *reyes católicos*, pursued false converts to Christianity from Judaism. Over the course of the sixteenth century, clerical inquiry into heresy on the Iberian Peninsula focused on a range of minority religious groups and heterodox communities, including not only converts to Christianity from Judaism and Islam, but also Protestants and *alumbrados*. Although civil authorities technically performed the executions of condemned and unrepentant heretics in *autos de fe*, ecclesiastical officials oversaw the entire legal process of identifying suspects, collecting evidence, and judging offenders. All accused parties were subject to clerical inquiry by virtue of their Christianity and the ecclesiastical nature of their alleged crimes. Whatever their theological errors, Muslims and Jews fell beyond the jurisdiction of the Church. Petty thieves of any faith faced local, civil judges rather than inquisitors.[24] The clarity of this jurisdictional schema, however, belied the practical challenge of defining who counted as a Christian and what the crime of heresy encompassed.

Addressing regional variation in religious practice and belief under the category *haeresis* facilitated identifying and prosecuting it as an offense. Yet by confusing such disparate voices, the Church hierarchy and political authorities made heretics of the late medieval and early modern periods seem more cohesive and menacing than they otherwise may have been. In a sense, Rome created heresy in order to defend more actively its monopoly on religious experience, and shifting techniques for reading the signs of heresy produced different kinds of heretics over time. Early modern inquisitors, such as the Dominicans Tomás de Torquemada and Diego Deza, drew extensively on the advice of their late medieval predecessors, who had systematized inquisition as holy method over the course of several centuries. *Practica inquisitionis hereticae pravitatis,* a thirteenth-century guidebook written by the Dominican inquisitor of Toulouse, Bernard Gui, along with *Directorivm inqvisitorvm,* a late fourteenth-century manual composed by the Dominican inquisitor of the Crown of Aragon, Nicolas Eimeric, were key models for formulating both the practice and the theory of inquisition in the late fifteenth and early sixteenth centuries.[25] Peninsular custodians of the Church employed these texts to read the rituals of the orthodox and heterodox alike. "It is evidently of interest to inquisitors," Eimeric wrote in *Directorivm inqvisitorvm,* first printed in Barcelona in 1503 and then republished and glossed by the canon lawyer Francisco Peña in multiple sixteenth-century editions, "to know who are the followers of the heretics and their sects, what is their life, their customs, and their rites and outward signs."[26] This is an obvious enough point, one that Eimeric went on to elaborate with an extensive taxonomy of stable, exterior markers of heresy. Eimeric's confidence in his ability to categorize heresy presupposed precisely the sort of literal reading of ritual that the Council of Madrid, teeming with representatives of the Holy Office, had celebrated. Eimeric cast the visible signs of heresy as legible to the trained inquisitor just as Cisneros and Guevara cast the mass Muslim baptisms as legible to the attentive evangelizer. These parallel claims to legibility are important because, as the anthropologist Deborah Root and others have argued, over time they produced an expanded conception of ritual in early modern Spain.[27] This sacralization of everyday life was an audacious effort to broaden the reach of inquisitorial power, even as the Crown continued to negotiate limits on the actual implementation of such expanded jurisdiction.

Royal and ecclesiastical officials recognized that this literal approach to reading the signs of heresy was a convenient legal fiction. Early modern inquisitors in particular acknowledged that the audible words and visible deeds of an accused party might not accurately reflect private orthodoxy or heresy in all cases. Gui and Eimeric knew that wily heretics might employ "guile" (*dolus*) and "ruses" (*cautelae*) when responding to an inquisitor's interrogation.[28] Torquemada and subsequent compilers of instructions for inquisitors understood that those "simulated and feigned" converts from Islam and Judaism presented even the most discerning of interrogators with a serious challenge.[29] Although Augustine had depicted this sort of hidden heresy as immaterial to the strictly legal question of ritual's efficacy, private heresy existed nonetheless. In other words, Augustine argued that while the moment of baptism itself established the Church's jurisdiction over the new convert, the forced repetition of the sacraments, combined with ecclesiastical vigilance, over time produced orthodoxy. Even Paul, as Augustine mentioned and others later approvingly cited, was first compelled to conversion on the road to Damascus and only subsequently taught by Christ. Augustine's rhetorical gambit in his writing about forced baptism was to use not only Jesus's parable of the banquet from Luke, but also the epistles and personal history of Paul, famous for his Christian universalism, to theorize a model of religious obligation that Paul himself, as recent commentators have pointed out, spent much of his lifetime criticizing.[30] In this view, faith was a product rather than a precondition of practice. Designed to identify and correct heresy in the present, inquisition was a necessary complement to Augustine's more sluggish behaviorism.[31]

In the most troublesome cases of hidden heresy, expert inquisitors advised lying in order to catch the heretic in his own mendacity. Among other sources examined below, Pope Gregory the Great's sixth-century distinction between the observable shell of language, misinterpreted by sinners, and the private kernel of the good Christian's holy intention, accurately recognized by God, provided the model for this sort of benign deception: "The ears of men [*humanae aures*] judge our words as they sound outwardly," wrote Gregory in his commentary on Job, the *Moralia*, "but the divine judgment hears them as they are uttered from within."[32] Gregory's opinion was widely known in subsequent centuries, not least because it was included in the collection of canon law called the *Corpus juris canonici*. Though Gregory was concerned specifically with divine judgment in the Job story, the twelfth-century Bolognese canon lawyer named Gratian, whose collection and commentary compose much of the *Corpus juris canonici*, presented Gregory's *humanae aures* phrase as a portable aphorism, not unlike Jesus's parable of the banquet. And he placed it in an extended discussion of perjury and ecclesiastical procedure. For early modern canon lawyers, as a result, dissimulation stood at the intersection of human judicial method and divine redemption. In manipulating the gap between signs and referents, the heretic sought to escape human punishment through subterfuge, while the inquisitor's divinely sanctioned deception served to exact divine punishment. No less than pious coercion, orthodox dissimulation was a weapon for fighting heterodox dissimulation. Sincere deception impeded New Christian insincerity and buttressed institutionalized ritual. From this perspective, coercion and dissimulation complemented each other.

While properly reading the signs of heresy demanded a stable taxonomy of heretical practices, effective lying required an awareness of changes in religious, cultural, and scholarly practices over time. Like modern specialists on the lookout for shifting forms of expression and categories of analysis, attentive inquisitors knew to historicize. In response to those who suggested that it was possible to identify crypto-Jews and Muslims solely by their eating practices, for example, Francisco Peña warned readers of Eimeric's *Directorivm inqvisitorvm* against oversimplification. Since not all stomachs bear any food or drink, Peña conceded in his gloss, dietary habits are not "conclusive evidence of heresy or apostasy."[33] Yet Peña also insisted that it would be "implausible" (*non videtur verisimile*) if the descendants of a converted Jew or Muslim continued to abstain from certain foods for reasons of health and taste. Why would they abstain, Peña reasonably asked, if not out of "respect and reverence" for the "wicked religions" of their progenitors?[34] Because variation in taste was universal, a lack of variation across several generations of converts provided evidence of heresy. Peña frankly noted that Eimeric's elaborate taxonomy of heresy sometimes failed, not because it was insufficiently exhaustive, but because it was methodologically inadequate. Like dissimulating, reading heresy required historical as well as legal and theological knowledge. In an example of what we might anachronistically dub inquisitorial interdisciplinarity, Peña's insight into the importance of history was itself historical. It was a product of several decades of experience with *conversos* and Moriscos whose religious and cultural practices were polyvalent. The Council of Madrid's insistence upon the efficacy of the forced baptisms produced all manner of reluctant or duplicitous New Christians, and inquisitors like Peña found it increasingly necessary to answer such duplicity not only with apologies for and applications of coercion, but also with their own brand of mendacity.

To demarcate Christianity through sacramental efficacy and inquisitorial torture while at the same time insisting upon the pastoral centrality of dissimulation may in hindsight seem like the height of cynical contradiction. When were the visible acts of faith what they seemed to be? How was it possible to distinguish between pious and impious deception? Who was to decide when to read bodies and texts naively and when to read them critically? Because disagreement about dissimulation and the conventions of interpretation had in the Christian context always been entangled with uncertainty about the efficacy of ritual, patristic sources figured prominently in early modern peninsular justifications for duplicity. Most important among these sources was a series of letters and commentaries on Paul's Galatians in which Augustine and Jerome debated both the legitimacy of dissimulation and the place of Jewish ritual practice in the emergent Christian community. This correspondence, to which, as we will see in chapter 6, participants in debates over the Morisco question returned again and again, focused on the famous "incident at Antioch," where the apostle Peter allegedly committed a grave evangelical error. Consider the episode: When Peter first arrived at Antioch, Paul tells us, he happily ate with the local gentiles, who did not follow the strict Jewish dietary laws. But later in his visit, when joined by a group of men who were circumcised and did follow these dietary laws—Jewish Christians, so to speak—Peter withdrew from the gentiles to eat with the newcomers. Paul eventually reached Antioch and became upset when he saw Peter eating apart from the gentiles. "If you, being a Jew, live in the manner of gentiles and not as the Jews," asked Paul in Galatians 2:14, "why do you compel [*cogis*] gentiles to live as Jews?"[35] Paul thought that the gentiles would interpret Peter's sudden decision to follow the Jewish dietary laws as a criticism of their rejection of those laws. Worried that the gentiles would as a result feel compelled to eat like the Jews in order to attain Christian grace, Paul publicly scolded Peter for his apparently hypocritical decision to dine with the gentiles only when no one observing the Jewish dietary laws was present. Paul's point was that by eating with the circumcised men rather than the gentiles, Peter had mistakenly given the impression that it was necessary for Christians to continue following the Jewish dietary laws in order to achieve salvation.

Despite his stern correction of Peter, Paul's understanding of Jewish ritual was in fact quite flexible. In Antioch, he drew a line between Jews and Christians by arguing that strict observance of Jewish law was not a condition of salvation in Christ, but elsewhere he had strived to make Jews feel welcome in the new sect by suggesting that Jewish ritual did not prevent salvation either. Augustine and Jerome understood both Peter and Paul to believe that Jewish ritual was ineffective, but Jerome alone wondered if Peter's observance of Jewish ritual in Antioch was a hidden strategy, some form of dissimulation, rather than a momentary pastoral lapse. While Augustine agreed with Paul that Peter had made a mistake at Antioch, Jerome denied that Peter, the father of the Church, could have erred so gravely. If Peter did not eat with the circumcised group out of confusion or hypocrisy, as Paul and Augustine maintained, he must have had some pedagogical or theological motive. The error of practice, Jerome speculated, must have been a performance meant to give fellow evangelizers, such as Paul, a public opportunity to educate potential converts from Judaism. According to Jerome, Peter's dissimulated observance of Jewish ritual presented Paul with the occasion to distinguish between the mistaken Jewish insistence upon the old law's ritual efficacy and the Christian allegorical conception of that law's force, which along with the Gospels suggested salvation by grace rather than acts. Neither Peter's observance of Jewish ritual nor Paul's account of the episode at Antioch was transparent.

This speculation about Peter's motives produced a crisis of exegesis as well as ritual. Jerome tried to explain the episode through parable and pedagogy, but Augustine thought that to defend such an overly wrought, figurative explanation was to accuse both Peter and Paul of mendacity. "I think it extremely dangerous," Augustine objected in a letter to Jerome, "to admit that anything in the sacred books should be a lie."[36] In his treatise on lying, *De mendacio*, Augustine had acknowledged that certain kinds of falsehood could, in limited circumstances, serve higher ends, but he refused to accept that scripture itself contained any untruth whatsoever. Such a concession, Augustine maintained, undermined all Christian epistemological certainty and institutional order. "If we once admit in that supreme authority even one polite lie," explained Augustine, "there will be nothing left of those books, because, whenever anyone finds something difficult to practice or hard to believe, he will follow this most dangerous precedent and explain it as the idea or practice of a lying author."[37] Holding the literalist line against Jerome was, for Augustine, a defense of both the integrity of scripture and the efficacy of Christian beliefs and practices. For Jerome, a figurative reading of Galatians paralleled Peter and Paul's dissimulation, which was a necessary feature of teaching and reading. By refusing to admit that Peter or Paul were dissemblers, in contrast, Augustine equated Jerome's figurative reading with a kind of scholarly deception. He insisted that the dual certainty of Jewish ritual's inefficacy and Paul's honesty demanded scriptural literalism.

Endorsing Jerome's defense of dissimulation and Augustine's apology for coercion, no less an early modern peninsular character than Antonio de Guevara fretted over the challenges posed by the new Morisco community. "I find so many things in need of correction among the New Christians," wrote Guevara in a letter from the 1520s, "that I consider it best to correct them in secret rather than to punish them in public."[38] As he traveled from Valencia to Granada in order to continue his pastoral work with converts from Islam, Guevara worried that to draw too much attention to New Christian apostasy was to risk scandalizing the simple folk and emboldening the sinful. It was professionally advantageous if legally dubious to convert by force, but to correct too aggressively the apostasy of the resulting New Christians was hazardous as well. Better, he thought, to be discreet. In hindsight, Guevara considered the previous decades' coerced baptisms "necessary, though maddening," but he came to perceive a new pastoral landscape in which it was "sometimes better to dissimulate than to castigate."[39] Reconfirming the transparent legibility and efficacy of the sacraments at the Council of Madrid, Guevara nevertheless also insisted upon the pastoral power of opacity. More than simply embracing the clash of holy and heretical deception, he understood that coercion had created the necessity for a gentler sort of dissimulation than the inquisitors tended to brandish. Even so, like many of his early sixteenth-century contemporaries, Guevara contributed to the Morisco debates as an apologist for both the coercive potential of ritual efficacy and the strategic importance of pastoral duplicity.

A facade of tolerance, to take Guevara's particularly charged example, should obscure a warranted but concealed coercion. In order to protect the Christian community, Guevara argued that the Crown and the Church might justifiably turn a blind eye to heterodoxy in the short term while seeking to cultivate orthodox practices in the long term. In this view, dissimulation was essential for shaping the social and institutional framework of Christian subjectivity. It was potentially dangerous to harbor scruples about employing dishonesty in both scholarly and pastoral circumstances, for there was a hardening perception that with each passing day false converts from Islam, armed with their own strategies of dissimulation, threatened to undercut the very legibility of Christian orthodoxy. Insistence upon the efficacy of the sacraments and transparency of Christian practice was an attempt to short-circuit the unsettling power of New Christian deceit. So too was the effort to theorize an alternative paradigm of orthodox dissimulation.

The historians John Bossy and Adriano Prosperi have argued that early modern theologies of discipline and dissimulation emerged from patristic debates as well as Rome's increasing emphasis on confession over the course of the late medieval period.[40] Formalized during the fourteenth and fifteenth centuries, penitent practices of devout self-consciousness provided a new foundation and justification for dissimulation while echoing a still influential disciplinary behaviorism. This was the behaviorism buttressing the ritual efficacy theorized by Augustine in the fifth century, promoted by Pope Innocent III in the thirteenth century, and reconfirmed by the Council of Trent in the sixteenth century. The Jesuit program of spiritual exercise, among other features of post-Tridentine religion, grew in part out of a renewed focus on the sacrament of penance, which provided individuals with incentive to police their interior lives, a process that required both discipline and dissimulation. But the mandate to pilot the winding tributaries of piety and impiety produced a need for navigational expertise. "Directors of conscience" helped kings and queens to reach their reservoirs of personal discipline, while the University of Salamanca professor of canon law Martín de Azpilcueta and his fellow casuists, those crafty practitioners of case-based moral reasoning, put pressure on the very idea of conscience.[41] Like inquisitors, confessors and casuists employed dissimulation to make sin detectable.

My argument thus far in this chapter has been that by offering tactics for teaching and deceiving alike, reedited inquisitorial manuals, patristic letters, and glosses on the *Corpus juris canonici* guided early modern experts in fostering disciplined action in both the sacramental and everyday contexts. The insistence that religious ritual, cultural practices, and daily comportment established the necessary conditions for Morisco belief produced a corpus of texts about how to celebrate the sacraments and regulate personal and social life. Debates about early modern peninsular conversion to Christianity from Judaism and Islam are thus an important if often overlooked piece of early modern Europe's broader intellectual and religious history. As we will see in chapters 5 and 6, by the beginning of the seventeenth century, post-Tridentine reformers and Morisco writers had crafted an ethics of charity from Manrique's professional aggrandizement and Cisneros and Guevara's pastoral calculus. For now, the important point is simply that through much of the sixteenth century, those charged with defining and regulating New Christian orthodoxy painted sincerity of faith as a fabrication and sought both to monopolize and to manipulate its means of production. Standing in the way of such a monopoly, however, were the Moriscos' own disciplinary practices and strategies of dissimulation.

MORISCO ACTS

"They baptized them by the herd in churches, throwing water on them with the baptismal cups," recounted the Morisco Jesuit Ignacio de Las Casas in his *Información acerca de los moriscos de España,* a collection of essays about the Moriscos addressed in 1605 to Pope Clement VIII. "And they so well understood what they received that many hid under the benches or covered themselves however they could, so that the water of holy baptism would not touch them."[42] Avoid the holy water, and avert conversion. In Las Casas's retrospective portrayal, the Muslims baptized by Cisneros and Guevara acknowledged the efficacy of ritual, even *Christian* ritual. No heretical crypto-Muslim, confident that his pious intention, or *nīyya,* as the Islamic jurists called it, would protect him, would hide from the baptismal water under the nearest church pew. He presumably would instead pretend to participate in the spectacle of Christian practice while guarding his purity of faith. He would, in a word, dissimulate. Over the course of the sixteenth century, many members of the Morisco community did manage to maintain a discreet connection to the religion of their Muslim predecessors through *taqīyya,* or dissimulation.[43] They developed strategies to take part in the life of the Church while at the same time passing down Islamic prophetic traditions and ritual practices to their children. They produced compendia of devotional and legal texts, which they hid in secret compartments in their houses' walls and floors, to be unearthed by renovators of the future. Learned Morisco jurists even managed to travel between Granada and Valencia, bearing copies of these *aljamiado* texts, or Spanish language works composed in Arabic script. In these and other ways, the Moriscos learned to keep flexible the relationship between the visible signs of their Christian experience and the private referents of their Islamic faith. Given this history of dissimulation and apostasy, Las Casas recognized that his audience found his account of the previous century's mass conversions difficult to believe. "I am not exaggerating," Las Casas nevertheless insisted, "since many firsthand witnesses, people who experienced the baptisms themselves, have confirmed this account, saying it to have been true."[44]

Having grown up speaking colloquial Arabic and been educated with other Morisco boys in the Casa de la Doctrina, a short-lived Jesuit school for the New Christians of Granada, Las Casas knew that the baptisms of his parents' generation were inadequate. The neophytes had converted without understanding either Islam's errors or Christianity's truth. Yet Las Casas echoed the Council of Madrid by arguing that hiding beneath the pews did not qualify as absolute resistance. Unlike many of his predecessors, however, Las Casas claimed that the converts hid from the holy water not because they were apostates in the making, but because they recognized the judicial authority, if not also the theological and cosmological power, of the holy sacraments. In Las Casas's view, baptizers and baptized both accepted the doctrine of ritual efficacy. At least in the moment, they acted as if contact with the baptismal water defined Christian identity, regardless of the various participants' contradictory or heretical intentions. For opponents of Morisco expulsion like Las Casas, the construction of a Christian community was contingent upon this mutually reinforcing obligation, initiated with the holy water of baptism. The flouting of these obligations for nearly a century did not render the baptisms invalid or unsuccessful. On the contrary, failure to fulfill the duties born of baptism required the discipline and reform of both New and Old Christians, a process that presupposed a shared conception of ritual efficacy.

Las Casas's darkly comic account of the peninsula's last *mudéjares* was a volley in polemical early seventeenth-century debates concerning Morisco history and expulsion, yet it was also an argument about the juridical origins of the Morisco period. By depicting the physical reactions to these baptism ceremonies, Las Casas acknowledged the Muslims' reluctance to convert while also undercutting the accusation that the ceremonies had inaugurated more than a century of religious duplicity. He aimed to replace the image of Moriscos and their inquisitorial adversaries locked in a battle of competing dissimulation with a subtler picture of the relationship between Morisco faith and Christian practice. Though they had subsequently wielded their *taqīyya* to powerful effect, in Las Casas's view, the converts nevertheless recognized the power of public ceremony and shared discipline to shape even the most private of religious identities. To study *taqīyya* only as a form of political defiance is to miss the religious history cleverly charted by Las Casas.

The Oran *fatwā*, a nonbinding legal opinion in defense of *taqīyya*, written sometime in the sixteenth century by an anonymous mufti of the North African city of Oran as a response to questions submitted by Iberian Moriscos, has come to be an emblem of this religious history. Specialists know this *fatwā*, which circulated in *aljamiado* manuscript versions, as the exemplary justification for Morisco dissimulation, but in fact it also outlined a program of ritual actions adapted to the peninsular situation. Even in the difficult circumstances faced by the Moriscos, private piety was not, according to the *fatwā*'s author, sufficient for complying with Islamic law.

The mufti argued, for instance, that it was impermissible to forgo the *ṣalāt*, or multiple daily prayers. It was, however, acceptable to comply with the prayer directive, "even if only by making some slight movement" (*aunque la hagays açeñando*).[45] It was necessary, he continued in a similar vein, to perform the required ritual ablutions, "even if only by plunging into the sea or river" (*haunque sea bañaros en la mar o en-el río*). Developing the important relationship between prayer and purity, the mufti argued that when pious Moriscos attempted at night to recoup *ṣalāt* missed during the day, it was still necessary to fulfill the ritual ablutions "even if it is just by rubbing your hands clean on the wall" (*aunque no podays sino con mashar con vuesas manos en las paredes*). In this last case, the mufti repurposed the term *tayammum*, which in Islamic jurisprudence refers to symbolic cleansing either when no water is available or when an individual cannot wash for health reasons. According to the mufti, religious persecution made "washing" without water permissible. Unorthodox night prayer justified a wider legal usage of *tayammum*, and this broader definition in turn sanctioned the Moriscos' nonstandard prayer schedule. Although the mufti did argue that devout intention was sometimes sufficient for fulfilling the obligations of a Muslim living under Christian rule, he at the same time maintained that even in difficult conditions like those faced by the Moriscos, there was often some way to render piety visible through action. The Oran *fatwā*, the preeminent extant elucidation of crypto-Islam, presented a case for ritual efficacy even while elaborating a theory of dissimulation. However heterodox the actual practices of Iberian Moriscos may have been in the wider Islamic world, this anonymous mufti of Oran defended their efficacy. As Las Casas underscored, effective ritual was as central to the Moriscos' vision of Islam as it was to peninsular canon lawyers' vision of Christianity.

With Morisco autonomy under threat in the mid-sixteenth century, moreover, the Moriscos began to disavow dissimulation. They claimed instead that because their participation in Christian ritual defined their religious identities, the Crown should allow them some degree of flexibility in the realm of cultural practices. Orthodox discipline became a scalpel for carving out a secular sphere. This decisive shift in approach came on New Year's Day of 1567, when the Chancellery of Granada, a local civic body, sought to publicize and enforce the *nueva pragmática*, or new law, approved the previous year by an assembly in Madrid.[46] This group of canon lawyers and court advisors had gathered to reassess the royal policy toward the Moriscos that had first been formalized at the Council of Madrid in 1525. The resulting regulations prohibited Moriscos from using their native Arabic, wearing their traditional clothing, bathing in public bathhouses, keeping their Moorish surnames, and engaging in a number of other daily practices that distinguished them from their Old Christian neighbors. These restrictions echoed the policy suggestions of several previous committees, including not only the Council of Madrid, but also a regional synod organized in 1554 by Bishop of Guadix Martín Pérez de Ayala and a provincial council headed by Bishop of Granada Pedro Guerrero in 1565. As I have already noted, although through much of the sixteenth century Crown and Church alike considered Morisco culture as Christian heresy, enforcement of the *nueva pragmática* in 1567 marked the first official application of this theory in practice. The period of dispensation threatened to expire. When the Granadan Morisco negotiator Francisco Núñez Muley went to argue his community's case for reversing or delaying the *nueva pragmática* before Don Pedro de Deza, a judge and auditor for the inquisition then serving as president of the Chancellery of Granada, he presented Morisco dissimulation as a product of faulty civic and ecclesiastical policy. Seeking to counter the trend toward persecution through sacralization, Núñez Muley implied that the Granadan Chancellery should protect its shrinking civic sphere of authority from further ecclesiastical encroachment. He argued for a clearly circumscribed notion of ritual efficacy in order to guard against the accusation of apostasy.

In his treatise, Núñez Muley aimed to transform Old Christian anxiety about Morisco identity into a meditation on the distinction between religion and culture. Drawing on his personal experience of those first years after the capture of Granada by the *reyes católicos*, he insisted that the subsequent regulation of Morisco daily life had produced heresy where there had previously existed only local Christian diversity. Among his extensive evidence, Núñez Muley offered an anecdote from his days working as a page for Hernando de Talavera: In 1502, Talavera journeyed into the Alpujarras Mountains to celebrate mass with his new Morisco flock. Núñez Muley vividly recalled in his petition how Talavera allowed the "zambra," a form of popular music prevalent among Andalusian Muslims, "in the choir with the clerics."[47] There were no organs up in the mountains, so Talavera improvised. A Morisco folk mass, musically speaking, was an apt metaphor as well as a compelling historical example for Núñez Muley's argument. We might sing in a certain way, he maintained, but since not all celebration is religious in nature, there is no contradiction between our songs and our Christianity. The reasoning extended to the language of Christian ritual as well: "During mass, some words were spoken in Arabic—in particular, when the holy priest said, 'Dominus Bobispon' [*sic*], the congregation responded,

'Ybara figun.' I remember this like it was yesterday."[48] As Vincent Barletta has suggested in his recent English translation of Núñez Muley's petition, the garbled rendition of the Arabic phrase "yabārak fīkūm," or "God be with you," stood in for "Et cum spiritu tuo," the conventional Latin response to the priest's liturgical call of "Dominus vobiscum."[49] While Talavera distinguished between religion and popular culture as part of a limited pastoral agenda, Núñez Muley presented his theological concerns in a broader political and cultural context. He described the Moriscos as sincere though imperfect Christians who should enjoy the same freedoms and protections as any other community of Christians. This charitable reading obscured the history of *taqīyya* for an Old Christian audience without directly attacking the Islam to which some members of his community undoubtedly continued to subscribe. Whatever his personal religious beliefs or political motivations, Núñez Muley was managing multiple allegiances. The argument that emerged from this balancing act was that a more narrowly defined religious sphere would preserve local Morisco autonomy and safeguard Christian orthodoxy.

If New Christian folk music and Arabic language once found a place in church, then surely, Núñez Muley contended throughout his petition, Morisco forms of dress, celebration, bathing, and expression should be equally unproblematic. He maintained that these cultural forms and everyday practices were not in any way "ceremony" (*çerimonya*), the word he employed to describe religious as opposed to cultural practices.[50] Rather, like variations in accents and rhythms of speech, they were geographically and culturally specific social markers. If Christians in Malta speak Arabic and dress like Turks, Núñez Muley reasoned, then New Christians in Granada should be able not only to celebrate with the *zambra*, but also to wear traditional clothing like the *almalafa* or to bathe in the shared *ḥammām*. Núñez Muley insisted that the royal and ecclesiastical pursuit of cultural uniformity in the name of religious orthodoxy was inconsistent. His petition to Deza was an attempt to unveil this inconsistency by distinguishing between variable, nonbinding cultural customs and religious obligations.

To convince his Old Christian interlocutors that hygiene, fashion, and language were cultural rather than religious in nature, Núñez Muley marshaled both Christian diversity and, more surprisingly, Islamic theology. As evidence, Núñez Muley offered another story about the *zambra*: A late fifteenth-century king of Granada, accompanied by musicians, dancers, and assorted revelers, was once heading from his city residence to the countryside for an afternoon of festivities. The impious but prudent monarch quieted his *zambra* musicians while passing through the Albaicín neighborhood, where many pious judges and jurists lived. Given this notorious account, Núñez Muley plausibly demanded, "How can one claim that the instruments and *zambras* are Islamic?"[51] Charting the boundaries of a peninsular civic sphere by invoking Islamic law, Núñez Muley argued that the *nueva pragmática* put the judges and bureaucrats responsible for the Moriscos in the same epistemological dilemma as the Moriscos themselves. It was impossible for inquisitors to prove that suspected heretics were engaging in particular practices as "çerimonya," just as it was impossible for Moriscos to prove that they were simply participating in local cultural life. Moreover, to negotiate the essence of Islamic ceremony was also to determine the boundaries of Christian ceremony. This was the question of jurisdiction that the Council of Madrid had addressed fifty years prior. Sanctifying and policing everyday life as holy practice may have produced legible conversions, but the cost of this legibility was steep: Were modes of daily washing to be as "effective" in the production of Christians as the sacraments themselves? The enforcement of the *nueva pragmática* in 1567 made the distinction between everyday life and religious ritual a question of degree rather than kind. As a result, the decrees forced Moriscos to theorize their own religious experiences before the law of the Church while at the same time turning inquisitors into amateur scholars of comparative religion. In Núñez Muley's view, such a division of definitional labor was cause for grave concern. He understood perfectly well that personal and institutional religious expertise did not meet on equal footing. An individual Morisco's explanation of the difference between his religious and his cultural practices stood no chance against the inquisitor's expanded jurisdiction.

Núñez Muley failed to convince Deza and the rest of the Granadan Chancellery of his community's position, and the *nueva pragmática* went into effect some months later. This was a crucial setback whose grave consequences are the subject of chapter 5. But the outlines of Núñez Muley's insistence upon the centrality of practice as a way to defend a distinction between the religious and the civic spheres informed the approach of Las Casas and other reformers writing in subsequent decades. It serves as a connective tissue linking debates about conversion, assimilation, and expulsion. Moreover and equally importantly, Núñez Muley's petition teaches modern scholars to look for discourses of the secular in seemingly improbable places like early modern Spain. For Núñez Muley and his successors, to demarcate and police the shifting boundaries of Christianity was to theorize a new and problematic civic space of cultural diversity, one that was possible to imagine only by reconsidering the history and meaning of the early sixteenth-century forced conversions. And in ways that are both surprising and illustrative, Moriscos themselves joined peninsular canon lawyers and inquisitors in employing the logic of ritual efficacy both to demarcate the boundaries of the religious sphere and to characterize what occurs within it.

GLOBAL FICTIONS OF CONVERSION

It should come as no surprise that conceptualizing peninsular Christianity's coercive inclusiveness in the sixteenth century entailed grappling with the contemporary history of New World evangelization as well as the origins of the Morisco period.[52] Though early modern scholars of all stripes admired the mendicant friars working on behalf of Christianity abroad, many nevertheless worried that this increasingly global evangelization had come at the cost of negligence at home. Anticipating the alarmist language and jingoistic sentiment of expulsion advocates such as Archbishop of Valencia Juan de Ribera, the anonymous author of the undated *Discurso antiguo en materia de moriscos*, for example, argued that those who departed for distant missions were irresponsible and rash. Like adventurers who abandoned their wives and children to houses full of "vipers and scorpions" in order to "hunt lions or ostriches in Africa," such men had allowed the Morisco problem to persist and intensify.[53] Evangelization abroad put at risk the existence of peninsular Christianity.

Abandonment of Old World responsibility to the Moriscos and their Old Christian neighbors was a common trope by the end of the sixteenth century, but opponents of expulsion, such as Ignacio de Las Casas and Pedro de Valencia, did more than join their intellectual adversaries in bemoaning the detrimental effects of distant evangelization. They also blamed the failure of Morisco assimilation upon the arrogance of missionaries who returned from the outlying territories of the Spanish empire with astonishing accounts of pastoral success. By narrating the conversions of the past and imagining the conversions of the future, these missionaries sought to control the narrative of early modern evangelization and imperialism and to celebrate their essential role in these accounts. Valencia wrested this triumphalist story from the traveling missionaries by including a short story of his own in his early seventeenth-century treatise against Morisco expulsion, *Tratado acerca de los moriscos de España*, the text with which I began this book. Quoting a refrain from Aesop's fables, Valencia challenged his countrymen to prove that Spain's global religious and political influence was more than the tall tale of a boastful people:

> An old refrain says: "Hic Rhodus, hic saltus." The story goes that someone was boasting with excessive flippancy about his jumping ability, and he said that he had achieved a jump of many lengths in Rhodes, a distance far greater than what was believable. Those present disputed, and he insisted on his story. An astute man got up and told him the words of the refrain: "There is no need to insist; pretend you're in Rhodes and complete another jump, and we will have to believe you." This can be said to us Spaniards: Let us complete the jump here that we achieve in China and Japan, and let us realize the miracles in our fatherland that we are said to realize in such strange and distant provinces.[54]

If conversion and assimilation abroad is easy, then why has it been so difficult on the peninsula? By looking back on the early sixteenth-century forced conversions and implying that reports like those penned by Cisneros and Guevara were inventions, Valencia marshaled the power of such dubious accounts to stimulate genuine evangelical action. He mocked the will to fiction narrated in this parable even as he employed it as a call to action. Let us repeat those miracles that "we are said to realize" (*que se cuentan que hacemos*), and let us address ourselves as we address the arrogant athlete, "pretending" (*hacer cuenta*) that Spain is Rhodes. These two uses of the verb *contar* highlight the concomitant power and danger of fiction, which may stimulate an audience to emulate exemplary models or obscure egotism. In Valencia's able hands, dissimulation eventually became a tool for compelling peninsular clergy to abide by their own duplicitous standard of miraculous achievement.

During the long period stretching from the first forced conversions celebrated by Cisneros to the 1609–14 expulsions opposed by Valencia, evangelization and conquest in the New World was more than a useful fiction in the Old World. It was also a topic of controversy and crisis. Debates in Madrid, Valladolid, and Salamanca as well as in Granada and Valencia tested the relationship among the various elite practices of interpretation that had long determined the legibility of Christian orthodoxy. As canon lawyers and theologians marshaled their methods of dialectical argument and defenses of ritual efficacy to resolve the issues raised by conversion, they also sought to expand the audience and scope of scholastic inquiry. Learned treatises on ritual and faith in a growing empire, consulted by solicitous monarchs and antagonistic classicists alike, reinvigorated a model of religious expertise that in other parts of Europe had begun to look outdated. But what, exactly, were the guardians of that expertise saying and writing about conversion in Granada and New Spain, and how did the intertwined debates about peninsular Jews and Muslims and New World indigenous peoples shape their opinions? Describing the *conquista* as an extension of the *reconquista* may have been an astute and persuasive strategy for a pioneering explorer like Christopher Columbus, who sought royal funding for a risky voyage, but how did the overlapping legitimacies of reconquest and conquest inform each other in Columbus's wake? For by the middle of the sixteenth century, to render legible the Muslim conversions of previous decades was to grapple with an increasingly global fiction of conversion. It was also to recognize that the tallest of conversion tales and the most cynical apologies for religious tolerance were to be found in the austere lecture halls of the scholastics. Inquisitorial and New Christian insights into the power of ritual served there not only to correct heretics, negotiate the frontier between religion and culture, or defend professional influence, but also to reimagine the ethical potential of coercion itself.

CHAPTER TWO

Glossing Faith

"The king can justly order the expulsion of the Saracens from our country if they pose a probable threat of subverting the faithful or overturning the homeland," argued the Dominican theologian and University of Salamanca professor Francisco de Vitoria in a mid-sixteenth-century lecture on Thomas Aquinas's *Summa theologica*. "He may legitimately do this because, even if he knows that it may cause them to be converted to the faith, they are not thereby forced [*nec per hoc compelluntur*] to convert."[1] The king's responsibility for administering his realm's secular affairs and protecting his Christian subjects from heterodoxy outweighed minority communities' rights to practice their religion and retain ownership, or *dominium*, over their peninsular possessions. Nevertheless, in Vitoria's view, conversion must not be the deliberate objective of burdensome taxes or expulsion threats. It should be instead the product of pastoral dedication and patience—"how it should be done," Vitoria stated.[2] At the very least, conversion must be the supplementary consequence of good governance. Vitoria's point here was twofold. On the one hand, he argued that the previous decades' Muslim conversions, both driven and reinforced by the expulsion-or-conversion decrees of 1502 (Castile), 1525 (Valencia), and 1526 (Aragon), were legitimate and binding. This opinion echoed the 1525 Council of Madrid and the seventh-century Council IV of Toledo, which Vitoria cited approvingly. On the other hand, Vitoria highlighted the manifest truth that no harmonious and orthodox Christian society had yet emerged from those baptisms celebrated by Francisco Jiménez de Cisneros in the late 1490s and early 1500s and by Antonio de Guevara in the 1520s.

Marshaling the contemporary failure of assimilation as evidence, Vitoria disputed the view of the late thirteenth-century Franciscan theologian Duns Scotus, who had defended the forced conversion of nonbelievers living under Christian rule so long as any negative consequences arising from such conversions were avoided. Because of the future's inscrutability, warned Vitoria in response, it was always dangerous to pressure nonbelieving subjects into baptism, even if such pressure were only indirect and thus technically licit. The recent peninsular conversions underscored Vitoria's concern about unforeseen consequences. Those conversions had angered Muslims throughout the Mediterranean, damaged Christianity's reputation, and generated all manner of New and Old Christian dissimulation. The consequences of coercion are "confirmed by experience; we see that Saracens never become Christians; no indeed," Vitoria claimed, before shifting from Latin into Spanish in order to mock the Moriscos. "They're just as Islamic now as before" (*Confirmatur, quia experientia videmus quod sarraceni nunquam sunt christiani, immo tan moros son agora como antes*).[3]

In this same section of commentary on matters of faith, Vitoria addressed another class of nonbelievers: those not living under Christian rule. Here his example was the indigenous communities of the Americas. In Vitoria's view, because the king of Spain had no more power over those people than any individual has over his neighbor, it was and remained illicit to compel them to accept Christianity. Once again, Vitoria was concerned about the consequences of coercion. He worried that to employ physical violence, destroy indigenous idols, and demand onerous tributes was to inspire indignation rather than stimulate New Christian faith. As was the case concerning peninsular Muslims, however, there were important exceptions to this prohibition on violence against nonbelievers. Vitoria argued, for instance, that if nonbelievers infringed upon the rights of their neighbors, either by limiting their ability to trade and preach or, more macabrely, by killing and eating them, as Vitoria knew some communities on "Terra Firma" to do, then it was valid to force those nonbelievers to follow natural law, even if it was technically illicit to compel conversion. Intervention was justified in such situations not simply because nonbelievers circumvented natural law itself, and even less because they were engaged in heretical practices. Intervention rather served to protect each commonwealth's freedom to control its own secular affairs. The clearest justification for compulsory conversion, argued Vitoria the theologian, was the safety, security, and prosperity of the state.

Throughout this discussion about the coercion of different classes of nonbelievers, Vitoria returned repeatedly to the recent history of peninsular

Muslims and Moriscos. This part of Vitoria's commentary on Aquinas's inquiry into "unbelief in general," located in the *Secunda secundae* section of the *Summa theologica*, was at its core a meditation on the intricacies of peninsular reconquest and evangelization. Occasional references to the New World served as points of comparison and contrast. This balance was reversed in Vitoria's later and more famous inquiry into imperial violence, a lecture entitled *De indiis*, or *On the American Indians*, which he presented in early 1539 to Salamanca students and faculty. In this lecture, the experience of peninsular Muslims was the counterexample that rendered New World conquest comprehensible, while Vitoria's inquiry into indigenous conversion abroad underscored the binding nature of Morisco conversions back home. Unlike his regular academic lectures, or *lectios*, which focused on either the *Summa theologica* or the more conventional scholastic pedagogical text *Sententiarum libri IV*, or *Sentences*, of the twelfth-century theologian and bishop of Paris Peter Lombard, *De indiis* was one of Vitoria's special relections, or *relectios*, on topical issues unsuited to his conventional courses. Over his twenty years as the senior professor of theology at the University of Salamanca, a position he assumed in September 1526 after teaching for three years in Valladolid's Colegio de San Gregorio, Vitoria presented twelve relections, eleven of which survive. Major university gatherings, these relections were opportunities both for the expansion and revision of points introduced over the course of the academic year and for the display of Thomism's flexibility and interpretive power. In the opening to *De indiis*, Vitoria underscored this point. He explained that his inquiry into the legal and epistemological status of the indigenous peoples of the Americas grew out of the above discussion of forcible conversion on the peninsula. And at several points in his analysis of the politics and ethics of New World violence, Vitoria invoked those "Saracens who live amongst Christians" and those "Saracens, Jews, or other unbelievers," none of whom, in Vitoria's sunny account, had ever been despoiled of their possessions simply for their unbelief.[4] That peninsular Islam became for Vitoria the paradigmatic example for a consideration of the sources and limits of imperial power in the Americas highlights a keen sense for his Salamanca audience's immediate frame of reference.

As I argue in the first half of this chapter, for Vitoria and his colleagues at the University of Salamanca, this debate about coercion, faith, and power in the New World was both a commentary on the peninsular conversion project and a conversation about the practices and presuppositions of theology itself. Reframing peninsular reconquest and New World conquest as issues of conscience rather than colonization, Salamanca theologians Domingo de

Soto, Melchor Cano, and others joined Vitoria in arguing that the Thomist discourse of natural law had a legitimate claim not only on scriptural exegesis, Church administration, and moral and natural philosophy, but on history and politics as well. This was in part an attack on jurists and humanists such as Juan Ginés de Sepúlveda, the foil to Vitoria's Dominican brother and New World evangelizer Bartolomé de Las Casas in the celebrated Valladolid debate of 1550–51. The extension of the Holy Office's jurisdiction in the early sixteenth century and subsequent cooption of inquisitorial law by court humanists and Morisco defenders alike were one way that dispute about New Christian conversion and assimilation drove peninsular religious reform in the early modern period. Dominican inquisitors, university professors, and evangelizers, however, took for granted that, in the hyperbolic words of the prologue to Vitoria's earliest surviving relection, *De potestate civilis*, or *On Civil Power*, "the office and calling of a theologian is so wide, that no argument or controversy on any subject can be considered foreign to his profession."[5] As a result, Vitoria's glosses on the boundaries of orthodoxy and Bartolomé de Las Casas's defense of religious discipline did not only concern the troublesome intersection of institutional jurisdiction and epistemological consistency, the principal concerns of those Dominicans who dominated the Holy Office. As I show in the second half of this chapter, Las Casas followed Vitoria in seeking to reimagine scholastic practices and social customs as the sturdy foundation for Christian faith, an intellectual project in which Mediterranean Muslims and New Christians both on the Iberian Peninsula and in the New World played exemplary roles. Despite criticisms subsequently leveled by the historian and evangelizer José de Acosta and examined in the chapter's concluding section, Vitoria and Las Casas successfully defended the dialectical method of Aquinas, who not coincidentally was also a fellow Dominican, even as they questioned the Crown's imperial policy. By insisting that scholastic methods of *lectio* and *relectio* should serve as a paradigm for the ritual efficacy of Christian ceremony in an increasingly global evangelical project, they made the case for glossing faith anew.

SCHOLASTIC PEDAGOGY AT THE EDGE OF ORTHODOXY

The first section of Peter Lombard's *Sententiarum libri IV*, or *Sentences*, the compilation of patristic interpretations and biblical citations upon which theology students from the late twelfth to early sixteenth century honed their interpretive skills, opens by establishing a distinction between things and signs. Citing the second book of *De doctrina christiana*, or *On Christian Doctrine*, Augustine's guide to hermeneutics, Lombard introduced this dichotomy between things and signs only then to follow his predecessor in further differentiation. Some signs, such as the sacraments, do not only signify, but also "hold something else," Lombard explained.[6] In his opinion, these sacramental signs were irreducible to their signifying role. Such initial *distinctiones*, a term that refers both to the scholastic method of argument and the particular division of Lombard's commentary into chapters, underscore the organization of the project as a whole. They serve as a kind of prose index. But even at the conclusion of the first book, Lombard continued to raise ever more precise conditions and distinctions in his vocabulary and argument. Certainly "there is some difference," Lombard frequently contended, between types of faith, levels of knowledge, and aspects of the sacraments.[7] Lombard was demonstrating that reading entailed the formulation of distinctions.

The neophytes to whom the *Sentences* were addressed must have wondered where these distinctions eventually led. What conclusion or content, what *sententia*, did this approach yield? The French historian Alain Boureau has claimed that medieval theology was a "machine for producing divisions."[8] Learning to participate in Lombard's reading machine marked students as theologians. In other words, division and subdivision was more than a method of critical engagement or doctrinal definition. It was also a pedagogical ritual. Unlike monastic reading practices, which emphasized meditation rather than argumentation, scholastic acts of critical distinction were performed in the classroom.[9] Students copied down dictations, converting the complex and carefully prepared glosses of their teachers into manuscripts for circulation and study. They then submitted their own *lectios* of Lombard's *Sentences* as part of their formation as intellectuals. I am not suggesting that theology students and their teachers in late medieval and early modern universities were unconcerned with the content of their arguments, but rather underscoring the extent to which argumentation in the form of glossing was a rite of passage, the beginning of a scholastic career.

In his own famous commentary on Lombard's *Sentences*, Aquinas explained that distinctions were a tool of necessity rather than choice. They were essential because of man's imperfect ability to perceive relationships among different categories of things and fields of knowledge. While God's science "remains one, not becoming many, while it considers diverse things," man's limited understanding is divided according to "genus and species" (*genere et specie*), and as a result, each field must be studied "distinctly and in diverse books" (*distinctim et in diversis libris*).[10] Aquinas understood the marking out of disciplinary differences as a flawed but indispensible way to approximate divine awareness of mutual contingency. His wager was that by revisiting well-trod theological texts, reassessing the analytical categories presumed by previous authors, and testing the boundaries separating theology, philosophy, rhetoric, and grammar, man might overcome his partial knowledge and approach God's universal understanding. If Lombard directed the ritual of distinction production toward conclusions, Aquinas aimed at ever more precise questions. Early modern critics of ecclesiastical elitism and profligacy, such as Erasmus and Luther, countered that by the mid-sixteenth century these scholastic methods of inquiry, as well as the institutions that supported them, had become academic in the pejorative sense of the term: inaccessible, dull, and irrelevant to the new religious reform movements taking hold north of the Pyrenees.[11] What Erasmus, Luther, and their intellectual heirs failed to see, however, was that their adversaries in the universities understood scholastic method as part of a "scalable" pedagogical method. In their view, scholastic rituals of glossing supported rather than hindered a broader religious renewal.

Following the models of his former teacher in Paris, the Flemish Dominican Peter Crockaert, and his like-minded Neapolitan elder, the theologian Thomas Cajetan, Vitoria began to integrate lectures on Aquinas's *Summa theologica* into his courses on Lombard as soon as he started teaching at the University of Salamanca. At first a contravention of university regulations, Vitoria's loosening of Lombard's monopoly on the syllabi of aspiring scholastics had become by the mid-1530s a part of the university's formal protocol. Melding Lombard's formulation of distinctions with Aquinas's more dialectical discourse of natural law, Vitoria drove the revival of peninsular Thomism in the age of Renaissance humanism and Christian reform. Like Aquinas before them, Vitoria and his colleagues and students at Salamanca were concerned, in the words of two modern specialists, "to take into account the interconnection of all areas of human knowledge and to contribute to a unified understanding of the world and its laws."[12] Establishing these lines of filiation among traditionally distinct fields of inquiry required, according to this Salamanca school of theologians, Aquinas's interrogative and dialectical approach. Such an approach was part of an attempt both to make the scholastic search for interconnection relevant to communities of intellectuals and political advisors outside of theology faculties and to mount a public case for Dominican expertise over and against the traditionally Franciscan tradition of Lombard commentary. This Thomist revival was a thoroughly educational affair. Because Vitoria himself taught several thousand lay and clerical students during his time at Salamanca, and, moreover, because his Dominican colleagues and successors on the peninsula's theology faculties followed his example by giving Aquinas a central place in their own classrooms, it is no exaggeration to say that Vitoria's pedagogical innovations and scholarly interests transformed the intellectual culture of the Iberian Peninsula.[13]

Because none of his *lectios* or *relectios* was printed during his lifetime, Vitoria's first audiences were all attendees at live events. Manuscript notes and transcriptions of these presentations, some of which Vitoria himself corrected, subsequently circulated within and beyond the university. Not surprisingly, there are discrepancies among these texts, and the twelve extant manuscript versions of Vitoria's gloss on Aquinas's *Secunda secundae* are no exception. Among other differences, for instance, the most complete text of these lectures, transcribed by the university student Francisco Trigo during the 1534–35 and 1536–37 academic years, does not contain the sarcastic aside and extended discussion about the Moriscos with which I opened this chapter.[14] Those passages are from a manuscript now held in Madrid's Biblioteca del Palacio Real, whose rubric refers to a course from 1542–43, when Vitoria covered similar material. But as the Spanish historian and editor Vicente Beltrán de Heredía has argued, because transcribers sometimes drew on multiple sources when compiling and revising their notes, it is impossible to date definitely particular *questios* within these compilations, irrespective of the apparently clear dates of the manuscripts and courses themselves. Vitoria's student transcribers filled in textual gaps born of tardiness or absence with notes from related lectures, not only from the early 1540s and mid-1530s, but also from the 1526–27 and 1528–29 academic years, when Vitoria inaugurated his professorship with lectures on the *Secunda secundae*.[15] Although Vitoria eventually came to dictate his pre-prepared classes, from year to year he nevertheless presented new riffs on old glosses, tailoring his lectures to the concerns of the moment. It is perfectly plausible, in other words, that Vitoria's extended discussion of peninsular Muslims and Moriscos dates to the 1520s, when debate about Muslim conversion in Valencia and Granada was particularly strident. Regardless of the exact date and historical context, however, it is clear from the manuscript record that Vitoria hewed a middle way between timely references to current events and reprises of familiar scholastic commentary. This balance between variation and repetition was a major element in Vitoria's case for the political relevance of scholastic inquiry.

This relationship between theology and contemporary politics and history was, according to Vitoria, the result of the shared conditions of theological knowledge and New Christian faith: both were the product of habit. Just as students climbed the rungs of the scholastic hierarchy by participating in the pedagogical rituals of the university lecture hall, ordinary Christians, New Christians, and, as we will see in moment, nonbelievers too ascended a parallel ladder of faith. Vitoria and his interlocutors were less concerned with demarcating a rigid hierarchy among different types of faith than with emphasizing the human capacity to move from one level of faith to another. Like Augustine, Vitoria recognized the power of practice to create faith and community. But unlike Augustine, who affirmed the necessity of violence in the disciplining of Christian apostates, Vitoria emphasized the importance of patience. In Vitoria's view, it was the very naturalness of this ability to learn and change that buttressed scholastic inquiry and pastoral imperialism. The university may have been a laboratory space for honing the physical and mental rituals that together produced professional expertise and learned faith, but the true measure of habit's potential was to be found out in the world.

Lombard, Aquinas, and others had made similar points about the relationship between faith, practice, and pedagogy. In book 3 of the *Sentences*, for example, Lombard investigated the faith of the ancients and uneducated, drawing in part on the story, recounted in Acts 10, of the Roman centurion Cornelius, whom Saint Peter assured salvation even before having confirmed his faith.[16] "There is some measure of faith," Lombard argued in this discussion, "without which salvation was never possible," even as he also affirmed that "faith made progress with the passage of time, just as knowledge did."[17] According to Lombard's teleology, faith changed over time. The necessary conditions for salvation were variable. Navigating contradictory source texts, Lombard attempted to address the tension between the unfolding of world history and Christian eschatology. He insisted both upon the necessity of distinctions among different kinds of faith and types of faithful individuals, and upon the human potential for development.

In his treatment of Lombard's taxonomy of faiths, Aquinas argued that while the Christian community as a whole should not strive merely for the "implicit" faith of the ancients or uneducated, such as Cornelius, neither should this community demand of all the "explicit" faith of the pious and knowledgeable.[18] Though he initially insisted upon the importance of faith even for natural knowledge and maintained that certain articles of faith must be believed explicitly, Aquinas eventually softened his argument by wondering whether "all are equally bound to have explicit faith."[19] Like Lombard, Aquinas concluded that faith and knowledge of revelation were dynamic and porous categories. Just as "divine revelation reaches those of lower degree through those who are over them, in a certain order," he maintained, "so too, men of higher degree, whose business it is to teach others, are under obligation to have fuller knowledge of matters of faith, and to believe them more explicitly."[20] Aquinas described a variable faith, one that knowledge and experience might transform. Even theologians, he implied, began their formation not on the podium or pulpit but as students sitting on benches in the lecture hall, when their knowledge and faith were less complete or "explicit." Employing personal and pedagogical language rather than Lombard's lofty historical rhetoric, Aquinas linked the question of faith to his own privileged role as a teacher. The distinction between implicit and explicit faith, along with the various shifting categories of faith between these two extremes, established a parallel between scholastic education and evangelical practice. An individual's climb up this hierarchy of faith paralleled Christianity's progress toward judgment day. For Aquinas, the catechism of recent converts and the formation of theologians were parables of Christian history. They were also models for quarantining anxiety about New Christian dissimulation: in his view, explicit faith was a result of practice.

Vitoria theorized the power of rituals both pedagogical and sacramental by examining the histories of peninsular Islam and New World nonbelief. He articulated the case for ritual efficacy through an explication of the different levels of faith found in diverse populations and locales. His basic question, again in his gloss on the *Secunda secundae*, was a radical one: Was faith even necessary for salvation? Taking a baptized infant as his first example, Vitoria asked whether this child, if he suffered an early death, would achieve grace despite the fact that he had not yet developed the faculty of reason. The question assumed the perspectives of Aristotle and Aquinas, who agreed that reason was a precondition for exercising agency, which in turn was necessary for individual faith. Vitoria argued that the faith necessary for salvation varied according to the identity of the individual, and so agency too was relative. This was why it made little sense to hold an infant to the same standard as an adult.

Though children and New World nonbelievers possessed reason naturally, an argument that Vitoria reprised in *De indiis*, it was unfair to assume that they could deduce the articles of Christian faith uninstructed. Even so, according to Vitoria, they may come to live ethically without knowing

Christ, which was sufficient cause for divine grace. In a crucial chapter entitled "Whether it is necessary to believe anything beyond natural reason in order to be saved," Vitoria examined what Dante scholars and other medievalists will recognize as the "virtuous pagan" question:

> He who has never heard about faith can be in God's grace, and grace is sufficient for salvation. But this man can have this without faith, which is to say without believing. Therefore faith and believing are not necessary for salvation, which has been previously demonstrated. This man may come to the use of reason, he who never had any kind of knowledge but through natural light; he resolves to live well [*bene vivere*]. He would now be in grace, because he does all that he can to be good and for good living; and nevertheless he does not have faith [*tamen non habet fidem*], which is to say he does not believe. The proof: He does not know anything about the articles of the faith. Neither is it possible for him to know. Therefore believing is not necessary for salvation [*non est necessarium ad salutem*].[21]

By highlighting a common capacity to "live well," Vitoria appeared to follow Aquinas and contradict Augustine in defending the innocence and educational aptitude of nonbelievers. The origins of this dispute over the possible salvation of righteous non-Christians dates to the early Christian period; Vitoria's concerns here, however, were decidedly contemporary. Unlike the Old World's Muslims and Jews, not to mention peninsular Moriscos and *conversos*, uninformed nonbelievers might, in this generous view of the New World's pastoral prospects, employ their natural rationality to ethical ends. The very potential of indigenous peoples in the Caribbean or New Spain underscored the limitations on peninsular New Christians, who were kept from the natural possibility of a moral life by centuries of accumulated heresy. This argument, as Vitoria's readers certainly recognized, was a step toward establishing the ontological status of the New World indigenous peoples as full humans, capable of rational thought, political governance, and material ownership, protected by established legal conventions, and potentially able to enjoy the eternal rewards of salvation. By way of contrast, however, it was also a subtle reprisal of his Morisco mockery, which hinged upon a frank acknowledgment of New Christian apostasy.

Yet the textual evidence for Vitoria's strong version of this argument about the varied capacities of different groups of nonbelievers to cultivate their explicit faith and knowledge from the seeds of implicitness is equivocal at best. In MS 49 of the Biblioteca Universitaria de Salamanca, for instance, the student copyist of this section of Vitoria's commentary on Aquinas does not even mention the fact, recorded above by the student Francisco Trigo in MS 43 of the same library, that nonbelievers can obtain salvation merely by ethical conduct and natural reason. Instead, the copyist records the opposite view: "It is an error," he has Vitoria argue, "to say that in order to attain glory faith is not necessary."[22] Upon closer examination, even the fair copy of Trigo's manuscript provides contradictory and unstable textual evidence, which the modern published volume, cited above, obscures. The phrase suggesting that an individual is able to attain salvation despite not being a faithful Christian—"et non habet fidem"—occurs twice in this short passage of the manuscript, though Trigo, Vitoria, or some other corrector crossed out the first instance.[23] The grammatical problem in the passage is one of emphasis. To keep the decisive phrase at the end of the sentence describing the conditions for salvation was to underscore the key point: This individual "does all that he can to be good and for good living," and "*nevertheless* he does not have faith, which is to say he does not believe" (*et tamen non habet fidem, id est non credit*) (emphasis mine).[24] In subsequent commentary, Vitoria reiterated this textual ambiguity by retreating in a more familiar way from the strong version of his argument about the relative, even superfluous nature of faith. That is, he introduced a further distinction. Nonbelievers who believe implicitly may achieve grace, he claimed, but eternal salvation remained beyond their grasp.[25] By establishing a new distinction between "sufficient grace" and "salvation," Vitoria undermined precisely the controversial argument toward which he had seemed to be building.

However frustrating, this material and theological indeterminacy reflects, in my view, one of Vitoria's most important lessons, which he fittingly sought to demonstrate rather than to explain: theology is method as well as wisdom. Vitoria knew perhaps better than any of his contemporaries that the process of formulating increasingly fine theological distinctions could never produce decisive conclusions. There always existed new material for further distinction. Though variable over the length of Christian time, the points of faith and rules for practice that the scholastics helped to determine for their contemporaries mattered, of course. But my point is that scholastic commentary was an artifact of scholarly ritual as well as a doctrinal authority. It was a ceremony of community formation and a form of pedagogical discipline. The consequence and meaning of Vitoria's glosses on New Christian faith cannot, in other words, be determined only by paleographic analysis or close reading, however important these approaches might be. Vitoria's decades-long exchange with his students and colleagues about the boundaries of orthodoxy and the legitimate uses of religious coercion was a method for reimagining and reforming what we might in retrospect call the discipline of theology. It was a living, breathing apology for what Aristotle described in the *Nicomachean Ethics* as "habituation" (*ethismos*), or the power of habit to shape moral action, and what Augustine, as we have already seen, somewhat more cynically articulated in his writings on the Donatists as "coercion," or the power of the Church to expand its membership and then regulate its adherents.[26]

In their successive *lectios*, Domingo de Soto, Melchor Cano, Diego de Covarrubias, and other Salamanca colleagues chose to respond to Vitoria's argument that explicit Christian faith is unnecessary for salvation, sometimes in order to counter it. De Soto, for instance, eased the force of Vitoria's claim by distinguishing between categories of faith and definitions of natural knowledge, thus limiting the scope of Vitoria's assertion. He agreed with his predecessor that some kind of faith was a precondition for salvation, but he equated such faith with that which he imagined an unbeliever might reasonably be able to deduce about the cosmos on his own: "knowing that God exists and that he is the judge."[27] Having established this single condition for salvation, De Soto then claimed that it was not possible to arrive at this natural knowledge of God except with supernatural help. Contradicting Vitoria, De Soto insisted upon a more rigid notion of necessity than his predecessor while defending a similarly flexible definition of faith. Cano instead retreated unequivocally from Vitoria's stance, underscoring the conventional Aristotelian position that in order to direct one's will toward something, it was first necessary to possess elevated knowledge of it. He also drew a further distinction, not pursued by Vitoria in this context but explicit in Aquinas's gloss, between unequal levels of natural knowledge. Even so, Cano's gloss on Vitoria was a defense of institutionalized reason rather than a return to an ideal personal faith; as he put it in a droll attack on the *alumbrados*, it was best not to "leave the North Star of reason to navigate in the sea of faith."[28]

By Cano's death in 1560, Vitoria's method for resolving doubts about New World authority may have "become something of an orthodoxy," as Anthony Pagden has suggested, but this evidently did not mean that the ongoing scholastic conversation thus came to a tranquil standstill, even within the University of Salamanca.[29] On the contrary, Vitoria's successors recognized that however desirable a loose scholarly consensus might have appeared, conclusiveness constituted a grave institutional danger, which is why they found ways to sharpen their teacher's points. They kept Vitoria's arguments relevant through disagreement and his method animated through the invention of further distinctions.

Vitoria and his Dominican colleagues are central to peninsular intellectual and cultural history because they sought to transform the disciplinary conditions of scholastic inquiry. I am arguing that they accomplished this through an investigation into the parallel between theological knowledge and New Christian faith. In examining this parallel, these scholars defended the view that their inquisitor brothers had recently endorsed: given the difficulties of identifying and regulating the faith of ordinary Christians, it was prudent and necessary to pay particular attention to the practices that shaped knowledge and faith in the first place. Perhaps more than any other scholar of the period, Vitoria recognized that debate about the legitimacy of the late fifteenth and early sixteenth century's mass conversions was an opportunity to reinvent the methods that defined university theologians as an intellectual community. The sacramental formalism that structured answers to the Morisco question may have justified violence across the Spanish empire, but it also provided the logic and impetus for a newly engaged and critical canon law. Clamorous early sixteenth-century disagreement over the disciplining of recent converts to Christianity was a foundation for the subsequent transformation of scholastic pedagogy and argument. Yet to reinvent their discipline by staking a moral claim to political authority, theology professors had to step beyond the university walls and address court advisors, evangelizers, and civil lawyers, each with their respective claim to political legitimacy. It was one thing to rearticulate the Thomist tradition for a community of like-minded scholars and students, but it was quite another thing to impose academic conventions and jargon upon the public discourse of the period. We tend to think of the famous Valladolid debate between Juan Ginés de Sepúlveda and Bartolomé de Las Casas as a learned disagreement about the nature of Spanish power and the ontological status of the indigenous peoples of the New World, but it was also another open front in the early modern conflict over interpretive method.

VALLADOLID: A CLASH OF CONVENTIONS

According to the late twelfth-century theologian Peter Cantor, developing the scholastic skill of *lectio* was only the first step in a three-part pedagogical process for "the exercise of sacred texts" (*exercitium sacrae Scripturae*), a phrase that epitomizes my claim that scholastic pedagogy was both a kind of effective ritual and a missionary template.[30] Cantor argued that *disputatio*, the public discussion of questions arising from difficult passages, and *praedicatio*, teaching by preaching, followed learning to read. This final stage of scholastic formation and critical engagement presented reading as a universal and worldly process. Commentary, in Cantor's view, should help readers to approach divine understanding of an interwoven world. But it must also produce more Christians. Vitoria understood his performance of scholastic *lectio* as a model for imperial *praedicatio*. But as Cantor's three-stage vision of theological inquiry underscores, wedged between interpretation and evangelization was the crucial and highly charged moment of public debate.

In the medieval university, disputation provided an opportunity to participate in the unfolding of knowledge, drive forward understanding through questions and responses, and reaffirm the credibility of the whole scholastic enterprise. But the public performance of dialectical method should not be confused with a spontaneous and dynamic search for truth through dialogue. The master theologian, who both determined in advance the topic under discussion and summarized the debate after the fact, chose the student responsible for posing questions, the *respondens*. Even in the more flexible "quodlibetal disputation," in which audience members posed questions about any topic, the master still presented a final rebuttal and summary the following day, as he did as well in ordinary disputations.[31] Both types of disputations provided students with a structured opportunity to hone their argumentative skills, but the process ultimately confirmed the authority of the master and displayed the advantages of dialectical method.

The Valladolid debate of 1550–51 resembled a scholastic *disputatio*, with Bartolomé de Las Casas casting Juan Ginés de Sepúlveda as his *respondens*.[32] Sepúlveda did not at first recognize the nature of the event in which he participated; his presentation before the audience of scholars at Valladolid suffered from a failing of form. According to Domingo de Soto's summary of the events, while Las Casas "read" (*leyó*) his own voluminous *Apologia*, written in response to manuscript versions of Sepúlveda's defense of war against the New World indigenous peoples, *Democrates alter sive de justis causis belli apud Indos*, also known as *Democrates secundus*, Sepúlveda informally "recounted the main points of his arguments" and "established his conclusion briefly." As a result, De Soto continued in his summary of the Valladolid conversations, it is impossible to grant Sepúlveda "equal reason" to Las Casas.[33] De Soto linked his dismissal of Sepúlveda's position to his ill-chosen style of presentation rather than to his invocation of Aristotelian social hierarchy or his appeals to Pope Alexander's VI's bull *Inter caetera* (1493), which granted the Crowns of Castile and Aragon political and religious authority in the New World, and Pope Paul III's bull *Sublimis Deus* (1537), which attempted to encourage peaceful methods of evangelization.[34]

Sepúlveda unwisely sought to wield his courtier's spontaneity for an audience of scholastics, whose style of presentation and method of argument were considerably different from those of his usual interlocutors. Las Casas the theologian, on the other hand, treated his Valladolid presentation as a scholastic *lectio* on the authority of the Spanish monarchy to wage war. Las Casas's fellow Dominican, confessor to Carlos V, and one of the judges who heard the arguments at Valladolid in August 1550, De Soto was evidently a biased observer. Yet his account reveals the extent to which scholastic conventions of knowledge and forms of legitimacy shaped the legacy of the Valladolid disputation.

In *Apologia pro libro de iustis belli causis*, a short defense of *Democrates secundus* that appeared Rome in 1550 as a response to the refusal by committees of theologians from the universities of Salamanca and Alcalá to recommend its publication, Sepúlveda began to display an awareness of the importance of arguing as a theologian. *Democrates secundus* was a humanist dialogue in which the range of Sepúlveda's rhetorical skill and literary Latin was, as the Salamancan members of the editorial committee condescendingly noted, on full display. In the front matter to his *Apologia*, in contrast, Sepúlveda claimed that this text would instead conform to the "scholastic method" (*more scholastico*).[35] The *Apologia* is organized in dialectical fashion, with responses to the objections raised by previous critics presented in clearly delineated order and buttressed with citations from biblical, patristic, and scholastic sources. Although the *Apologia* has often been catalogued as a juridical document, as a formal summary, a "resumen" or "refundición" of *Democrates secundus*, there is material evidence that Sepúlveda thought of the work as a *summa* on the question of just war. Here was his attempt at theological inquiry based on the model of the medieval *summae*. For example, one version of the *Apologia*, contained in a manuscript that was edited by Sepúlveda himself, carries the scholastic-sounding title "Summary of the Questions on War against the Barbarians," or *Summa quaestionis ad bellum barbaricum*.[36] This was a short version of the *Apologia*, and it did not include the introductory address to Antonio Ramírez, the bishop of Segovia and friend and critic of Sepúlveda, or a concluding section, both of which are present in other versions. These absent sections were written in an informal prose unlike the scholastic register of the text's body, which would explain why they are missing from this particular manuscript. The theologians, Sepúlveda acknowledged both argumentatively and formally, had misunderstood his claims in *Democrates secundus* because they brought the practice of scholastic *lectio* to bear upon a humanist text designed to persuade rather than perform. The *Apologia* was Sepúlveda's attempt to engage his scholastic critics in their own terms.[37]

While De Soto underscored Sepúlveda's formal miscalculations in his writing and Valladolid presentation, for Las Casas the problem was argumentative as well as structural and stylistic. In his opinion, Sepúlveda's failures of argument and form were interconnected. Sepúlveda selectively cited biblical examples without taking into account scholastic glosses on these episodes; his solutions to juridical and evangelical conundrums generated rather than limited violence; and most importantly, he misconstrued the categories of religious difference structuring Christian thought at least since the time of Augustine. Sepúlveda claimed, for instance, that Augustine himself condoned violent punishment of both heretics and pagans, among other nonbelievers.[38] As you will recall from my introduction and chapter 1, when writing about the Donatists Augustine does mount a defense of coercion as a way of obligating Christian behavior. Yet in his interpretation both here and in his longer *Apologia*, Las Casas insisted that Augustine also limited such coercion to apostates like the Donatists, who were technically baptized Christians and thus subject to Church authority.[39] When Augustine did mention a more general class of nonbelievers, Las Casas claimed that he did so to mount the circumscribed argument that it was licit for a Christian sovereign only to prohibit idolatry among his own subjects, and not, as Sepúlveda suggested, to wage war on foreign idolaters. Prohibiting idolatry at home was not the same as pursuing war abroad, all nonbelievers were not parallel, and political authority was clearly delineated. Las Casas implied that to the properly trained scholar, these distinctions were utterly conventional. In his attempt to produce a recognizably scholastic argument, Sepúlveda was, according to Las Casas, at best intellectually negligent—"frivolous and false" are his words—and at worst purposefully mendacious.[40]

Las Casas's reading of Augustine was an instrument for combating Sepúlveda's model of just war, but Las Casas's interpretation of Augustine was undeniably a generous one. As the Council of Madrid's conclusions concerning the mass Muslim conversions of the early sixteenth century suggest, Las Casas and his Dominican brothers at Salamanca, who shared his reading of Augustine, differed from those shapers of imperial and evangelical policy examined in chapter 1. Like Sepúlveda, the Dominicans who dominated the Holy Office tended to draw on the Augustinian tradition in order to widen the scope and intensify the implementation of New Christian discipline and public coercion. In contrast, the mid-sixteenth-century University of Salamanca Dominicans, as well as the next generation of Jesuit scholastics and post-Tridentine reformers who learned from them, employed the very same discourse of discipline in order to drive scholastic innovation and mollify the violence that accompanied New Christian assimilation. As De Soto's account of the Valladolid dispute so clearly reveals, in both cases to take a position on the role of coercion was to define and defend a particular mode of scholarly inquiry and institutional legitimacy.

Though Sepúlveda was too stylistically cavalier, it is important to note that his conclusion about the justice of imperial war in the Americas was well within the early modern bounds of reason. Esteemed jurists and theologians, including the president of the Council of the Indies Cardinal García de Loaysa, Friar Domingo Betanzos, and others, agreed with him.[41] Moreover, like Vitoria's, Sepúlveda's concern with conquest and conversion in the New World grew directly out of his writings about religious conflict in the Old World, a topic that he addressed at the request of Pope Leo X. The pope had asked Sepúlveda, a scholar and translator at the papal court, to write a rebuttal to a group of Iberian agitators, based at the aptly named royal college of San Clemente de los Españoles in Bologna. These men were increasingly critical even of defensive wars, despite the fact that the medieval tradition of just war theory had always deemed such wars legitimate.[42] As Sepúlveda explained in his prologue to the first part of *Democrates,* which took anxiety about Turkish expansion as its point of departure, this was how he came to focus his attention in the early 1530s on questions of just war, military discipline, and Christian rule. What Sepúlveda did not say here, however, was that he had already dealt with some of these issues as early as 1529, when he published the little-studied *Cohortio ad Carolum V,* an exhortation to arms against the Turks addressed to Carlos V. Suleiman the Magnificent had laid siege to Vienna that same year, and debate about the possibility and acceptability of Christian princes' waging war against the Turks was occupying Erasmus and Luther as well as Sepúlveda.[43] Just as Vitoria presented *De indiis* as a development and expansion of previous glosses on peninsular Islam, Sepúlveda, through the common title, dialogic structure, and overlapping themes and characters, attempted to integrate his *Democrates secundus,* composed in the mid-1540s, into previous debate about Christian power and religious difference in the Mediterranean. This contemporary anxiety about Turkish expansion explains why both Vitoria and Sepúlveda peppered their texts about the New World with references not only to peninsular Islam, but also to Constantinople. Like Vitoria, Sepúlveda staked his claim to scholarly and political legitimacy by presenting his writing about religion and conquest in the Atlantic as an expansion of his concern with Islam in the Mediterranean, and as with Vitoria, implicit in this approach was a pragmatic defense of the conventions and methods that defined his own textual community.

Though Sepúlveda's intermingling of Old and New World concerns was a familiar approach to examining the limits of orthodoxy and empire, the consequences of his formal miscalculation in the disputation at Valladolid were grave. De Soto's summary of the Valladolid debate reiterated Las Casas's criticism of Sepúlveda's interpretation of Augustine. In De Soto's view, Sepúlveda botched his attempt to engage in the scholastic conversation; his reading of Augustine was inadequate, his style brazen, and his arguments faulty. It was for these reasons that De Soto gave Sepúlveda short shrift in his summary of the Valladolid debate, even though the episode itself ended without a clear resolution.[44] Despite this lack of consensus, De Soto nevertheless helped to produce a sense—still prevalent among some specialists—that Las Casas and his Salamanca allies prevailed over Sepúlveda.[45] Not only was Sepúlveda unable to publish *Democrates secundus*, but soon after the conclusion of the Valladolid disputation, Las Casas himself published De Soto's summary of the Valladolid debate along with his own short reply to Sepúlveda's arguments. In practice, De Soto's summary functioned as part of Las Casas's critical apparatus. Sepúlveda's own voice and claims were reduced to the status of straw man. An impulse of institutional and professional self-preservation drove this mischaracterization.[46] The Salamanca theologians presented political authority and violence in scholastic terms, examining the legal and political questions concerning conversion and empire using a method to which Sepúlveda's texts and education did not conform. This defense of particular forms of argument and expression against humanists like Sepúlveda is central to understanding the way in which sixteenth-century scholastics envisioned Christianity itself.

That Vitoria is best known today as a father of international law rather than as a scholastic reformer or theorist of religious discipline is a testament to the success of De Soto, Cano, and several subsequent generations of Salamancan students and faculty in drawing Thomism into the early modern public sphere. But as the conservative early twentieth-century political theorist Carl Schmitt famously argued, it is also the upshot of liberal historians' quest to salvage Vitoria's more secular-friendly arguments from their scholastic modes and institutional contexts.[47] An analogous division between form and content structures contemporary knowledge about Las Casas, whose *Brevísima relación de la destrucción de las Indias,* a short account of New World violence, is much more commonly studied than either his extensive response to Sepúlveda in the *Apologia* or his 1537 Latin treatise on evangelization, *De unico vocationis modo omnium infidelium ad veram religionem,* which I examine in this chapter's next and final section. It makes little sense to celebrate Vitoria and Las Casas as the fathers of modern international law and anthropology, respectively, while at the same time attacking them for their Eurocentric presuppositions and unabashedly evangelical agendas.[48] Avoiding this selective triumphalism, this chapter offers a different approach, one that focuses both on the pedagogical practices of the Salamanca scholastics and on the content of their arguments. My claim, in short, is that the mid-sixteenth-century resurgence of scholasticism and the explosion of debate over the boundaries of Old and New Christianity were mutually contingent processes.

REGULATING RITUALS, PREACHING FAITH

Bartolomé de Las Casas proposed a generous reading of Augustine's apology for coercion during and after his dispute with Sepúlveda at Valladolid, but like so many other peninsular intellectuals of the sixteenth century, he had internalized Augustine's disciplinary lesson. Las Casas was an experienced and pragmatic evangelizer who knew, as the parable of the banquet in Luke made explicit, that to overcome the coercive force of local custom was to exert a different kind of coercion in its place. In Las Casas's view, conversion required replacing indigenous religious practices with Christian ritual, a process that he hoped eventually would produce orthodox faith as well. Las Casas's model of *praedicatio* paralleled Vitoria's paradigm of *lectio* and De Soto's account of *disputatio* in this regard. Each entailed a set of pedagogical practices intended to demarcate community boundaries.

To elaborate the role of discipline in the evangelical context, however, Las Casas did not begin with Aristotle, Augustine, Aquinas, or even Jesus. He began rather with the Prophet Muhammad. In *De unico vocationis modo,* Las Casas maintained that until the invention of Islam, all religious traditions had recognized that it was important for potential converts to enter freely into the process of conversion.[49] Las Casas claimed that Muhammad's preferred method of conversion by the sword both failed to produce true converts and condemned the evangelizers themselves. While Paul served as Las Casas's pastoral model, Muhammad was his paradigmatic counterexample.[50] The Christian conquerors and *encomenderos* of the New World failed to emulate Paul; instead, they mimicked Muhammad and his followers, who had subjugated and converted much of the Mediterranean and

Middle East during the eighth and ninth centuries. Citing a dialogue from the *Speculum historiale,* a short text associated with the translation workshop funded by the twelfth-century abbot of Cluny Peter the Venerable, Las Casas reduced the expansion of Islam to a story of forced conversion.[51] He noted that although Muhammad's sanctioning of conversion by the sword may be self-defeating in the hereafter, the efficacy of the approach nevertheless inspired imitation among exponents of other faiths, including Christianity. In response to this unregulated economy of mimetic violence, Las Casas advocated a more disciplined process of evangelization.

The conditions of conversion itself are not the focus of *De unico vocationis modo,* however. Las Casas recognized the baptismal moment merely as the forgotten origin of a communal disciplinary process. He hoped that participation in the shared customs of a new religious community would obscure that crucial first decision, freely made or not, to pursue conversion. To be Christian, Las Casas argued in other words, was to participate in Christian rituals such that the participation ceased to require any daily decisions at all. Custom replaced decision making. Framing faith in terms of ritual and action, Las Casas recognized that successful evangelization helped neophytes to develop the habits that marked a Christian identity. As Las Casas described it, the goal of the preachers' performances was to lead New Christians into a new naturalness born of repetition: "Custom is a habit, or with the repetition of acquired acts it engenders a habit, which, if it is not nature [*natura*] of itself, it undoubtedly is a form of nature [*quasi natura*], since custom makes habitual acts easy, quick, and unencumbered, as if driven by nature itself."[52] Like the gap between the real and the verisimilar, the slippage between "natura" and "quasi natura" was useful from the pastoral perspective. Las Casas recognized the coercive quality of local custom, or *consensus gentium,* in shaping a sense of the natural, even as he attacked Muhammad's conversions by the sword. The "quasi" implied that the apparently stable and universal natural law, or *jus naturae,* so extensively theorized by Vitoria and his successors in Salamanca, was culturally contingent. No less than faith and understanding, Las Casas knew that law may appear natural, but it was subject to change over time. By describing how Christian practice might come to seem ordinary and ahistorical even for New Christians, he candidly acknowledged a potentially worrisome parallel among Christianity, Islam, and the indigenous religions of the New World: all faiths were habits with histories.

Among those who disagreed with Las Casas's view was the late sixteenth-century Jesuit missionary of Peru José de Acosta, who in pastoral matters insisted upon the importance of personal faith and individual agency over communal habit. Many indigenous New Christians, Acosta wrote in *De procuranda indorum salute*, his own influential treatise on evangelization printed in Seville in 1588 and written in Lima the year before, "pretend [*se simulent*] to be Christians only in view of the priest, and whenever they have the opportunity, they secretly return to their old superstitions."[53] While Las Casas had celebrated participation in Christian ritual and contact with the Christian community, however temporarily duplicitous it may be, Acosta demanded that the private mental lives of converts match the public ceremony from the start. For Acosta, who between 1588 and 1590 served as the Jesuits' *visitador*, or traveling inspector, to the provinces of Andalusia and Aragon, where he would have had the opportunity to see the failure of New Christian assimilation firsthand, the familiar peninsular anxiety about dissimulation was a problem in the New World as well. Worried by this apostasy, Acosta echoed Luther and the *alumbrados* in arguing that the material efficacy of the sacraments—the "something else," as Lombard would say—was contingent upon the intention or sincere faith of the participants in the ritual.[54] And he refused to accept that Christian customs and social practices themselves produced Christian orthodoxy. Alluding to an unnamed fellow Jesuit who doubted those who claimed to have successfully converted many Indians' souls, Acosta was consumed by the prospect that indigenous conversions merely served appearances, just as the peninsular Muslim conversions had.[55]

Acosta thus argued that any flexibility in regard to faith should be a temporary and passing step on the path toward an even more explicit and dogmatic Christian universalism. He agreed with Vitoria and Las Casas's emphases on the role of teaching in the transformation and development of individuals' faith, and with Lombard and Aquinas on the teleological arc of faith through religious history, but he differed with them on details of pastoral policy. To recognize even momentarily the legitimacy of nonbelievers' implicit faith was, according to Acosta, to risk excusing lax catechism and unmotivated proselytizing. The eschatological potential of good-living innocents rapidly turned into the intransigent dissimulation of the Moriscos. But the disagreement between Acosta and his scholastic predecessors also concerned the limits of scholastic distinction as a critical method. Distinguishing between categories of faith was useful up to a point, Acosta admitted, but Vitoria and Las Casas had gone too far. Contradicting Vitoria's strong argument about faith's inessential role in salvation, Acosta insisted that faith without knowledge of Christ was "nothing but knowingly expressing craziness."[56] The Roman centurion Cornelius invoked by Lombard may have acquired some vague sense of Christian faith by studying with the Jews before the appearance of the Gospels, but, in Acosta's view, the standards of faith necessary for salvation were lower then. In the sixteenth century, "without faith in the mystery of Christ, no one can be saved. So taught Saint Thomas a long time ago, and so decreed the Council of Trent."[57] Similarly, Acosta added, claiming that an Inca from the Peruvian sierras could, like Cornelius, intuitively identify with the Christian story was no different from "claiming to know the *Aeneid* or the *Odyssey* without ever having heard the names of Aeneas or Odysseus. Who could resist laughing?"[58] Although Acosta evidently benefited from the Jesuits' renowned training in classical languages and comparative philology, a subject of chapter 3, he grew frustrated with what he saw as the remoteness of scholastic inquiry from the practical concerns of global evangelization.

Acosta acknowledged that not all Christians and Christian faiths were alike, but he sought to historicize these categories of subjectivity and belief in ways that might help him as an evangelizer. He took a more critical stance vis-à-vis Vitoria, Cano, and De Soto than his Jesuit brothers Luis de Molina and Francisco Suárez, two stars of the late sixteenth-century generation of Jesuits who dominated peninsular theology faculties.[59] To Acosta, who studied theology at the Jesuit Colegio in Alcalá de Henares, one of many institutions founded by the education-minded Jesuits in the sixteenth and seventeenth centuries, salvation through Christ was part of an eschatological story beginning with creation and ending with final judgment. Salvation required sincerity. I have included a reading of Acosta's *De procuranda indorum salute* at the end of this chapter because it offers thoughtful criticisms of Vitoria and Las Casas's defense of coercion and custom as foundations of scholarly practice and Christian orthodoxy. But Acosta's reliance on sincerity presupposed a stable correspondence between the sign and the truth of the New Christian. As Augustine had acknowledged long before, such stability was impossible to maintain, particularly at the borders between religions and empires. This impossibility explains why the intertwined efficacy of scholarly and pastoral practices became so important in early modern Spain, despite the concerns of Acosta and others: it was possible to fine-tune the shared pedagogical conditions of New Christians' faith, even if faith itself remained forever in doubt.

Acosta was right that in their struggle to deal with the example of peninsular Islam, Vitoria and Las Casas had in some sense written faith out of Christianity. Their position suggested an effort of scholarly accommodation.

Even in the context of debates about conquest and conversion in the New World, this formalist approach to defining the boundaries and essence of Christianity was shaped both by the still pressing question of Morisco dissimulation and by the impulse to reimagine the discipline of theology. This emphasis on the force of habit may have emerged as a contingent response to the epistemological challenges posed by New Christianity, but it came to inflect the reproduction of canon law and, in turn, the definition of orthodoxy. Even so, to articulate the relationship between form and content in the context of anxiety about New Christian heterodoxy and imperial legitimacy was not simply to rise to an erudite theological challenge. To read and teach the New Christians' myriad new languages was also to struggle to separate the heresy of nonbelievers' sacred texts and traditions from their linguistic forms of expression, to grapple with the translatability of Christian scripture and ecclesiastical vocabulary, and to reimagine the boundaries of comparative philology in a newly global early modernity. Like law, language too was up for debate.

CHAPTER THREE

Polyglot Forms

The theologian Martín Pérez de Ayala, a former student of Francisco de Vitoria in Salamanca who later served as a Spanish representative at the Council of Trent, bishop of Guadix, and archbishop of Valencia, opened his posthumously published teaching text, *Catechismo para instrvccion de los nveuamente conuertidos de moros*, with a fictional dialogue about the challenges posed by New Christian conversion: "Tell me the truth, if you desire it from the heart," says an Arabic-speaking teacher to his Muslim interlocutor concerning a possible conversion to Christianity. "Because coming to the Christian religion, so holy and perfect, is like coming to God; he wants the heart of him who approaches to be simple, without duplicity [*sin doblez*], or any fiction, and he does not tolerate [*no sufre*] being one way in the heart, and another in the tongue and in exterior acts."[1] The teacher's uneasy insistence upon his student's sincerity underscores Pérez de Ayala's awareness in the 1550s, when he composed this text with collaborators while serving as bishop of Guadix, that the forced conversion and failed assimilation of previous decades had destabilized the legibility of New Christian faith. This was one of the lessons that Pérez de Ayala's successor as archbishop of Valencia, Juan de Ribera, who eventually became an opponent of Arabic language evangelization and a forceful advocate of Morisco expulsion, aimed to convey when he oversaw the revision and publication of the *Catechismo* in 1599, more than thirty years after its composition and just a decade before the Morisco expulsions actually began.[2] By then, compulsory participation in the life of the Church, though designed to eliminate heterodoxy, instead had produced the intensity of indecipherability that would lead eventually to expulsion. No multilingual evangelizer could remedy this situation with a humble appeal to New Christian sincerity. The canon lawyers, court advisors, scholastic reformers, and missionaries examined in the previous two chapters responded to this epistemological dilemma by defending ritual efficacy and pedagogical discipline. These candid answers to the fact of New Christian duplicity aimed to harness the power of habit in the reconstruction of religious subjectivity and scholarly method. They were products of Francisco Jiménez de Cisneros and Antonio de Guevara's coercion on the Iberian Peninsula and of several generations of violent conquest in the New World. As the bodily imagery of Pérez de Ayala's dialogue suggests, however, the gap between a private heresy of "the heart" and a public orthodoxy of "the tongue" was not simply a theological or political issue. It was also a philological one. The familiar breach between public ritual and private faith corresponded to a second troubling chasm between word and meaning.

Debates about the assimilation of New Christians transformed the conventions of comparative philology along with the uses for canon law and the nature of scholastic training. One of these transformations was conceptual. In his Latin and Castilian grammars, the renowned humanist and Salamanca professor Antonio de Nebrija had outlined rules for correct communication while arguing that all languages shared key syntactical and morphological features. But as Pérez de Ayala and others working in the pastoral trenches of the Old and New Worlds came to realize some decades later, successful evangelization, if not language teaching in general, hinged upon neither a rigid model of correct expression nor a fiction of linguistic universalism. The foundation for the evangelical project was rather real communication on the ground. Their revised goal was to establish and maintain the contact out of which linguistic fluency and Christian faith might emerge. As a result, despite anxiety about New Christian dissimulation, some evangelizers and language teachers argued that to dismiss the power of "the tongue" was shortsighted, for even the most superficial communication might lead over time to knowledge and faith. Similarly, the notion of corrupt or nonstandard usage was beside the pragmatic point, an insight that grew out of longstanding disagreement among peninsular scholars about the relationship between classical and comparative philology, on the one hand, and the exigencies of language education, on the other hand. In reaction to Nebrija's prescriptive standard of linguistic purity, there emerged a new documentary and descriptive focus on linguistic usage, a tension that structured the discipline of linguistics in the twentieth century as well as the early modern period. This descriptive approach to comparative philology implicitly celebrated the diversity and elasticity of language, learned through active engagement with other speakers, just as the Jesuits' pastoral *accommodatio* celebrated the suppleness of Christian subjectivity, formed and reformed through exercise. Underlying this philological and pastoral formalism was Augustine's now familiar notion that ritual practice could produce Christian beliefs and identity just as communication could produce meaning. In this view, there existed a grammar of faith no less than a grammar of Arabic, Hebrew, or Latin. As Jerome warned in his criticisms of Augustine, however, to overstate the explanatory power of grammars both literal and metaphorical was to miss the fact that such formalism functioned as a convenient fiction as well as a normative claim. Like culture and history, language was local. Now a dangerous apostasy, now a charitable teaching method, the fiction of formalism served many masters, not least the hard-nosed defenders of Jerome's Vulgate. This mutual definition of grammar and evangelization is the subject of the first part of this chapter.

The second transformation in the conventions of comparative philology over the course of the sixteenth century was historical and institutional. Alfonso de Zamora, Juan de Vergara, and other *converso* Hebraists from the team of scholars that worked on the Complutense Polyglot Bible, published by Francisco Jiménez de Cisneros in the 1510s, had helped to cultivate in Alcalá and Salamanca Christian communities of Hebrew and Aramaic scholars. The roots of this peninsular Hebraism stretch back to the previous century, particularly to the intellectual circles of the bishop of Burgos Alonso de Cartagena and the Hieronymite friar Alonso de Orpesa, but the publication of the Complutense Polyglot Bible was a turning point for what since the nineteenth century has been known as comparative Semitic philology.[3] This is in no small part because Cisneros brought to the risky Complutense editorial project his credibility as a disciplinarian in Granada and Inquisitor General in Castile. Though many of the newly printed volumes were lost at sea en route to Italy, and Alcalá's Colegio Trilingüe, the intellectual and social home of the publishing venture, was destroyed during an antimonarchical uprising known as the Revolt of the Comuneros, in subsequent decades peninsular Hebraism found its footing. Zamora's student, the Cistercian Hebraist Cipriano de la Huerga, trained in Alcalá the next generation of comparative Semitic philologists, which included the editor and librarian Benito Arias Montano, the poet Fray Luis de León, and the Hebraist Martín Martínez de Cantalapiedra.[4] During his time as librarian in the Escorial, Montano in turn guided a tightly knit group of scholars that included Pedro de Valencia and the Hieronymite historian José de Sigüenza, both of whom you have met in the preceding pages. The peninsular record of Arabic philology is inextricable from this history of Hebrew study, for until the early seventeenth century the two languages were taught jointly.

Even so, these eminent sixteenth-century Hebraists boasted only intermittent Arabic knowledge, which, I argue, is paradoxically why such knowledge was so useful to them as a lever of disciplinary reform. Like the Moriscos, who transformed classical Arabic and redefined the nature of their religious and cultural identities by writing in *aljamiado*, experts in Hebrew language employed their Arabic to demarcate the shifting boundaries of philological inquiry. As the second half of this chapter demonstrates, by trafficking in an Arabic intended for display, decoration, and easy translation, avant-garde Hebraists put their limited bits of Arabic knowledge to use as markers of a new kind of professional expertise.

Neither the pastoral story of Arabic in Granada and Valencia nor the scholarly story of Hebrew and Arabic study in Alcalá and Salamanca fit neatly into conventional accounts of peninsular philology, which tend to chart a rising tide of Orientalist rigor over the course of the early modern period.[5] As Mercedes García-Arenal and Fernando Rodríguez Mediano have rightly argued, an "erudite space" for an increasingly comparative philological and theological inquiry did emerge at the end of the sixteenth and beginning of the seventeenth century, primarily through the effort to transcribe, translate, and interpret the Sacromonte lead books, which are the subject of the next chapter.[6] Yet the transition from the fitful Arabism of Hernando de Talavera's Granada to the learned inquiries of seventeenth-century polymaths was plodding and erratic. Like Hebrew, Arabic did eventually become an instrument of Christian hermeneutics and antiquarian imagination, but the initial goals of those pioneers at Alcalá and Salamanca were more modest, their knowledge of Arabic by and large middling. These circumstances were at first a product of inquisitorial restrictions on Semitic language study and ubiquitous anxiety about New Christian apostasy. Students and teachers of language distinguished between benign Arabic and Hebrew signs and their potentially heretical referents in order to justify comparative interests during a period of sectarianism and suspicion. As the chapter's brief concluding section on Francisco Sánchez de las Brozas's 1587 Latin grammar *Minerva sive de causis linguae latinae* shows, however, over time this strategic distinction between form and content matured into a powerful instrument of intellectual inquiry.

PHILOLOGY AT THE LIMITS OF ORTHODOXY

Soon after assuming his post as Granada's first archbishop, Hernando de Talavera invited the peninsula's few scholars knowledgeable in Arabic to

Granada in order to aid in communication with the local population and to lead language classes tailored to the pastoral endeavor. "It was really something," related José de Sigüenza in his history of the Hieronymites, "to see such a dignified and elderly archbishop, occupied with so many tasks, go to class and learn the Arabic case endings and conjugation, only for the benefit of those souls."[7] As part of this effort to cultivate Christian Arabic study and Muslim conversion, Talavera's confessor and fellow Hieronymite, Pedro de Alcalá, set to work at Talavera's request on an Arabic-Castilian lexicon, grammar, and bilingual catechism. In his *Vocabulista in arabico* and *Arte para ligeramente saber la lengua arauiga*, both published in 1505 at the Granada printing press established by Talavera, Alcalá along with his colleagues from Talavera's circle aimed to provide doctrinal and linguistic uniformity in a region where knowledge of spoken Castilian, not to mention familiarity with Church Latin, was sparse if not nonexistent.[8] An effort to facilitate the new converts' knowledge of basic Christian doctrine along with Christian missionaries' linguistic acumen, the *Arte* included Arabic versions of the Ave Maria, Pater Noster, Credo, and Salve Regina, each transliterated along with the rest of the grammatical material into Latin letters. In Talavera's view, so pressing was the need for these sorts of teaching texts in those first years after Granada's reconquest that the archbishop himself was known to voice his willingness to "happily trade an eye" for proficient knowledge of Arabic, which he nevertheless failed ever to attain.[9] Unlike the *reyes católicos*, who supported teaching Christian liturgy and doctrine to the Moriscos in Castilian and Latin but not in Arabic, Talavera saw Arabic catechism and communication as the key to conversion. As the dark humor concerning his own linguistic ineptness suggests, he was circumspect concerning the impediments to such an ambitious program of bilingual evangelization.

In contrast to his colleague and patron, Alcalá explained in the prologue to the *Arte* that he expected students accustomed to Latin grammar to recognize the commonalities between Latin and Arabic, thus facilitating quick mastery of the latter. For this reason, he did not organize his *Arte* according to the models of grammarians from the Arabophone world. He followed instead the example set by Nebrija, whose *Introductiones latinae* and *Gramática de la lengua castellana* were first published in Salamanca in 1481 and 1492, respectively. Reprinted many times in subsequent decades, Nebrija's texts' principal objectives were to identify and normalize proper speaking and writing, in what one historian has recently dubbed a "pedagogical *reconquista*" of infelicitous barbarisms.[10] Such dedication to exactitude was an important innovation in the study of Romance vernaculars such as Castilian, which, unlike Latin, Greek, Hebrew, and Arabic, had never before been the subject of professional philologists' systematic attention. By elevating an erudite register of Castilian in this fashion, Nebrija sought to provide a foundation for vernacular scholarship and global empire. According to Nebrija's account from the *Gramática*'s prologue, it was none other than Talavera, then serving as confessor to Queen Isabel, who foresaw the project's intellectual and political importance and encouraged his patron to support it.[11] Like Nebrija's texts on Castilian grammar and orthography, Alcalá's *Arte* was both a symbolic first step in the history of peninsular comparative philology and a product of Talavera's vision. Not published until three years after Cisneros had replaced Talavera's pastoral irenicism with a more combative approach to conversion in Granada, however, the *Arte* arrived too late to serve its purpose there. Moreover, Alcalá's prescriptive and Latinizing approach rendered it marginal to the worlds of Semitic language scholarship that later took shape elsewhere. As we will see below, biblical commentators working in late sixteenth-century Salamanca, Rome, Leiden, and Antwerp produced their own philological apparatuses rather than rely on the inadequate texts of their predecessors.

Among the first scholars to question Nebrija and Alcalá's model of comparative philology was the *converso* humanist and religious reformer Juan de Valdés. A contradictory figure deeply influenced by Erasmus and later associated with the *alumbrados*, Valdés mocked Nebrija's view of Castilian as a grammatical *arte* taught in books rather than a lived form of communication. Nebrija's "gramatiquerías," as Valdés sardonically dubbed such *arte* in his *Diálogo de la lengua*, a conversation between a group of curious Italians and their Iberian interlocutor composed in the 1530s, consequently missed the truly dynamic aspect of spoken Castilian, replete with popular refrains and nonstandard usage.[12] Like true Christian faith, lived language was to be found in the experience of the people rather than in the books of the learned, a point that Valdés reiterated in his most widely read work, *Diálogo de doctrina cristiana*, published anonymously in 1529.[13] In response to the Italians' request in *Diálogo de la lengua* that their Iberian informant, an eponymous Valdés, justify his linguistic choices in Castilian by employing Latin grammatical terms, Valdés countered with one of his many digs at Nebrija's doctrinaire method: "I have learned the Latin language by art and book, and the Castilian language by use," he responded. Though it was possible to account for Latin knowledge by scholarly study, Valdés continued, facility with Castilian, a living artifact, was born of "the common use of speaking."[14] Like Nebrija, who in 1517 published a Castilian spelling guidebook entitled

Reglas de orthographia en la lengua castellana, Valdés did sometimes convey his Castilian orthographic or lexical preferences, but unlike his predecessor, he most often did so only to highlight and explain the extant cornucopia of actual expression.[15] In other words, Valdés offered examples of the ways that native Castilian speakers employed ambiguous phrases, chose among synonyms, and distinguished between geographic and class-specific registers. In articulating a descriptive counterbalance to the prescriptive strategy of Nebrija, Alcalá, and other imitators, Valdés popularized the characterization of Nebrija as an insufferable pedant. As early as the 1560s, it was possible to state as a matter of historical record, as Martín Pérez de Ayala did in his autobiographical "*Discurso de la vida*", that Nebrija's insistence upon linguistic exactitude was a longstanding source of scholarly stultification rather than a remedy for linguistic and doctrinal inconsistency.[16]

Pérez de Ayala's views on language pedagogy and comparative philology were shaped by his experience with the Moriscos, whom he came to know as bishop of Guadix, a diocese of Granada. He was appointed the city's bishop in 1549 thanks to the support of Carlos V, who believed that previous time spent as a professor in Granada had afforded his favored candidate the requisite pastoral experience and linguistic and cultural knowledge. Nevertheless, Pérez de Ayala acknowledged upon accepting the position that he was neither "accustomed to preaching" nor "knew anything about either the language or customs of the Moriscos."[17] He was a quick study of both the Moriscos' needs and the ways to fulfill them in Guadix, though, where he remained as bishop until 1560. In the 1554 Synod of Gaudix, for instance, Pérez de Ayala and his colleagues reiterated previous, unenforced prohibitions on the Morisco use of Arabic, even though they conceded the Pauline necessity of preaching and administering confession to the Moriscos in their own language, at least in the short term.[18] During the decades before the adoption in 1567 of a definitive ban on Arabic, Pérez de Ayala supported linguistic accommodation while validating the Crown's anti-Arabic stance. Accommodation, he hedged, would lead eventually to Arabic's disappearance.

During his time as bishop of Guadix, Pérez de Ayala and his Arabic interpreter, the beneficiary priest Bartolomé Dorador, composed a series of teaching texts, including the above-mentioned *Catechismo* eventually published by Juan de Ribera and a bilingual Arabic-Castilian *Doctrina christiana,* which appeared in 1566. Pérez de Ayala and Dorador followed Alcalá in culling the Arabic translations of Christian liturgical and doctrinal vocabulary from Islamic practice, performing the inverse operation of Robert of Ketton, who employed biblical language in his twelfth-century Qur'an translation.[19] Echoing as well the descriptive approach outlined by Valdés in the *Diálogo de la lengua* and put into New World practice by the Franciscans Andrés de Olmos, whose *Arte de la lengua mexicana* of 1547 was the first Nahuatl grammar, and Pedro de Molina, whose *Vocabulario en la lengua castellana y mexicana* of 1555 was the first printed Nahuatl lexicon, the *Doctrina* focused in particular on the challenges of Arabic pronunciation and transliteration.[20] While Alcalá dedicated only a brief chapter to the enunciation of Arabic sounds, Pérez de Ayala and Dorador saw drama in phonology, which they addressed in detail at the end of the *Doctrina*. These "rules for knowing how to read the Arabic words in this doctrine" offer vignettes of contemporary Castilian, Hebrew, and Greek speakers in acts of contorted elocution. To the authors' ears, for instance, the aspirated Arabic *ḥa'* "is formed in the throat itself, as when someone hawks, or removes phlegm from his chest. In this same way the Hebrews pronounce their *chet* and the Greeks their *chi*."[21] Their effort to describe the Arabic letter *'ayn* and its effects on the pronunciation of surrounding vowels similarly reckoned the limitations of the Castilian glottis before surrendering to the need for native speakers: "Although [the *'ayn*] is pronounced in the throat, it is not aspirated like the *ḥa'*, but rather softly turns over in the throat, and it seems to have a bit of the sound of a *g*. In sum, to pronounce Arabic correctly, you must hear it from a native speaker."[22] Though Pérez de Ayala and Dorador highlighted phonological parallels between Arabic and other languages, they were more interested in tools of communication than in abstract standards of linguistic universality. Moreover, these phonological-focused sections of the *Doctrina* underscore the distance traveled since Alcalá's struggles to formulate an Arabic vocabulary of Christian orthodoxy.[23] By the mid-sixteenth century, that is, Pérez de Ayala could afford to take the translations of Christian terminology for granted. He paid attention instead to the necessary positioning of the tongue, throat, and teeth in the enunciation of Christian prayer, as well as to a wider corporeal grammar of faith. The "summary of the ceremonies, and the composition of the body maintained during Mass," an appendix that precedes the *Doctrina*'s phonological guide, underscores Pérez de Ayala's view that faith was the fruit of well-cultivated physical and linguistic habit. In contrast to the *Catechismo* and its bilingual teacher's appeal to the sincerity of faith, the *Doctrina* presented a more pragmatic guide to the production of faith and fluency alike. To learn the sounds and gestures of Christian ritual was a necessary first step toward orthodoxy. Taking the long view, Pérez de Ayala insisted that the converts would "come to know the rest of the doctrine with the passage of time."[24]

In his *Información acerca de los moriscos de España*, composed, as you will recall from chapter 1, at the turn of the seventeenth century, the Morisco Jesuit Ignacio de Las Casas worried that Pérez de Ayala's confidence in the power of pronunciation could be dangerous as well as beneficial. In his view, the familiar issue of New Christian dissimulation was at its core a philological problem, one that might be resolved with parish priests knowledgeable in Arabic. However, unlike Talavera and Pérez de Ayala, who tried to encourage New Christian participation in Christian ritual even if such participation was in Arabic rather than in Latin or Castilian, Las Casas supported Arabic study primarily for Christian missionaries, who would consequently be capable of monitoring the Moriscos' orthodoxy. Las Casas fretted that the Moriscos had learned over the course of the sixteenth century to turn the vernacular version of Pérez de Ayala's formalism into a new kind of linguistic heresy. Consider Las Casas's humorous evidence of the need for Arabic-speaking pastors, who might catch the Moriscos in their puns:

> When we say "Jesus," they say "Chichigi," which means "chickens," and when in Valencia they hear said, "Señor ver Deu," which means "Lord the true God," naming the sacrament of the Eucharist, they sneer with laughs, because in their language, "verdeu" means "nag" or "mule," and when "sanctified be your name" is said, they say "holy sin, you man," and instead of saying "he will come to judge the living and the dead," they say, "he will come to play at eggs and gardens," along with other much worse things; and if they reproach them, they deny it by saying that they don't know or understand what they say and do.[25]

These and similar "scandals of language," as the Aragonese expulsion advocate Pedro Aznar Cardona called them, were pernicious because they appropriated the sounds of Christian ritual to derisive ends.[26] They highlighted the conventionality of the mass's physical and oral grammar, but as ridicule rather than piety. Las Casas here acknowledged the strongest counterargument to the sort of philological and pastoral formalism that served as the foundation for Jesuit *accommodatio* and angered José de Acosta, as well as generations of *erasmistas*, *alumbrados*, and other sixteenth-century proponents of religious renewal: demonstrations of orthodoxy were sometimes shams. As the Jesuits Order's pedagogical record suggests, to turn a blind eye to apostasy and miscommunication could be a successful pedagogical strategy in the long term, but it relied upon a charitable pastoral stoicism in the present.

Elsewhere, though, Las Casas was more sanguine about the tenuous linkage between word and meaning, which allowed not only jokes at evangelizers' expense but also communication among speakers of different dialects. In a brief text copied together with an early seventeenth-century letter to the provincial head of the Jesuit Order in Castile, Cristóbal de los Cobos, Las Casas underscored the intelligibility of Arabic's three-letter root system, accentuating the populist stance staked out by Valdés in his explanation of Castilian usage. The overlap between Valdés's and Las Casas's views is not coincidental. The *Diálogo de la lengua* remained unpublished until the eighteenth century, largely because Valdés's first readers were more concerned with his religious renewal project than with his philological polemics, but many of Valdés's fellow *conversos* made their way into Jesuit circles in the 1540s and 1550s, and so it is likely that Las Casas, along with Ignacio de Loyola, Juan de Polanco, and other early Jesuits concerned with pedagogical and philological method, came across the *Diálogo* in manuscript form. In any case, Las Casas reserved a particularly Valdesian enthusiasm for the capacity of Arabic roots to ease communication across regional and religious lines. These roots facilitated comprehension of literary or legal texts and stimulated communication with those diverse speakers who mixed and mangled the language's formal register into myriad local dialects, just as Romance language speakers had mixed and mangled Latin. "I could not make myself easily understood in our language if it were not thus," Las Casas maintained in defense of the root system of Arabic and Hebrew. "We recognize this word 'bread' whether we hear a stranger ask for 'brode' or 'brade,' and the same is true of 'wine,' 'wone,' or 'wane,' etc."[27] In Las Casas's view, the Arabic grammatical rules, at least as a student of Latin or Castilian might imagine them, were necessary only to understand learned texts and the Qur'an. Beyond such elite registers, Las Casas claimed with his own populist pun, "grammar is on vacation."[28]

In privileging real-time communication among Moriscos, Las Casas and his fellow Jesuits, such as the Granadans Juan de Albotodo and Jerónimo Mur, echoed one of Loyola's first and dearest pastoral priorities, which was the spiritual conquest of the Islamic world. Even as subsequent Jesuit missionaries like Francisco Xavier and Matteo Ricci traveled beyond the Atlantic to the Pacific Ocean, this interest in Mediterranean Muslims was not completely eclipsed. To catechize peninsular Moriscos with tolerable dialectical fluency was no simple endeavor, but Muslims beyond the peninsula demanded even deeper knowledge of written as well as spoken Arabic. Las Casas's show of optimism concerning the intelligibility of spoken Arabic disguised his weaknesses as a reader and writer. Mur apparently suffered from a similar shortcoming, for he was unable to accept a professorship of Arabic at the Jesuits' Roman college because his own formal Arabic was not up to snuff, and after remaining for some time in Rome, he instead traveled to Valencia at Martín Pérez de Ayala's request to help with the evangelization of the Moriscos there.[29] To remedy his own linguistic deficiencies, Las Casas, for his part, journeyed precisely to that Roman college abandoned by Mur, where Giovanni Eliano, one of the few Jesuits who possessed advanced knowledge of both Arabic and Hebrew, finally began to offer Arabic language courses in 1562.[30] Such courses had been a priority since the 1550s of another Roman Jesuit, Jerónimo Nadal, who saw the Roman college as a place to experiment in untangling the most challenging of pedagogical knots, Arabic or otherwise. It was Nadal's hope that teachers in the Jesuits' far-flung institutions would then implement the tried-and-true techniques from the Roman laboratory.

Even as the Jesuit Order became famous for its evangelism and comparative philology, however, its reputation rested upon its strict and extensive Latin study. As hundreds of Jesuit colleges aimed to integrate classical poetic and historical texts into religious education, the philological formalism described above began to take shape. In his 1572 Latin teaching grammar, *De institutione grammatica*, the Jesuit Manuel Álvarez followed Valdés, Pérez de Ayala, and other pastoral linguists in privileging pedagogy of practice over theology of exactitude. Álvarez's grammar remained popular for decades, in part because the *Ratio atque institutio studiorum Societatis Iesu* of 1599, a much-debated and revised document that systematized the first half-century of Jesuit pedagogy, instituted rigid Latin-only communication among young students and their teachers in Jesuit colleges. In short, *De institutione grammatica* and the *Ratio* mandated that students learn languages by using them.[31] Even if these students did not completely understand the grammar they partially and oftentimes incorrectly employed, and even if teachers initially let misunderstandings and miscommunications pass without comment, the wager was that to develop the habit of communication was to speed acquisition. Like piety, language fluency required practice. Advanced aptitude nonetheless required much else in addition to this ability to use the target language, particularly when it came to missionary languages like Arabic or Nahuatl. Deep knowledge of the cultures in which the language was embedded, a diachronic sense of the language's grammatical and lexical history, and, perhaps most importantly, an ability to switch between elite and popular registers depending upon the context and interlocutor all required a balance between abstract knowledge and daily usage.

The *Ratio* fine-tuned the approach to Latin instruction for the Jesuit Hebrew classroom, where it was necessary to address the unique set of dangers posed by studying the holy tongue of the Jews. The section of the *Ratio* that outlined this curriculum stressed the importance of the distinction between the sound and shape of Hebrew words, on the one hand, and the potentially heretical meanings articulated by Jewish commentators and poets, on the other hand. Even Hebrew scripture posed hermeneutic peril, as suggests the persistent myth of the linguistically corrupt Hebrew and Greek Old Testament as a Jewish fabrication. At the beginning of the sixteenth century, Cisneros and Nebrija had shared a good laugh over this notion that medieval rabbis had either invented out of whole cloth or deliberately miscopied and circulated Hebrew and Greek manuscripts of the Old Testament in order to mock their Christian antagonists. But the publication delays and tepid papal reception of so monumental a work of Hebrew scholarship as the Complutense Polyglot Bible gave later Hebraists reason for concern, even if their authority as scholars nevertheless grew out of the project. This anxiety was evident in the *Ratio,* which instructed professors of Hebrew language to separate for their students the useful linguistic shell from the dangerous heretical nut: "When he is interpreting the sacred books, he should not spend as much effort on pondering the meaning [*sententiis*] as on taking note of the power of the words, and the special idioms distinctive of the language, and the grammatical rules according to the actual usage [*usum*] of the authors."[32] Although Hebrew study was reserved for advanced students previously trained in biblical exegesis, the leaders of the Jesuit Order tried to shelter these students by circumscribing class discussion, a decision that undoubtedly facilitated knowledge of basic Hebrew while stunting more advanced proficiency. This was the cost of understanding the Hebrew text as a collection of grammatical conventions and sayings in need of parsing, rather than as a potentially rich and contentious reservoir of meaning.

Censorship as well as pedagogy shaped this approach to comparative philology. Despite the allowances of the *Index of Prohibited Books* examined below, the very presence of Hebrew and Arabic script rankled those inquisitors charged with rooting out New Christian apostasy. By publicizing their lack of interest in semantic questions, the successive teams of Jesuit pedagogues who composed and revised the *Ratio* under the nominal direction of Claudio Acquaviva tried to insulate their teachers and students from the accusation as well as the allure of apostasy.[33] Even the most ardent early modern defenders of the *artes liberales* beyond the narrow world of Semitic philology struggled with this methodological dilemma. The question concerned how to interpret and quarantine the heresy of the ancient Greeks and Romans while integrating their philosophical insights and literary sophistication into a Christian context. Though Erasmus proposed the dual answers of allegorical interpretation and readerly sincerity, the Jesuit teaching program instead skirted the central issue by employing Christian, Latin, and Greek texts in classes on theology and selecting ancient secular literature to teach classical grammar. Hebrew registers and genres offered no such dichotomy between art and religion. Even the medieval Hebrew odes to wine and women, from King David's Psalms to the bawdy poems of the Andalusian Jewish scholars Moses Ibn Ezra and Judah Halevi, displayed a striking biblical intertextuality. As a result, the authors of the *Ratio* determined that there was no choice but for students to direct their attention toward the Hebrew Bible, which despite its sacredness as a Jewish text at least also held a fundamental place in the Christian canon. Neophytes limited their analysis to the observable aspects of the language while ignoring the problematic "power of the words," which more highly trained theologians would gloss in other contexts. As we have already seen, Las Casas was more nonchalant about the possibility that the Qur'an might corrupt students of Arabic than his Jesuit brothers were about the possibility that the Pentateuch would corrupt students of Hebrew, because in his view the chief goal of peninsular Arabic training was oral communication rather than textual comprehension or grammatical hairsplitting. Arabic and Hebrew shared many grammatical features and in some ways presented parallel risks to orthodoxy, Las Casas acknowledged to opponents of Semitic language education. But because Arabic was a living language in a way that Hebrew was not, in Las Casas's view the pedagogical aims and evangelical payoffs were dissimilar. While the reality of Latin and Semitic language education was in practice less tidy than the *Ratio* mandated, this insistence upon a clear distinction between form and content in the Hebrew classroom is a crucial nugget of historical evidence because it came to characterize the Jesuit approach not only to language education, but also to missionary work more generally.

Jesuit evangelizers justified doctrinal and philological flexibility in terms borrowed from the fifth-century disagreement between Jerome and Augustine and employed by Francisco de Vitoria as a tool of scholarly reform in Salamanca: "In the early Church," insisted Bartolomé Roboredo, a Jesuit working in China, for instance, "the holy apostles dissimulated and permitted many Jewish and gentile ceremonies in order not to distance gentiles and pagans from the law of Christ."[34] Some degree of duplicitous permissiveness during the first stage of evangelization was necessary. In Roboredo's gastronomic idiom, to rush into complicated doctrinal questions would be "too hard a bite for those new to the faith" (*bocado duro para principiantes en la fe*).[35] My argument here is that the descriptive approach articulated by

Juan de Valdés, practiced by Martín Pérez de Ayala, and uniquely visible in the Jesuit Order's approach to comparative Semitic philology served as the foundation for pastoral *accommodatio*. The *Ratio* formulated this point in a section devoted to the teaching of Christians: "where neither the teaching of the faith nor moral purity is at stake, a prudent charity [*prudens caritas*] demands that Jesuits accommodate themselves [*se illis accommodent*] to those with whom they are associating." Roboredo and others extended this idea to nonbelievers as well, arguing that it was necessary to "accommodate [*acomodarse*] to the manners, ceremonies, and political customs" of local converts or potential converts.[36] Produced in Mexico, China, Salamanca, and elsewhere, the manuscript material dealing with the global Jesuit project of evangelization circulated widely in the Hispanic world, shaping pastoral conventions as well as modes of philological inquiry.

The Jesuits became a flashpoint for tensions between universal prescriptivism and local descriptivism that in scholarship on the Romance vernaculars first emerged with Nebrija.[37] For them and other evangelizers charged with integrating and educating New Christians, to formulate an approach to language education was to take a stand on religious ritual and renewal. Language teaching and evangelization were interrelated processes, often pursued in tandem by the same individuals. Like the moral behaviorism and scholastic pedagogy examined in the previous two chapters, comparative philology in pastoral situations presupposed the power of habit to shape subjectivity. Among the benefits of submission to a philological regime focused on communication, mimicry, and repetition was not only the resulting multilingualism itself, but also an intensified attention to pedagogical method. Through this philological lens, it is possible to see more clearly the polyvalence of coercion. In the realm of language education, some degree of coercion was a feature of effective instruction. That coercion created the conditions for new knowledge and improved communication was an insight born of comparative philology at the pastoral edge of empire and orthodoxy. At the centers of peninsular education, however, the story of comparative philology unfolded differently.

ERUDITE FORMALISM

In the late tenth century, Moses Ibn Ezra asked his friend and contemporary, the Zaragossan author Abū Ibrahīm Iṣḥāq Ibn Barūn, to send him a copy of the latter's comparative grammar and lexicon *The Book of Comparison between the Hebrew and Arabic Language*, or *Kitāb al-muwāzana bayn al-lugha al-'ibrāniyya wal-'arabiyya*. After reading the text, Ibn Ezra's response was ambivalent. In some poems, he lavished praise on his friend's work, but Ibn Ezra also thought that comparative research on Hebrew and Arabic could be profoundly dangerous, writing at one point that *The Book of Comparison* was "as honeycomb to the pure of heart, but as poison to the hypocrites."[38] Throughout the text, Ibn Barūn cited the authoritative Hebrew grammars of the tenth-century Jewish scholars Sa'adiah Gaon and Ibn Janāḥ, traditional Jewish works such as the Mishnah and the Masoretic texts, and, more surprisingly, Arabic sources, including a translation of the Pentateuch, passages from the Qur'an, examples from the oral *ḥadīth* tradition, and pre-Islamic lyric from the *Mu'allaqāt* of Imrū'al-Qays.[39] Systematic comparative research of the kind pursued by Ibn Barūn demanded this co-mingling of sources across ecumenical lines. Despite powerful traditions of profane prose and poetry in both Hebrew and Arabic, the exemplary language that Ibn Barūn set out to study was located in holy text and its glosses. To ignore these texts would have been disingenuous, but, as Ibn Ezra acknowledged, to study them in this comparative context was to risk heresy. He worried that some readers would insist that the very act of employing noncanonical texts and another tradition's holy language to parse sacred Hebrew text was heretical regardless of the interpretive result. Yet because similarities between Hebrew and Arabic might help elucidate ambiguous passages or vocabulary in Hebrew scripture, knowledge of Arabic language and familiarity with Islamic sources were, at least in theory, potentially useful tools for Jewish commentators.

This medieval history of scholarship on Hebrew and Arabic, some of which was accessible in the sixteenth century through the writings of the eccentric linguist and astronomer Guillaume Postel, the Hebrew printer and teacher Elia Levita, and the peninsular biblical commentator Pedro de Palencia, served as a model for comparative philology in the early modern period. Even in this scholarly as opposed to pastoral milieu, inquisitorial pressure structured philological method. Although Catholic censors officially outlawed all rabbinic commentaries and Jewish versions of scripture, some strictly philological texts were permitted to circulate freely among Christian commentators. The *Index* did not prohibit, for instance, the late twelfth- and early thirteenth-century rabbi and philosopher David Kimhi's study of Hebrew and Arabic roots, scattered grammatical works by the German cartographer and Hebraist Sebastian Münster, and related research by a few other well-regarded sixteenth-century scholars.[40] This was a systematic effort on the part of the Church to distinguish between permissible formal analysis and suspicious engagement with heretical content, especially during the period after the Council of Trent. The fiction of such a distinction between language and meaning was prudent pedagogy in Pérez de Ayala's Valencia or the Jesuit *colegios* scattered around the peninsula and beyond; it was also a mechanism for negotiating the new boundaries of Christian Hebraism. In this way, the claims and concerns of those medieval Jewish scholars dedicated to comparative Semitic philology filtered into early modern debates about language, orthodoxy, and coercion.

The *Index*'s exceptions for certain kinds of comparative philology helped to foster Hebrew teaching and publication, both on the Iberian Peninsula and in other European printing centers whose Jewish populations swelled with *converso* émigrés in the sixteenth century. Using elegant Hebrew stamps, Daniel Bomberg and Robert Estienne had by the mid-sixteenth century published complete editions of the Talmud, works by Maimonides, and texts by other medieval and early modern Jews, including both Ibn Ezra and David Kimhi. Despite Christian anxiety about rabbinic deception, diverse groups of Protestant and Catholic scholars made use of these Jewish texts and traditions in their effort to reexamine the language of scripture, contemplate the history of the Israelites, and, as the historians Eric Nelson and Guy G. Stroumsa have recently shown, reconsider the nature of political community and scholarly practice.[41]

Arabic study during this transitional period for comparative Semitic philology was inseparable from Hebrew scholarship, as it had been in various ways for centuries. Late medieval Christian evangelizers and polemicists interested in converting Muslims and Jews had understood the importance of integrating Arabic education into textual communities with strong extant curriculums in Hebrew and Greek. Under pressure from the Dominican jurist Ramón de Penyaforte and his younger contemporary, the polymath Ramón Llull, the *inter sollicitudines* decree of the 1311 Council of Vienne mandated the establishment of scholarly chairs for Arabic at Salamanca, Paris, and Rome. Similarly, the 1431 Council of Basel unambiguously called for the education of Christian preachers competent in Hebrew, Arabic, Greek, and Aramaic.[42] Despite both the Church's seal of approval and a tradition of peninsular Arabic study by thirteenth-century Christians located, among other places, in Castile and Sicily, Arabic was not taught in a systematic way until the middle of the sixteenth century. When the Flemish grammarian Nicolas Clénard came to Salamanca to study Arabic in the 1530s, already nearly a half-century after the fall of Granada, he was sorely disappointed at the lack of Arabic expertise, pedagogical materials, and interested students that he found there. Clénard managed only to organize informal Arabic tutoring sessions with Hernán Núñez de Toledo, a widely respected Greek specialist who collaborated with Cisneros on the Complutense Polyglot Bible. After having spent some ten years on the Iberian Peninsula, however, first in Salamanca and then as a tutor to the future King Henrique in Portugal and as professor in Braga and Évora, Clénard left for Granada and then Fez in search of broader Arabist infrastructure and pastoral opportunity.[43]

This sorry state of Salamanca Semitic philology began to change, however, with the establishment of the "professor trium linguarum Salamanticae," or university chair of Hebrew, Aramaic, and Arabic. First occupied in 1543 by Cipriano de la Huerga's student, the Hebraist Martín Martínez de Cantalapiedra, the position's formation marked a new phase in the integration of Arabic language education into Hebrew pedagogy. The result was a shift in the conventions of peninsular Hebraism. However counterintuitive it may seem, the most important impetus for the improvement of peninsular Arabic education in the mid-sixteenth century was not the evangelization of the Moriscos or the economic and political challenges posed by Mediterranean piracy, but rather the growing interest in and institutionalization of Hebrew study.

To display a bit of Arabic knowledge became a way for *converso* Hebraists to convey both their comparative philological interests and their dedication to transforming contemporary standards of scholarly expertise. Few of these Hebraists, Martínez de Cantalapiedra included, were actually able to read Islamic holy texts like the Qur'an or classical collections of *ḥadīth*, not to mention medieval philosophical works by Ibn Sīnā or Ibn Rushd. This gap in Arabic knowledge was in part a result of material circumstances. Inquisitorial censorship and intimidation, on the one hand, and an absence of first-rate stamps for printing in Arabic script, on the other hand, made acquiring Arabic texts difficult. The Italian Arabist Giovanni Battista Raimundi and his wealthy patron Ferdinando de' Medici founded the two Roman centers of European Arabism, the Maronite College and the Typographia Medicea publishing house, only in the 1580s.[44] Even so, expert Hebraists had recognized long before that knowledge of Arabic was a potent tool of Christian exegesis and eschatology as well as Hebrew commentary. At once instigating and undermining innovation in comparative philology, these contradictory forces produced a thriving economy of distinctly inexpert Arabic. As I argue, this inexpert Arabic was not simply an inconsequential pause in an inexorable ascent toward the philological erudition of the mid-seventeenth century. It may not yet have been particularly useful as a tool of holy hermeneutics, but it did serve as an object of professional exchange and marker of intellectual like-mindedness. In other words, when the Hebrew teacher Martínez de Cantalapiedra, the poet Fray Luis de León, and the classicist Francisco Sánchez de las Brozas displayed even a nascent interest in the Arabic language, they were redrawing the intellectual networks that together defined early modern peninsular Hebraism. My objective is not to reduce these scholars' Arabic study only to a way of claiming professional prestige, but rather to examine how gifted and engaged thinkers incrementally transformed their disciplines by stepping beyond their comfort zones at a particular historical moment. Although Hebrew sources ranging from comparative grammars to medieval philosophy and history served an array of political and theological purposes throughout Europe in the early modern period, it was only with these mid- to late sixteenth-century peninsular Hebraists' efforts to integrate Arabic study into Hebrew education that the previously secure religious moorings of Jewish sources began to loosen.

What did Arabic education actually entail in the Hebrew classroom? For Martínez de Cantalapiedra and his Salamanca students, there were only two available printed Arabic grammars, Alcalá's *Arte* and Guillaume Postel's *Grammaticum arabicum*, published in the 1530s. While Alcalá's text was designed for use among Moriscos rather than for study in the library, Postel aimed at a more scholarly audience by organizing his inquiry according to Arabophone models and including amongst the Latin explanation more Arabic script, however rudimentary the stamps. The *Grammaticum arabicum* represented an improvement over Alcalá's basic handbook, but as the paucity of extant copies in peninsular libraries suggests, it did not circulate widely there. As Luce López Baralt has demonstrated, Martínez de Cantalapiedra instead relied heavily on manuscript teaching materials, organizing his Arabic instruction around a grammar entitled *Al-jurumiyya*, named for its North African author, Muḥammad Ibn Dawd a-Jurrum.[45] Unlike both Alcalá's and Postel's works, this text was composed completely in Arabic; it was designed for students already familiar with the Arabic alphabet, lexicons, and specialized grammatical concepts. Used by generations of beginners, first in manuscript copies and then in the Typographia Medicea's handsome expanded edition, this grammar was a favorite of students. At least one extensively annotated copy of this printed edition, now bound in a codex containing miscellaneous Arabic pedagogical material from the late sixteenth and early seventeenth centuries, suggests that even well after the discovery of the Sacromonte lead books in the 1590s students continued to struggle through this text with word-to-word Arabic-Castilian translations and accompanying multilingual notes.[46] Arabic-only grammars, in other words, did not produce a Salamanca pedagogy of linguistic immersion like that cultivated by Jesuit pedagogues laboring on the pastoral frontier. Instead, they created a need for Castilian and Latin study guides, which subsequent Orientalists collected and preserved as evidence of their discipline's tottering early modern origins. Whatever the bold claims of curriculum reformers and innovative polyglots, neither a polemical interest in Islamic theology nor an evangelical dedication to communicative preaching drove Arabic instruction in mid-sixteenth-century Salamanca. Even the most motivated of students and teachers instead struggled, oftentimes without much success, to acquire basic Arabic competency as part of their formations in Hebrew and biblical studies. The ostensible aim of this formation was to be able to read the Hebrew Bible with the eye of a comparatist trained in Aramaic and Arabic, but the unevenness of the enterprise suggests that Arabic "expertise" served a host of other functions as well.

Benito Arias Montano, invited for his exegetical prowess by Martín Pérez de Ayala to attend the late sessions at Trent in 1562, was a rare exception to this amateurish Arabism.[47] Even so, his use of Arabic in the Plantin Polyglot Bible aptly illustrates how the language came to serve decorative and professional ends in addition to hermeneutic ones. Although the Flemish publisher Christopher Plantin was the motivating force behind the Polyglot Bible and King Felipe II chose Montano as editor-in-chief, Montano put his own imprint on the imposing eight-volume set in a variety of important ways. He worked closely with Plantin to resolve the typographical and formatting challenges presented by a text in Hebrew, Greek, and Latin script. He helped to choose the project's international team of editors and translators, which included Guy Le Fèvre de la Boderie, a celebrated Syriac specialist, and Francis Raphelengius, a respected scholar of Greek, Hebrew, and Arabic. And he wrote a series of prologues that explained the importance of studying the holy text in its original languages and contextualized the ambitious editorial endeavor within the history of the Complutense Polyglot Bible.[48] But he put a more literal imprint on the edition too, ending each book of the Pentateuch, contained in the first of eight volumes, with a curious, multilingual colophon. On the final pages of each book, Montano followed a printed version of his signature by a decorative flourish and the word *talmīd*, composed in Arabic script and meaning "scholar" in Hebrew.[49] On the page containing the Hebrew text, Jerome's Vulgate, and the ancient Aramaic translation, Montano offered his Hebrew initials followed by this "talmīd" moniker, and on the subsequent page containing the Greek Septuagint, its

Latin translation, and a Latin version of the Targum Onkelos, Montano again followed his signature, this time in Latin, with the same out-of-place Arabic word.

These colophons at the end of each Pentateuch chapter are the only Arabic text in the entire eight-volume polyglot set. Montano was displaying his comparative philological interests for knowledgeable readers and obscuring them for another audience unfamiliar with Arabic script. The moniker included in the Biblia Regia, as the Plantin Polyglot is also known, easily could have been mistaken by nonspecialist readers for an extension of his decorative flourish, a common feature of Iberian "rúbricas" of the period. My contention is that Montano signed his name with this Arabic moniker in order subtly to underscore his identity as an inventive and forward-looking Hebraist. Given the inclusion in the final volume of the Biblia Regia of several contentious treatises on biblical exegesis, this formalist aspect of Montano's comparative interests makes sense. Indeed, he later became infamous for a reading practice so focused on the forms of sacred letters and words that he was accused of tending toward the Kabbalistic.[50]

The Biblia Regia was probably the text in which Montano's colophon had the most extensive circulation, but learned interlocutors from the European republic of letters would have known about Montano's moniker even before the final edition of the Polyglot Bible began to circulate. He often signed correspondence this way, even when writing about matters unrelated to Hebrew or Arabic philology to non-Orientalist interlocutors ranging from Juan de Ovando, the president of the Consejo de Indias and university reformer, to King Felipe II.[51] The Stockholm and Antwerp archives containing the letters Montano sent to his colleagues in northern Europe after returning to Spain contain many similar signatures. Both Raphelengius and Plantin, with whom Montano exchanged weekly letters for decades, would have particularly appreciated this "wink-wink" among specialists in Hebrew, Aramaic, and Arabic. Nevertheless, Ovando and Felipe II, as well as more conservative scholarly adversaries like the Salamanca classicist León de Castro, also accurately recognized this Arabic moniker as a sign of a new and potentially dangerous kind of philological expertise, even if they had doubts about its precise meaning. When Castro, who was irked that Felipe II passed him over as editor of the Biblia Regia, denounced Montano to the Holy Office of the Inquisition and claimed that his scholarly focus on Hebrew scripture crossed the line into heresy, he also accused Montano of publicly signing his name as "rabí" (rabbi).[52] Perhaps Castro was mistakenly reading "talmīd" as "rabbi" rather than "student." It is possible that Montano himself aimed to present a subtle, bilingual wordplay along these very same lines—the nearly identical word "Talmud," which designates the collection of rabbinic commentary outlining the rules and regulations of an orthodox Jewish life, comes from the same Semitic root. Castro, who undoubtedly hoped to point inquisition officials to what he saw as Montano's heretical commitment to reading Jewish sources, missed or ignored the joke, however. For Castro, the confusion of Hebrew and Arabic etymology was a way to settle old scores and protect his professional status. Although Castro and Montano harbored contradictory motivations, the one seeking to undermine comparative Semitic philology and the other to defend it, they both nevertheless portrayed Arabic study as part of a complete formation in Hebrew language.

Scattered in peninsular archives are parallel examples of how this economy of expertise worked in practice. In the 1550s, for instance, Montano shared his translation of the biblical love poem the Song of Songs with his friend Fray Luis de León. Such translations of scripture into the vernacular were prohibited, and such intellectual exchange dangerous. Montano, who as librarian of the Escorial enjoyed access to all manner of forbidden printed editions and manuscript material, however, was not one to abide by such prohibitions in private, and neither, apparently, was Fray Luis. Though both ended up under inquisitorial suspicion when their shared notes went missing and Fray Luis's translation of the Song of Songs began to circulate, it was Fray Luis who paid the greater price for the transgression. Inquisitorial representatives arrested him in 1572 because of this unapproved translation. Fray Luis's depositions before the Holy Office, which arrested Martínez de Cantalapiedra and another Salamanca colleague, Gaspar de Grajal, as well, reveal a curious detail about Montano's borrowed Song of Songs manuscript: "At the end of said book," Fray Luis admitted during questioning, "are two lines written in Greek, and a line and a half in Arabic."[53] Needless to say, Fray Luis's inquisitors found this unapproved vernacular biblical text and its multilingual annotations particularly worrisome. Did Castro's anti-Hebraist smear campaign, the source of Montano, Fray Luis, Martínez de Cantalapiedra, and Grajal's woes, have some truth to it? Did these men constitute a secret Hebraist cell at the very heart of the peninsular scholarly community? Or were they simply trying to make sense of their source texts with new philological tools? Since Montano was in the early 1570s overseeing the production of the Biblia Regia in Antwerp, several inquisitors planned to contact Montano's correspondent, Juan de Ovando, who, as we know, would have easily recognized Montano's handwriting, in order to see whether Fray Luis was telling the truth about this little borrowed book.

Unfortunately, the manuscript itself has disappeared, and Fray Luis's trial documents contain no copy or translation of the Arabic lines, and so it is impossible to know the content of this marginal material. Yet this manuscript lacuna strengthens rather than hinders my argument, which is that the content of those lines was as beside the point for their first readers as it is inaccessible to us. For Fray Luis and Montano, the very presence of multilingual script confirmed the intimacy of their relationship and their shared conception of Hebraist inquiry; for their inquisitorial adversaries, it heightened the suspicion of heresy. In each case, the meaning of the words was secondary.

All the same, it is a fair speculation that these short verses were some sort of innocuous blessing, farewell, or aphorism. Extant letters from contemporary Hebraists in northern Europe occasionally contain marginal Arabic notes that resemble those described in Fray Luis's inquisition record.[54] Because Montano was so well integrated into this wider community of scholars, it is unsurprising that he included similar sorts of marginalia in his own correspondence and manuscripts. Like Montano's moniker, this Arabic served decorative and social rather than substantive ends. The goal was to display a shared interest in comparative Semitic philology, even if, as the prominent philologist Isaac Casaubon and his contemporaries Joseph Scaliger and Ignacio de Las Casas agreed, knowledge of Hebrew did not lead inexorably to knowledge of Arabic. These hearty scholars were bonding over the challenges of learning a famously tough language.

Following the Iberian trail of Fray Luis's Song of Songs reveals further evidence of how this exchange of learned sociability and marginalia worked in practice in the peninsular context. As part of the terms for his release from Valladolid's inquisitorial prison, Fray Luis agreed to write an authorized Latin version of the Song of Songs, along with an updated Latin version of his commentary. The resulting text, published in 1580 and expanded in 1589, was itself a revision of his illicit Castilian translation, precisely the work that he was writing when he consulted Montano's curious manuscript.[55] At the beginning of his explanation of the second chapter of Song of Songs, Fray Luis clarified the meaning of the Hebrew word *shoshanat*, or "lily," a term that appears in the first verse of the poem's second chapter. He explained that the word referred to a particularly beautiful "lily of the valley," which grows in humid environments and has seven leaves.[56] The Real Academia de la Historia owns an exemplar of Fray Luis's text, which contains marginal commentary by Francisco Sánchez de las Brozas, and in his short, marginal note beside the underlined word *shoshanat*, Francisco Sánchez pointed out the relationship between the Hebrew word and what he thought was its

Arabic cognate: "From the Arabic *açucena*," wrote Francisco Sánchez.[57] Like Fray Luis, Francisco Sánchez here attempted to clarify the meaning and etymology of *shoshanat*. But the word Francisco Sánchez cited is the Castilian rather than the Arabic cognate. The classical Arabic word for "lily of the valley" is *sausan* in the singular and *sūsan* in the plural, which does share a root with *shoshanat*, but this is not the term in Francisco Sánchez's gloss.[58] Francisco Sánchez knew that the Castilian word was an importation from Arabic, and he knew that this word was related to the Hebrew word under discussion by Fray Luis, but he did not actually cite the Arabic cognate. He referred to the tripartite division of Hebrew and Arabic parts of speech in the opening chapters of his Latin grammar, *Minerva*, and so he certainly was interested in the etymological and morphological pathways connecting the Semitic languages. But in this instance Francisco Sánchez sought primarily to display his sophistication as a comparative philologist.[59] He aimed to make it seem that he was tracing the lexicographic connections directly between Hebrew and Arabic, but in fact he was doing so via Castilian.

Hebrew and Arabic were the two languages that separated the run-of-the mill sixteenth-century theologian or classicist from the cream of the philologist crop. And by the early seventeenth century, Semitic content as well as form began to matter. The peninsular theologian Pedro de Palencia and many other Hebraists and biblical scholars argued that fellow Christians must attempt to address comparative philology's imbrication in ancient and religious history. They should listen to those nimble contemporary and medieval rabbis who introduced philological knowledge from outside Judaism into their interpretations of Jewish holy texts. Historicizing the use of rabbinic glosses, Palencia pointed out that the Israelites and their prophets had borrowed many words from other languages, and that these words became common usage. "Wise rabbis now do the same thing," reasoned Palencia, "following only this [Hebrew] proverb: 'leshon ha-qodesh mebulal,' which means [the holy tongue is] scrambled and mixed up with words from other languages."[60] Palencia insisted that if Hebrew was necessary for understanding the Bible, then so too were Aramaic and Arabic. This lucid justification for comparative Semitic philology marked a shift in Oriental studies from the networks described above. Material changes both produced and strengthened this shift. The Typographia Medicea in Rome had recently developed an improved set of Arabic stamps and published the first interlineal Arabic-Latin version of the New Testament and an Arabic book of Christian prayers. Over the course of the 1590s they also published pedagogical material such as a Latin-Arabic *Alphabetum arabicum*, Arabic-only texts by

Ibn Sīnā and others, and a new edition of the *Al-jurumiyya*. In 1617, Thomas Erpenius came out with his own version of *Al-jurumiyya*, which went by the Latinized title *Giarumia*, and in 1626 he edited an interlineal Latin-Arabic version of the medieval Iberian chronicle known as the *Crónica saracina*. These peninsular-related projects underscore the extent to which the late sixteenth century's tentative and improvised Iberian Arabism influenced the Orientalism of the next century.

Though the Arabism of Benito Arias Montano and Fray Luis de León emerged from different social and institutional contexts than the pastoral Arabism of Martín Pérez de Ayala and Ignacio de Las Casas, they both exhibited a striking disregard for semantic meaning in favor of a focus on form. To maintain the gap between sign and referent served pastoral and intellectual ends. It produced the distinction between Semitic languages and Semitic heresies; it was an instrument for cultivating both New and Old Christian multilingualism; and it aided the reconceptualization of pedagogical discipline and scholarly innovation. In these diverse and counterintuitive ways, the history of peninsular philology is inextricable from the history of Jewish and Muslim conversion to Christianity in the fifteenth and sixteenth centuries, as well as subsequent debates over how best to assimilate and police the converts.

GRAMMARS OF FAITH

No less than New Christian assimilation, effective language education and scholarly reform hinged upon a cultivation and manipulation of custom. As I highlight in this chapter's brief concluding section, fluency and faith alike came to be seen as products of shared rules and conventions. Like Castilian or Arabic, Christianity had a grammar. When Augustine read Galatians to argue that faith was a product of ritual, and Jerome countered that such interpretive literalism and moral behaviorism were sometimes too blunt a pastoral instrument, they were disagreeing over this grammar's capacity to guarantee the correspondence between the signs and the referents of orthodoxy. Unlike Jerome, who defended pastoral dissimulation through an allegorical interpretation of the incident at Antioch, Augustine refused either to blur the visible boundaries of the Christian community with talk of private intentions or to undermine scripture with inventive interpretations. To put their debate in philological terms, Augustine insisted that grammar produced meaning, while Jerome maintained that both grammar and meaning were contingent. This disagreement among theologians about the relationship between the general rules and particular circumstances of orthodoxy was a problem too for early modern philologists, who sought to clarify the relationship between the universality of grammar and the particularity of spoken and written language. Anticipating the Port Royal grammarians, for instance, Francisco Sánchez de las Brozas sought to systematize and reaffirm humanistic exegesis by positing what he called the *ratio grammatical*, or universal grammatical reason. The test case for Francisco Sánchez in this regard was the grammatical enigma of ellipsis, and one of his key examples of ellipsis was a phrase in which the absent word was "faith." Did Latin grammar definitely conjure the word, as Augustine thought ritual produced the thing itself? Or did Francisco Sánchez's inflexible reading merely lend a false sense of grammatical consistency, as Jerome found Augustine's view of Galatians to do?

In *Minerva*, Francisco Sánchez defined ellipsis as "the absence of one or more words in a correct construction, such as 'I want a few [words] with you.'"[61] Although the word "words" is absent from the example, readers and listeners would have understood the implied meaning because of the grammatical structure of the phrase. Previous writers, ranging from the first-century Roman grammarian Quintilian to the English Renaissance humanist Thomas Linacre had treated this problem of omission under various different names, but Francisco Sánchez accentuated the importance of the idea by devoting an entire section of his grammar to cataloguing examples. Moreover, unlike Linacre, who argued that it was possible to deduce the omitted word or phrase either from comparable phrases by the same author or from the remaining words in the particular sentence—either by historicizing or close reading, we would now say—Francisco Sánchez claimed that it was the *ratio grammatical* that provided a third, definitive tool for making sense of the omission. Consider the following example culled from Francisco Sánchez's alphabetical list of missing words, in which proper knowledge of grammar confirmed the meaning of the phrase:

> Faith. Terence, *Phormio*: "By the immortal Gods," in which Donatus says there is ellipsis, and "faith" or something similar is necessary. Cicero, *Œconomico*: "And so, by the immortal Gods, what did you first teach to this one?" Terence: "By the Gods and the faith of men."[62]

The exclamation "pro Deum inmortalium," taken from Terence's second-century BC play *Phormio*, is missing a word or phrase, which the fourth-century commentator Aelius Donatus suggested could be *fidem*, or faith. According to the logic of Donatus and Francisco Sánchez both, the genitive plural construction "of the immortal Gods" produced an ellipsis, which explained how the grammatically incorrect or incomplete phrase might be, in fact, correct and whole. The missing accusative might be visibly absent, but its implicit presence was a condition of grammatical correctness and precise meaning. Despite his apparent hedging about the missing word ("'faith' or something similar"), Francisco Sánchez was sure enough of this reading to categorize it under "F" in his chapter on ellipse, which is structured alphabetically according to the first letter of the various absent terms. In his view, the absence was evidence of ellipsis, and the presentation of the missing words was both a gloss on the ambiguous Latin passage and evidence for the existence of a universal *ratio grammatical*.

In formulating this reading of Terence and theory of grammar, Francisco Sánchez ignored possible counterarguments from the realms of literary criticism and cultural history: Could this apparent ellipsis be the product of a careless scribe? Was Terence the poet disrupting or obeying the grammatical conventions of his day? How universal was this Latin literary register? Echoing Augustine's theology of the sacraments, Francisco Sánchez argued that grammar produced meaning, but he ignored the cultural and historical specificity of grammar itself, Jerome's principal concern. In Francisco Sánchez's effort to theorize a universal *ratio grammatical* from the building blocks of Latin literature, he overlooked the particularities of his examples. He pretended to pursue a descriptive approach to language, cataloguing turns of phrase and parsing curious syntax, but in fact he practiced a boldly prescriptive method, reconstructing the normative rules of Latin from the varied classical evidence. This was Noam Chomsky's criticism of Francisco Sánchez, to whom the former was drawn as a possible forerunner to his own twentieth-century model of deep or universal grammar. Chomsky eventually rejected Francisco Sánchez's concept of ellipse because he found it insufficiently broad and portable. Unlike the Port Royal grammarians Claude Lancelot and Antoine Arnaud's philosophy of language and mind, in which Chomsky saw a clearer connection to modern linguistics, ellipsis did not offer a deep enough access to human intelligence. Yet Chomsky's criticism of Francisco Sánchez was later leveled at Chomsky himself, an inversion that underscores the impossibility of escaping from the particular into the general.[63] Universal grammars exist on a linguistic horizon whose approach is always blocked by political, historical, and material specificity. Augustine's theology ensured that ritual overdetermined faith, while Francisco Sánchez employed grammar in a parallel way. The goal in each case was to eliminate contingency. Yet like Jerome, who depicted Augustine's literalism as a mere fiction for combating apostasy, Francisco Sánchez could not entirely ignore literary and linguistic specificity. Through Francisco Sánchez's failure to prove the existence of a *ratio grammatical,* it is possible to see the extent to which debate over the relationship between form and content was a tool for controlling the course of assimilation and reimaging the boundaries of orthodoxy.

This aspect of philology was not lost on the New Christians themselves. We have already seen how *conversos* leveraged their Hebrew knowledge into a new kind of comparative philological expertise. Moriscos accomplished something similar by making the case that Arabic was an essential tool for reading Christian scripture. They did not simply argue, like the wise rabbis cited by Palencia, that lexical and syntactical parallels among Hebrew, Arabic, and Aramaic might clarify obscure passages in the Hebrew Bible or correct Jerome's Vulgate translation. Instead, they made an even stronger case, based on new and confounding scriptural evidence unearthed in the hills outside of Granada. At the intersection of the pastoral and the erudite stories narrated above, Arabic translators converted this peculiar evidence into the familiar and authoritative form of Christian holy text. That sacred authenticity could be a product of an institutional process and human editors did not strike Benito Arias Montano, Pedro de Valencia, Ignacio de Las Casas, and the texts' other opponents as strange, for they knew from experience the contingent quality of historical truth and philological knowledge. But they urged caution in the case of this Sacromonte episode, lest the discoveries' defenders turn the sacred processes of truth making into a mockery. The gap between sign and referent had served inquisitors and evangelizers well for nearly a century. It was now time for the Moriscos to seize their opponents' weapons and employ them to their own ends.

CHAPTER FOUR

Heterodoxy in Translation

Over the course of the 1590s, laborers, children, and treasure hunters discovered twenty-two Arabic etchings falsely attributed to a first-century Christian martyr in the hills behind the Albaicín neighborhood of Granada. Along with these lead books, a series of relics and Latin plaques also appeared in the network of caves on the hillside, which soon became known as Sacromonte, the holy mountain. When the first major findings were reported, some of Granada's residents rejoiced in the city streets; others performed barefoot pilgrimages to the discovery site. But scholarly rows and institutional wrangling soon colored this initial excitement, as a gaggle of theologians and philologists struggled for decades to translate and interpret the polysemous documents, which celebrated the Arabic language while emphasizing points of agreement between Christianity and Islam.[1] Should the texts be read as the lost narrative of an early Christian saint, which, as Pedro de Valencia, Benito Arias Montano, and Ignacio de Las Casas pointed out, required overlooking an anachronistic Arabic and Spanish lexicon and a jumbled account of early Islam? Or, as Archbishop of Granada Pedro de Castro, Granadan jurist Gregorio López de Madera (not the editor of the *Siete partidas*), Roman Arabist Bartolomé Pectorano, and Marqués de Estepa Adán Centurión all suggested, could there be a divine explanation, a miracle that might confound such philological and historical objections?

The Sacromonte lead books, along with the Turpiana manuscript—a multilingual parchment found with various other relics during the 1588 renovations of the former minaret of the Nasrid Great Mosque—provided an appealing Christian history to a medieval Muslim city.[2] Moreover, because the lead books advocated the principle of the Immaculate Conception of the

Virgin Mary, a subject of intense argument among Franciscans and Dominicans in late sixteenth- and early seventeenth-century Andalusia, the documents filtered into mainstream theological discourse as proponents of this doctrine cited the discoveries to support their position.[3] At the same time, educated Moriscos, such as the court and inquisition translators Miguel de Luna and Alonso de Castillo, two of the few people on the Iberian Peninsula capable of reading and, as several scholars have argued, *writing* the lead books, would have appreciated not only the prestige associated with translating and glossing the texts, but also the flexible Christianity articulated within them. In sum, these forgeries provided a sense of local, Christian identity, played an influential role in theological debate, and transformed early seventeenth-century Arabic and Oriental studies in Spain.[4]

Defenders of the texts found them handy for the consolidation of local power, wealth, and prestige. Modern historians, like early modern detractors, have concentrated on exposing the "plomos" or "libros plúmbeos," as the lead books and Turpiana manuscript collectively were known, as forgeries. I do not focus here on the fact of forgery, confirmed by Pope Innocent XI in 1682, when he declared the texts "pure human fictions, fabricated for the ruin of the Catholic faith."[5] The first half of this chapter studies instead the interpretive processes and material history that made the unveiling of forgery necessary in the first place. Only through an audacious process of transformation could the strangeness of the Arabic paleography and the ambiguity of the theological content disappear from the lead books. In quickly translating the texts, Miguel de Luna and Bartolomé Pectorano, whose works I examine closely below, sought to parse troubling Islamic passages as Francisco Sánchez de las Brozas had parsed snippets of classical literature: they posited a grammar both linguistic and religious in order to harden the discoveries' meaning. Several decades after the initial discoveries, the philological and codicological evidence of the early translators' hesitancy had evaporated, replaced by an ever more strident editorial confidence and rich manuscript production. The history of this transformation is a history of the reception and meaning of the lead books in particular, but it is also an account of how early modern peninsular scholars reinvented philological expertise in the process of negotiating the boundaries of orthodoxy. No less than to become Christian through conversion and assimilation, to become scripture through translation, edition, and interpretation was to adhere to conventions both material and hermeneutic. The men who sought to accomplish this invention of scripture submitted the lead books, themselves, and their audiences to a regime of scholarly discipline.

Their attempt to appropriate the power to canonize, for this is what controlling the definition of authenticity and the boundary between fiction and scripture meant, ultimately failed. But as I argue, the contested nature of their failure demonstrates an early modern Spanish conviction that textual and theological form might still produce sanctity.

The second half of the chapter turns to learned handwringing over the history of the Spanish language. The lead books contained a mixture of sixteenth-century Spanish, classical Latin, and postclassical Arabic, a paradox that detractors often invoked as evidence of falsification. Attempting to demonstrate that Spanish and Latin could have been in simultaneous use in first-century Iberia, defenders of the texts like Gregorio López de Madera pointed out that a mingling of languages had always accompanied ethnic and cultural miscegenation. As a result, López de Madera and his allies saw no reason why the Turpiana manuscript's hodgepodge of different languages or the lead books' anachronistic Arabic should arouse particular suspicion, especially since they hailed from a region famous as an imperial crossroads. López de Madera's contemporary, the historian of the Spanish language Bernardo de Aldrete, however, was unsure that the multilingual *plomos* served as sufficient evidence to rewrite the histories of language and empire. Conflicting models of skepticism characterized this disagreement over what we now call diachronic linguistics, a field of inquiry that in the Spanish context was influenced by decades of dispute over the Sacromonte discoveries.

Defenders of the lead books formulated and employed their glosses on the discoveries in ways that may now seem pious only to the most cynical of observers. Such an observer might argue that piety in this context was but an instrumental fiction or naive error. In this view, those thousands of pilgrims who venerated the Sacromonte texts and martyrs were blind to their coercion by the discoveries' educated apologists. To be sure, to create the conditions of Sacromonte piety was not to coerce in the manner of the previous three chapters' inquisitors, scholastics, and philologists, who revolutionized law and language by debating the legitimacy of compulsion in a variety of pastoral and pedagogical circumstances. The Sacromonte episode displays a different sort of coercion, for the lead books' translators and commentators tampered with textual sources rather than bodies and souls. The scholars in this chapter forced the lead books through the process of canonization rather than the rituals of conversion and assimilation. Moreover, they were frank about the professional interests that informed their attitudes toward orthodoxy and discipline. Such instrumentalism was not a telltale defect of institutionalized hypocrisy. It was rather an integral feature of religious practice. By examining the contentious debate about how a series of mysterious and multilingual texts like the *plomos* nearly became Christian scripture, we are able to see that, like religious orthodoxy or linguistic fluency, scripture and sainthood were products of juridical conventions, interpretive practices, and institutional power.

BECOMING SCRIPTURE, CONTAINING FICTION

The diverse glosses and translations of early modern readers of the lead books seemed to convert the Arabic etchings into sacred texts. In fact, two different versions of the lead books emerged from these manuscripts and printed materials. Foreshadowing the language of the papal rejection, the documents' detractors attacked the discoveries as dangerous and heretical fictions. Their commentaries circulated across the Iberian Peninsula with copied or translated sections of the original documents. Because Archbishop Pedro de Castro jealously guarded the lead tablets themselves in Granada until the middle of the seventeenth century, when he reluctantly sent them first to Madrid in 1631 and then on to Rome in 1642, critics of the discoveries saw themselves as condemning an archeological curiosity rather than a proper text.[6] The dubious material history of the tablets proved the skeptics' critical point: a truly authentic religious text would have been cited in other ancient sources; it would have been copied and codified by some studious early saint; it surely would have become, over the course of fifteen centuries, a sacred *book*.

Defenders of the discoveries acknowledged this problem, and they set about producing such a recognizable and aesthetically beautiful holy text. They circulated both manuscripts and printed secondary sources, replacing the lead etchings with paper and ink. To accompany this formal and material repackaging, they formulated a scholarly apparatus affirming the Arabic etchings' Christian orthodoxy. The Islamic elements were either purged from the Spanish and Latin translations or circumscribed by a web of commentary. Once translated into Spanish and Latin, contested Arabic theological terminology fit seamlessly into authoritative, now Christian manuscripts. The "Solomonic" Arabic script, identifiable by separated, angular characters conducive to etching quickly on metal but unusual in the history of Arabic paleography, disappeared behind a layer of conventional Spanish and Latin writing. By the time Pope Innocent XI declared the lead tablets forgeries, there existed a decades-old textual history attesting to their early Christian orthodoxy. The heretical fictions had, at least in this second tradition of commentary, ceded the way to gospel.

Although Christian authors from Augustine to Renaissance defenders of poetry attempted to demarcate history from fiction, most found the uniqueness of scripture to be self-evident. By the sixteenth century, the long effort to portray the methods for distinguishing scripture from other narratives as a set of divine hermeneutic laws had succeeded in making defense of canonic texts seem redundant to a Christian audience.[7] However, those charged with interpreting new texts, especially those whose authorship and material history were dubious, faced the more complicated challenge of a positivist interpretive process. A text's newness itself was associated with deception, which it was the responsibility of translators, editors, and interpreters to control and explain. Simply categorizing a text as fiction did not quarantine its potential danger, for many learned readers considered fictions, particularly contemporary fictions, to be at best a frivolous waste of time and at worst a disruption of social and religious order. Despite the presumption that scripture was different in kind from these other potentially dangerous narratives, theological concern about forged or apocryphal religious texts paralleled this anxiety over fiction's mimetic power.[8] Unorthodox religious representation might mislead a pious but naive populace.

Notwithstanding debate over the differences between history and fiction, early modern critics, for theoretical and strategic reasons, often did not distinguish between the dangers posed by untruthful heretics and those posed by inventive poets. They thus inadvertently revealed the confused boundary between religious and literary narrative. Pedro de Valencia wrote in 1607 to Archbishop of Toledo and Inquisitor General Bernardo de Sandoval y Rojas to attack the lead books, attempting to employ these fraught boundaries to his advantage. Valencia claimed that the texts reminded him of many other "fictions from books made by heretics, as well as other deceits with which they are forged and sold," highlighting his concern both with the problem of blurred narrative categories and with a purposefully heretical intent to pass off an invented text as an integral part of religious history, even if only for entertainment or profit.[9] Like that of Ignacio de Las Casas, Valencia's legitimacy as an opponent of Morisco expulsion rested in part upon his integrity as a critic of the lead books. For this reason, it is impossible to gauge attitudes toward the Moriscos by the Sacromonte episode alone. Las Casas and Valencia demarcated the line between fiction and forgery in the *plomos* even as they defended, as we will see in chapter 6, a renewed program of New and Old Christian mixing. In contrast, Archbishop Pedro de Castro recognized his own unique reliance on Morisco translators in his effort to defend the forgeries as authentic, and so he joined the lead books' critics in opposition to Morisco expulsion. Despite the historical significance of these scholarly and political debates, the thousands of pilgrims who began to venerate the Sacromonte martyrs paid little heed to the critical opinions sent by naysayers from Madrid, Salamanca, and elsewhere. However dubious its textual foundation, their pious devotion was real, its effects enduring.

That a diverse audience saw these discoveries as a miracle whose reward was a hitherto unknown canonical story obliged the Church to reach a judgment. The pilgrims' wonder was produced through a mimetic process, but determining whether this was a scripturally or fictionally driven imitation would be decided only after a century of exasperating, perhaps purposely slow institutional decision making. And even then, the simple papal dismissal of the lead books as "human fictions" belied a complicated history that included not only rejection, but also cooption and canonization. The papal formulation itself underscores the broader hermeneutic problem concerning the relationship among fiction, scripture, and heresy, for the modifier "human" remained tellingly present in the rejection, suspended between a theological contradiction in terms (a divine fiction) and a tautology (all fictions are human). This anxiety over how to portray the distinction between holy and heretical narrative, palpable throughout the Sacromonte debate, drew attention to both the instability of linguistic meaning and the complex balance of hermeneutic power to determine and sanction that meaning. While epistemological doubt about legal and literary documents was a pressing political affair, challenging the boundaries of scriptural canonicity and questioning the very language of holy text were, many theologians vociferously argued, an eschatological matter. Despite such attempts to distinguish appropriate reading practices for different kinds of texts, conflict over the lead books' meaning focused either on obscuring the disturbing parallel between these various hermeneutics or developing formal modes for undermining it.

Take as examples two pieces of evidence from the Sacromonte controversy, Miguel de Luna's 1595 translation into Spanish of the two most famous and theologically important lead books, *Kitāb qawā'id al-dīn* (Book of the Foundations of Religion) and *Kitāb fī-l-dāt al-karma* (Book of the Essence of God), and Bartolomé Pectorano's interlineal Latin and Arabic version, *Sol veritatis* (The Sun of Truth), finished around the time of the pope's 1682 judgment.[10] Miguel de Luna, whose translation was commissioned by Archbishop Pedro de Castro and supported by King Felipe II, succeeded his colleague Alonso de Castillo as Arabic interpreter to the Crown. He also wrote *La verdadera historia del Rey Don Rodrigo*, which reimagined for a late sixteenth-century audience the Muslim conquest of the Iberian Peninsula in terms sympathetic to the conquerors. Importantly, Luna claimed to have merely translated *La verdadera historia*, attributing it to (who else?) an "Arab historian" in order to lend the text authority and deflect criticism.[11] Pectorano, on the other hand, was one of the Arabic interpreters charged by Pope Innocent XI with translating the lead books. Professor of Arabic at the University of Naples, he was famous for supposedly having converted the son of the emperor of Ethiopia to Christianity during his travels through the Middle East and Africa. In 1658 Pectorano came to Spain, and King Felipe IV wanted to make him archbishop of the Italian city of Reggio in Calabria, then under Spanish authority. Determined to mount a defense of the lead books, Pectorano refused the offer and instead took a position as the first canon of the Abbey of Sacromonte, where he set to work on his transcriptions and translations.[12]

Because codicological conventions such as binding, decoration, and layout nudged readers toward particular interpretive assumptions, to produce an elegant manuscript was to engage in theological dispute. While Luna's text remained an unbound draft meant to spur initial interest in and satisfy preliminary doubts about the lead books, the material and formal details of Pectorano's interlineal translation made his loftier goals self-evident.[13] The final folios, for instance, provide an index of names—amazingly, in transliterated Solomonic Arabic, transliterated classical Arabic, conventional Arabic script, and Latin—and a chart comparing specific passages in the laminates to both orthodox sources and heretical confutations. Although Pectorano himself figured prominently in his text's introductory story of the Sacromonte lead books' discovery and translation, he let the conventions of theological commentary and the materiality of early modern manuscripts authorize the rest of the text. The manuscript's formal elegance leaves the impression that an orthodox consensus on the status of the lead books has already formed and that Pectorano was simply and piously making it available to readers. As a papal scholar, a member of the clergy, and a celebrated guest in Spain, Pectorano wrote from a position of professional security, and so unlike Luna or Castillo, he could afford to be definitive in his translation. Writing earlier than Pectorano and from the complicated position of a Morisco Arabist funded by Felipe II, Luna had to tread more carefully. His wariness is evident in the top and bottom margins of every page, which are filled with signatures and crosshatching, a notarial convention designed to protect the integrity of the text and, in turn, the trustworthiness of the author. Waiting both for consensus and for a lead book manuscript tradition to coalesce rather than offering a definitive fair copy, Luna tried to guard his reputation as an expert Arabist and avoid inquisitorial suspicion.[14]

Kitāb qawā'id al-dīn, the first Arabic text discovered in the Sacromonte caves, relates in paratactic prose the histories of Adam, Eve, and Jesus. A colophon on the final laminate reveals the author to be Thesiphon Aben Athar Arabi, who later lead books divulge was the brother of Saint Cecilius, the mythical founder and first bishop of Granada. Luna's Spanish version of *Kitāb qawā'id al-dīn*, which he calls *Libro de los fundamentos de la ley*, served the dual function of solidifying the lead books' theological meaning for a broader audience and enticing Felipe II, to whom the manuscript was sent in 1595, to support translation of the remaining discoveries.[15] Although at first glance the text seems to be a reasonably orthodox account of early Christianity, Luna nevertheless proceeded carefully in his translation. He hedged the body of his text with hundreds of footnotes, transliterated specific Arabic words that might raise suspicion, and referred to the opinions of Alonso de Castillo, who was at the same time working on his own, separate translation. Archbishop Pedro de Castro, who like Adán Centurión learned Arabic to read the lead books, closely regulated Luna, Castillo, and the other early translators.[16]

Pedro de Castro and the notary officials who validated the Sacromonte translations attempted to mitigate the dual dangers of inquisitorial suspicion and unreliable translators by making sure Arabic experts signed formal agreements, or *juramentos*, before beginning their work. Luna agreed not only to translate accurately, but also to do so "word for word, *verbum ex verbo*, loyally."[17] Charged with producing a lexicon in prose, Luna constantly defended his word choice by referencing the range of possible meanings in the Arabic original. For example, when translating a phrase located in the passage that introduced Jesus to the story—clearly an important narrative moment—Luna faithfully rendered the Arabic sentence "fa-inā amthala laki al-tawhid al-muthalātha" (Verily I exemplify to you the three-part unity) into Spanish as "y assi exemplificar os quiero la unidad trina."[18] Letting such a theologically decisive moment go unaccounted for would have invited philological questions, so Luna offered a note explaining the translation. Yet the language he used to reiterate his certainty regarding this translation revealed an insecurity that the note was meant to obviate. Composed in a mixture of Spanish, Latin, and Luna's own transliterated Solomonic Arabic, the citation is short but authoritative: "The Arabic word 'mutalata' *id est* three-part, and this adjective is given just as in the Arabic."[19] Luna provided the Arabic evidence for his faithful translation and highlighted the theological trustworthiness of *muthalātha* by linking it to his Spanish translation with the authoritative Latin connector *id est*, or "that is." In most instances Luna remained satisfied with the less commanding vernacular *quiere decir*, but when specifically defending Spanish translations of potentially tricky Arabic words, he preferred a formal Latin terminology that carried both the force of classical grammar and the prestige of the Church's language.

Luna's hedging largely disappeared from later versions of the lead books. In *Sol veritatis*, Pectorano rendered the Arabic phrase cited in the previous paragraph, "Verily I exemplify to you the three-part unity," in Latin as "narrabo tibi unitatem Trinitatis" (I narrate to you the unity of the Trinity).[20] The Arabic term for the Christian Trinity, *thālūth*, unsurprisingly comes from the same root as the word for "three-part," but this was not a mere confusion of vocalization on Pectorano's behalf: the words for "Trinity" and "three-part" do not resemble each other in Arabic. Rather, his translation was a gloss on the more flexible Arabic vocabulary, from which the actual word *Trinity* is noticeably absent. Pectorano did provide a margin note at this line in his text, not in order to explain his translation of *muthalātha*, but rather to revise his choice of "narrabo." With this word, "I narrate," the text shifts from a third-person, omniscient account to the first-person voice of Thesiphon, supposedly martyred in the Granadan hills where the tablets were discovered. Perhaps dissatisfied with this poetic language of narration, Pectorano replaced "narrabo" with "exemplificabo" in the recopied sentence of a margin note, thus following Luna's version. While Pectorano's language of exemplification implied the doctrinal truth of the Trinity, the Arabic root of the original in fact carried the explicit literary connotations (as in "narrabo") of representation, metaphor, and resemblance. First designed to erase the literary language of narration, this gloss had by the end of the volume become a scholarly marker of the lead books' orthodoxy. That is, the very first reference on the comparative doctrinal chart found in the final folios of *Sol veritatis* was the Trinity. While a host of traditional sources supported the doctrine of the Trinity, Pectorano made clear that Muslims, Gnostics, and other mistaken peoples denied it.[21] Readers were supposed to recognize that the text of the lead books should no longer exist in this middle ground of theological debate, but pass instead, according to the chart's spatial logic, to the left-hand column of established and authoritative sources. The table recording the lead books' alleged mention of the Trinity refers, of course, to precisely the page examined above, doubly obscuring Pectorano's sleight of hand, for it was there that he had inserted the word *Trinitatis* in the first place.

Pectorano's scholastic method similarly concealed the allusive quality of Mary's inclusion in the lead books' account of a tripartite God. Thesiphon explained the "three-part unity" with the metaphorical image of a father who looks into a mirror illuminated by the Holy Spirit (*rūḥanī al-muqaddas*) and sees his son. "The father is the first person. The son is the second person. And the Holy Spirit is the third person," he elaborated. "Three people in one essence, and thus Mary was the mirror."[22] By reproducing God's representation as Jesus, Mary was the reflecting surface that made the three parts visible. For many Old Christians, Mary was indeed such an intercessor. She was a nurturing figure capable of mitigating the harsh judgments of a retributive God. Stories about Mary provided a proximate and familiar point of entry into the confusing theology of the Trinity, a way for worshipers across the Hispanic world, especially recent converts, to participate in local Christian practice.[23] While the various poetic genres were dangerous for their disruptive mimetic potential, narratives such as those about Mary's life helped to produce pious action. The art historian Felipe Pereda has taken this argument about the relationship between Marian devotion and conversion a step farther, arguing that evangelizers themselves recognized the usefulness of Mary iconography for the Christianization project. Christian preachers and theologians emphasized Mary before a Morisco flock because they knew of Mary's acceptability within Islam. Devotion to the Virgin Mary and the *plomos* were mutually reinforcing modes of popular piety and local adoration over the course of the seventeenth century.[24] This connection emerged because one of the relics found in the same lead box as the Turpiana manuscript was half of the handkerchief Mary supposedly used to wipe her tears at the crucifixion of Jesus, and several important passages in the lead books feature Mary as a main character. Not only did Mary take a *mi'rāj*-like night journey paralleling Muhammad's, but in one of the found tablets she also described her dictation of the so-called *Libro mudo*, or mute book, another set of etchings that no translator was able to decipher but whose eventual decoding, Mary predicted, was to occur at a final-judgment assembly on the island of Cyprus.

In this end-of-days scenario, the processes of translating, editing, and glossing the *libros plúmbeos* would transform the Christian scriptural canon as a whole. Sacromonte philology was destined to reveal a universal theological truth. In another lead book entitled *Kitāb tara'ij haqīq al-aynīl* (Book of the History of the Truth of the Gospels), Mary posed a series of metatextual questions to Saint Peter about the future discovery and interpretation of the lead tablets. In response, Peter outlined the decipherment of the *Libro mudo*, praised the Arabic interpreters that would accomplish the text's translation, and predicted a definitive reading of the lead book corpus as a whole. This reading was to emerge from what Pectorano called in Latin a "great council" on Cyprus, and it was to occasion nothing less than Mediterranean religious harmony.[25] The gathering, which recalled both the Council of Trent and the many councils convened by Spanish bishops over the course of the sixteenth century to discuss Morisco affairs, was to feature several characters with striking early modern Spanish and Mediterranean parallels. In Adán Centurión's Spanish version of the episode, a "holy priest" (*santo sacerdote*), supported by the "king of the Arabs who will not be Arab" (*rey de los arabes y no será arabe*), was destined to encourage various privileged interpreters, led by a "most humble creature" (*humildísima criatura*).[26] As detractors of the lead books pointed out, these characters in the Cyprus assembly suspiciously resembled Archbishop Pedro de Castro (the holy priest), Ottoman Sultan Suleiman the Magnificent or one of his heirs (non-Arab king of the Arabs), the bilingual Morisco readers and learned Arabists (the interpreters), and the Virgin Mary herself (the most humble creature). The overwrought timeliness of this prophecy was suspicious, to say the least.

The lead books suggested that religious discord and violence would end not when the truth of one religious tradition had dominated all the others, but rather when religion itself came to be defined by shared iconographies, histories, and practices across traditional ecumenical lines. To craft religious similitude was to enable Morisco assimilation and counteract dissimulation. The emergence of this final harmony, Peter's prediction continued, would be preceded by an intensely contradictory, polemical, and violent debate over interpretation. Along with fornication and pride, Peter told the Virgin Mary that the "multiplication of ways of speaking with metaphors as well as dissimulated ridicule" was evidence that God's blessing had vanished from the world.[27] Dissimulation was the sign of a religious crisis that the Sacromonte lead books would bring to a happy conclusion.

The linguistic ambiguity and unstable theological grammar of the *libros plúmbeos* were nevertheless themselves part of this crisis. For the discovery of the lead books to mark an end to the metaphorical mode of reading that both detractors and defenders of the texts necessarily exercised, it was first necessary to parse the texts themselves. By celebrating in this way the role that readers played in establishing a definitive meaning of the lead books, the forgers both carved out a privileged social and religious place for the future interpreters (who they might have guessed would be themselves) and framed the formal and material transformation of the texts as part of a universal religious cosmology and Mediterranean political geography. Cyprus was, after all, a middle ground, an island between the Christian and the Islamic worlds. The lead books foretold the story of interpretation's end in a fit of material and epistemological clarity and religious harmony. The common features of Christian and Muslim religious lives would become unproblematic aspects of a universal faith rather than the contested terrain of a political and pastoral power struggle.

Despite this fiction of understanding among different religions, insistence on Mary's sinless birth, evident in both learned opinions on the lead books and the popular devotion the texts helped generate, transformed the Mary of Sacromonte from a narrative to a dogmatic tool within the Christian community. Franciscans and others employed the lead books in order to pressure the Vatican to decide upon the doctrine of the Immaculate Conception, declared dogma by Rome only in the mid-nineteenth century. Among the many seventeenth-century authors who cited the lead books in defense of the Immaculate Conception of the Virgin Mary was the prior of the Monasterio de San Jerónimo in Madrid, Fray Gerónimo de la Cruz. In his *Sacrarum virginum vindicatio,* a text addressed to Felipe IV that circulated with Sacromonte manuscript material, Fray Gerónimo attempted to separate the lead books' Mary rhetoric from its apparently Islamic material. Let's not throw out the evidence of Mary's Immaculate Conception with the bathwater of the Qur'anic references; we should be slow to judge such contradictions, insisted Fray Gerónimo, since defenders of the texts could rightly argue that "when faith discovered the world, the Catholic religion suffered even greater contradictions than the one that the lead books suffer today."[28] Fray Gerónimo's point was that orthodoxy changed over time. It became more or less secure depending upon a host of institutional, social, and political processes. Proving both Felipe Pereda and Fray Gerónimo's insights, Mary's presence in the lead books had a profound theological and social impact. Regardless of the allegedly heretical intentions of the lead books' authors, by gradually making certain popular forms of ritual and belief orthodoxy, the Vatican eventually coopted the Mary worship that the forgeries themselves had helped produce. A local Granadan council had declared the relics authentic in 1600, and as Adán Centurión cheerfully reminded his readers, the Tridentine rules for authentication and canonization left Rome with no other option but to accede. The pope could police the philological and theological boundaries of the Sacromonte texts themselves, but the Granadan judgment on the relics had to stand. As a result, devotion to Cecilius's remains and Mary's handkerchief continues to this day.[29]

As a final example of how the Sacromonte lead books put the institutional power to translate and canonize on display, consider this disagreement over a passage from the discoveries that mimicked the Islamic declaration of faith, the *shahāda*. Luna's version, which directly precedes the "three-part unity" passage, reads as follows: "No one understands God but God; and if we were to understand God, it would not be God, for man's understanding is weak."[30] Variations on "there is no God but God" (*lā ilaha illa Allāh*), a fundamental Islamic statement of belief, are scattered throughout the lead books. Defenders of the texts dismissed the Islamic referent by cataloguing parallel Hebrew and Latin formulations of God's singularity, insisting upon a Judeo-Christian context for the Arabic Sacromonte texts.[31] But it was difficult to avoid the reality that the texts were written in Arabic, and so comparing this repeated reformulation of the *shahāda* with parallels in other monotheistic traditions did little but provide evidence for a common grammar of God's oneness.

The controversy continued in subsequent pages. Just before the conclusion of *Kitāb fī-l-dāt al-karma*, which in most manuscript collections of the corpus follows *Kitāb qawā'id al-dīn*, there are two Arabic letters, a *mīm* and then a *rā'*. Preceding the two characters is another invocation of the *shahāda*, and following them is the word *Allāh*, which ends the chapter. In both the lead laminates and the manuscript versions, "seals of Solomon" (i.e., star of David diagrams) and an affirmation of God's oneness decorate the space below the end of the main text. As many modern readers have pointed out, thus repeating early modern scholarly insights, the second part of the traditional Islamic declaration of faith is *Muḥammad Rasūl Allāh* (Muhammad is the messenger/prophet of God).[32] It seemed reasonable, as Pedro de Valencia and others noted, to read the *mīm, rā', Allāh* as an abbreviation of this phrase, especially since it followed the first part of the *shahāda*, translated by Luna as "there is no other God but God."[33] Notwithstanding the obviousness of this reading, which served as evidence of the documents' heretical character, transcribers and translators of the texts immediately began transforming the abbreviation.

Luna followed his accurate translation of the first part of the *shahāda* with long dashes in the main text where the second phrase of the translation should be. He thus concluded the chapter with an erasure, explaining that after the final lines "four singular letters *littera proparte* follow, which for now are not understood" (*se siguen quatro lettras singulares littera proparte que por agora no se entienden*). This placeholder, *por agora no se entienden*, occurs in the margin notes of many folios of this early translation, and much like the *id est* mentioned above, it signals a particularly problematic passage or Arabic term. In a margin note specifically about this section's thorny "singular letters," Luna paraphrased the work of his fellow translator Alonso de Castillo, who claimed, "The Arabic says 'gua rabune alah,' which means and our creator God. The 'gue' is copulative and the 'rabune' is a noun meaning creator, combined with the plural pronoun, 'ne,' or our creator God, 'alah,' which means and our creator God."[34] It is possible that Castillo innocently confused the *mīm* for a *wāw*, which means "and" in Arabic, because although the Solomonic ductus of the former was slightly more angled than that of the latter, clear descenders identified both Arabic letters. But the explanation of the first-person possessive ending is at best irrelevant and at worst spurious, for the individual letters from which he extrapolated the meaning do not admit prefixes or suffixes. This overly wrought and ultimately faulty grammatical argument, apparently meant to buttress the paleographic claim, casts doubt on Castillo's gloss as a whole. Interpreting the letters as "and our creator God" is certainly more flexible than the clearly Islamic implications of "messenger of God," the most theologically weighty genitive construction, or *iḍāfa*, in the Arabic language. Moreover, Castillo's translation is four words, which would explain the discrepancy between the *two* hotly contested letters present in the Arabic manuscripts and the *four* letters Luna mentions. Was Luna's concluding observation of four mysterious letters an erasure of the two-letter Arabic evidence and a lie buttressing a translated acronym?

Invoking a paleographic defense for what he portrays as innocent uncertainty rather than outright deception, Luna explained that the letters on the original round lead tablet were elongated in order to keep the lines flush, making them difficult to decipher. Filling the textual gap with Castillo's tentative reading, Luna insisted on delaying a final decision about the characters' meaning with the evasive though strategically hopeful "por agora" of critical ignorance. Later translators were less timid. If the goal of the abbreviation in the first place was to encourage creative and multiple readings while at the same time subtly invoking a widely recognizable Islamic turn of phrase, then this *mīm* and *rā'* played their roles splendidly. Adán Centurión translated the final line as "There is no God but God, Jesus, the Spirit of God" (No hay Dios sino Dios, Jesús, Espíritu de Dios), adding in the Holy Spirit and Jesus for good measure. Centurión tried to defend this translation by reading the *rā'* as *rūḥ*, or "spirit," but he admitted that in other sections of the text he translated *rūḥ* differently, and he conveniently avoided mentioning the abbreviations at all.[35] Pectorano, for his part, translated the phrase as "There is no God but God; the Messiah is the Spirit of God" (*Non Deus nisi Deus Messias Spiritus Dei*), changing the Arabic text to fit his Latin translation by adding the words *mesīḥa* (Messiah) and *rūḥ* where, as he mentions in a margin note, only the "two solitary letters" (*duas l'tras solitarias*) once stood.[36] Although Pectorano, unlike Luna, at least managed to see the correct number of letters, he imagined an orthodox Latin translation, invented an Arabic phrase as the original, and relegated the troublesome remnants of synchronicity to the margins.

The forgeries seemed to breed yet more forgery. The apparently trivial *mīm* and *rā'*, which capture the hermeneutic problems posed by language as a whole, were theologically fundamental. At the same time, these letters were perceived to be inherently unreliable, even heretical, as Valencia implied by citing Paul in his letter on the lead books: "And so tongues are a sign, not for believers but for unbelievers," reads 1 Corinthians 14:22, "and prophecy is not for unbelievers but for believers."[37] Like Paul, Valencia was skeptical of any text that emphasized its status as a system of signs, even though his own scholarly authority rested upon the ability to parse language and recognize generic convention. Attempting to give the impression of antiquity, the paleographic and philological features of the lead books did foreground their linguistic peculiarity. Valencia was incredulous, carefully distinguishing mysterious though unreliable language from the prophecy, as Paul put it, of the believers. Along with his fellow critics of the lead books, Valencia either insisted upon the heretical Islamic language of this and similar passages or decried the shared theological syntax as a marker of the lead books' fictionality, dubbing it a crass attempt to please a broad audience.[38]

The Sacromonte lead books' advocates' emphasis on translation belied the theological insistence that these texts were, in fact, new revelations, thus contradicting the notion that scripture was untranslatable. The paradoxical nature of this argument, which resonates with the similarly paradoxical refusal to admit the translatability even of Jerome's Vulgate, itself a revision of earlier translations, reveals the institutional and formal conditions of possibility for the production of orthodoxy. There is an echo here both of Augustine's theology of the sacraments, which insisted upon a visible measure of orthodoxy, and of Jerome's defense of dissimulation, which acknowledged that some level of well-intentioned duplicity was sometimes necessary in order to achieve pastoral ends. It was critical to translate the Sacromonte texts expediently, thereby obscuring the suspect Arabic original.

Yet portraying Luna and Pectorano's textual decisions as deliberate censorship does not tell the whole story. The process of transcription and translation is, of course, editorial in nature, which is not to absolve Luna and Pectorano of their responsibility as interpreters, but simply to recognize that editors must make choices. Rarely is scholarly consensus so firm that such decisions seem commonsensical or objective. As Hans Ulrich Gumbrecht has argued, the editorial process entails both imaginative and scientific work.[39] Though Pectorano's choice to parse the Arabic acronym by writing the words he thought they represented in the main text itself might seem misleading or coercive in hindsight, these sorts of decisions provide insight into how the process of "canonization through commentary" functioned.[40] Faced with the impossibility of translating an Arabic acronym "word for word," Pectorano, more than Luna, made explicit an implied meaning whose divine apostrophe he understood to be directed at a universal audience. He claimed an authority we now associate either with editors of literary texts, who routinely fill in missing words and "correct" copyist errors, or with critics more generally, whose analyses produce sacred objects of a different order. Pectorano's editorial practice highlights the difficulty of using formal differences in hermeneutic strategy to track the boundary between the literary and the religious spheres. His insistence that an uncorrupted divine word might be contained in a corrupted text reveals a keenly modern awareness of scripture's literary quality and material historicity. Defenders of the lead books were not able to prove the texts' orthodoxy, but the terms of the detractors' attacks exposed a relationship between the heretical unreliability of fiction and the trustworthiness of scripture. Linguistic conventionality, after all, underpinned them both.

THE INVERISIMILITUDE OF REVELATION

In his *Tratado de la verdadera y falsa profecía* of 1588, Juan de Horozco y Covarrubias, who later held Martín Pérez de Ayala's old post of bishop of Guadix, tried to reinforce the distinction between fiction and scripture. Obscuring the way in which social practices and institutional authority produce orthodoxy over time, Covarrubias proposed a series of stable rules for distinguishing between true and false prophecy. Covarrubias argued that a principal marker of divine truth was familiar language. As Paul had suggested in Corinthians, theological reliability and familiar language were intimately connected. Foreign "tongues" might seduce a receptive audience and aggrandize the speaker, but linguistic difference was essentially a sign of superficiality. Critics of Covarrubias's brand of formalism did not candidly point toward popular piety or institutional struggle as driving forces in shifting the meanings and uses of sacred texts, as a modern historian might. Instead, they invoked a belief in divine power to undermine the apparently secure hermeneutic principles enlisted to preserve the dichotomy between revelation and literature.[41] God could change the textual and hermeneutic playing field, they insisted, simply by revealing a new text. To suggest that this new revelation must conform to the material and formal conventions of previous holy texts from the Judeo-Christian tradition was to limit the authority of God to subvert those conventions. Refusal to acknowledge this divine power of exception was a particularly humanist form of heretical hubris.

While an insistence upon the omniscience of God and the reality of the miraculous underwrote a reading practice even more radical than the humanists' scholarly doubt, defenders of the lead books articulated their own Pyrrhonic skepticism. Citing Ecclesiastes 8:7 on man's constitutive ignorance, but shifting the terms for debate from divine omniscience to limitations on historical knowledge, Gregorio López de Madera argued that the lead books' detractors held too secure a view of ancient times. In a brilliant inversion, López de Madera cited the Donation of Constantine, the exemplary early modern instance of forgery's enduring power to affect social, political, and even religious history, not as a warning about the danger of forgery, as his readers would have expected, but as evidence for the need occasionally to revise and correct centuries of accumulated error.[42] He echoed the skeptical arguments of his opponents, such as Benito Arias Montano, who in a letter to Archbishop Pedro de Castro loosely cited Cicero in order to urge scholarly prudence. "We must not treat the unknown as known and readily accept it," warned Montano.[43] López de Madera and Montano agreed about the need for skeptical inquiry even as they disagreed over how to chart the horizon of the known and the unknown in the first place.

What is more, López de Madera responded to the attack on the lead books as mere fiction in explicitly literary terms while nevertheless implying that the stakes of the representation were religious. Invoking classical literary theory and recalling Bartolomé de Las Casas's concerns about the Prophet Muhammad's evangelical coercion and deception, López de Madera argued that the lead books were not fictitious, because if the authors had wanted "to feign in them, they would have sought the verisimilar [*verosimil*]." Everyone seemed to agree, however, that both the content of the texts and the circumstances of their discovery were inverisimilar.[44] López de Madera read this implausibility as a sign of divine exception and proof of fiction's absence, for a plausible representation would have more effectively stimulated the audience's mimetic faculty.[45] In other words, if the authors of the Sacromonte texts were in fact dangerous heretics intent on spreading their mistaken beliefs and practices, then surely they would have marshaled the power of fiction by following its rules, rather than offering a representation that, in Madera's theatrical and religious vocabulary, witnesses viewed with skepticism. The audience of learned skeptics, rendered narrow-minded by the burden of its Aristotelian vocabulary, failed to perceive the Sacromonte truth that the pious pilgrims proved.

You will recall that like the pope after him, Pedro de Valencia attempted to use the term *fiction* as a theological dismissal. López de Madera responded as an aghast literary critic, condescendingly correcting inexact application of terminology. But López de Madera's answer was not completely disingenuous, for it was impossible to separate clearly a condemnation of apocryphal religious forgeries from conventional disapproval for traditional Renaissance literary forms such as, for example, chivalric romances. Writers of various stripes, including Juan Luis Vives, the Jesuit Gaspar de Astete, and Antonio de Guevara, who himself is famous for forged citations, disparaged these *libros de caballería* and other literary genres over concerns about readers' spiritual health.[46] Because of their alleged common capacity to corrupt through example and imitation, it is no coincidence that *libros de caballería*, like *conversos* and Moriscos, were prohibited from the New World.

Both the Sacromonte lead books and works like *Amadís de Gaula* were thus perceived to be dangerous because they might lead their respective audiences to confuse truth with invention. Cervantes, of course, poked fun at this Platonic concern, exploring not only the dangers but also the ethical potential of imposing imaginative worldviews upon a corrupt reality. Nevertheless, Don Quijote's misreading was a satirical exaggeration of this learned unease over mimetic danger, while popular devotion to the lead books, Saint Cecilius, and the Sacromonte Virgin actually came to structure religious life for many Granadans from the late sixteenth century to the present. Though fear of fiction's power motivated its critical condemnation, the potential for art to transform behavior and belief was, and perhaps remains, most clearly visible in the religious sphere.[47] In López de Madera's Aristotelian reading of the lead books, he circumvented this parallel between the effects of literary and religious mimesis, even while confusing the lines of heresy, fiction, and scripture.

Yet López de Madera did not simply invoke skepticism and then rest his case in defense of the lead books. Faced with the texts' mixture of sixteenth-century Spanish, classical Latin, and postclassical Arabic, he also proposed an elaborate genealogy of linguistic complexity. Attempting to demonstrate that contemporary Spanish and classical Latin could have been simultaneously in use in first-century Iberia, López de Madera argued that the Sacromonte discoveries provided evidence for a long history of peninsular multilingualism. Early modern speakers, he noted, employed different languages and registers depending upon the community and context, so why could the ancient inhabitants of the Iberian Peninsula not have done the same?[48] Moreover, López de Madera argued that the specific languages by which it is possible to identify nations over time are themselves mixtures, including borrowed words and phrases from an array of neighboring communities and warring empires, so why do critics find the Turpiana manuscript's mixture of Spanish, Latin, and Arabic so problematic? Individuals speaking different languages with shared imperial or biblical histories, such as Spanish and Portuguese, or Hebrew and Arabic, can sometimes understand each other perfectly well. So why, he asked, do humanist detractors of the *libros plúmbeos*, such as Pedro de Valencia and Benito Arias Montano, sanctimoniously point out that the texts were written primarily in Arabic even though the first-century Granadan addressees were not native Arabic speakers? López de Madera here drew on the same precedent as the early seventeenth-century theologian Pedro de Palencia, who, as you will recall from chapter 3, defended the use of rabbinic glosses among Christian commentators by charting a long history of Mediterranean linguistic cross-fertilization. Neither comparative philology nor diachronic linguistics offered definitive resolutions to the Sacromonte debates. On the contrary, the effort to gloss the Sacromonte discoveries laid bare the epistemological holes and unstable conventions characterizing language study around the turn of the seventeenth century.

Consider in this regard the relationship between the puzzling language of the lead books and Turpiana manuscript, on the one hand, and competing theories of the history of the Spanish language, on the other hand. As precedent for his argument that Spanish, Latin, and Arabic could have existed simultaneously in ancient times, for instance, López de Madera highlighted the shared features of various Near Eastern languages. Crediting Paul and Jerome with first recognizing the "common genealogy" (*propogacion misma*) of Hebrew, Chaldean, Syriac, and Arabic, López de Madera suggested that the "great closeness" (*mucha cercania*) among these languages was pregnant with theological meaning.[49] It was also paradigmatic of the similarities and differences among other groups of languages, such as the Romance vernaculars. Although he mistakenly concluded from this evidence of Semitic similitude that Spanish and Latin "could have since their beginning intermingled" (*puderion desde su principio mezclar*), López de Madera's concern with language families reflected an emerging late sixteenth- and early seventeenth-century scholarly interest in the shared features of *all* language.[50]

López de Madera's argument about the interrelated nature of the world's languages recalled how previous great comparative philologists, including Guillaume Postel and Joseph Scaliger, had first traced the common Hebraic origins of multiple Semitic languages. No less an intellectual than Benito Arias Montano had sought to expand the reach of the Semitic language tree by arguing that in addition to Arabic and Aramaic, Castilian too grew from the same trunk as Hebrew. The Hieronymite linguist Rodrigo de Yepes had subsequently developed this titillating idea in his 1583 manuscript study of peninsular topography and religious history, *Historia de la muerte y glorioso martyrio del Sancto Innocente*, which presented a strikingly Hebraic peninsular antiquity.[51] Overlapping histories of Semitic and Romance languages and the existence of a pre-Roman or "primitive" Spanish were important ideas in the Sacromonte context because, among other reasons examined above, they underscored the lead books' prophecy of religious harmony. An ingenious history of linguistic exchange made the future possibility of religious understanding imaginable.

Not everyone was buying this story, however. In his language study of 1606, *Del origen y principio de la lengva castellana, ò Romance, que oi se usa en España*, which five years later was published as the first part of Sebastian de Covarrubias's lexicon, *Tesoro de la lengva castellana, o española*, the canon of the Cathedral of Cordoba, Bernardo de Aldrete, forcefully countered López de Madera's claims. He correctly argued that the Spanish language emerged from corrupt, vernacular Latin.[52] Antonio de Nebrija had proposed a similar relationship between Latin and Spanish over a century earlier, but Aldrete was the first to document systematically the morphological and lexical transition. Although he never mentioned him by name, Aldrete's text was an attack on López de Madera's defense of the ancient lineage of Spanish, a position for which the lead books, if authentic, provided evidence. *Del origen y principio* triggered animated counterattacks by scholars such as Bartolomé Ximénez Patón, who found López de Madera's position convincing, and in his second book of 1614, *Varias antiguedades de España, Africa, y otras provincias*, Aldrete took a conciliatory tone.[53] In the prologue to this latter text, dedicated to none other than Archbishop Pedro de Castro, Aldrete professed belief in the authenticity of the lead books, and later in the volume he acknowledged that Sacromonte saints might have communicated in sixteenth-century Spanish with the appropriate divine assistance. Still maintaining that Spanish had descended from and postdated Latin, Aldrete nonetheless admitted the possibility of miraculous exception and implied that the *plomos* may be one such example.

Despite this concession, some have hailed Aldrete as the father of Romance philology.[54] Compared with foils like López de Madera or Ximénez Patón, Aldrete has come to be known more widely today not only because his linguistic conclusions turned out to be more accurate, but also because his argument about the relationship between the diachronic changes in language and the expansion of political power now strikes some scholars as excessively triumphalist.[55] All the same, both admirers and critics of Aldrete agree that his work represented an important shift toward a recognizably modern methodology of historical linguistics, even if they disagree over his imperialist agenda and tactical fudging. In any case, there is no doubt that the slippage between Aldrete's strong argument in *Del origen y principio* and his conciliatory claims in *Varias antiguedades* demonstrates that his conclusions were intimately shaped by the Sacromonte episode. The basic epistemological dilemma raised by language debates about the discoveries was clear and generalizable: To what extent should scholarly consensus function as the stable standard of evidence by which the authenticity of the lead books is determined, and to what extent should the lead books force a revision of scholarly consensus? Dispute between Aldrete and López de Madera over the development of the Spanish language, like related debates between Miguel de Luna, Alonso de Castillo, Bartolomé Pectorano, Benito Arias Montano, Pedro de Valencia, and others over how to translate and interpret the lead books, demonstrates that the very rules for reaching consensus on points of theology and philology were up for grabs.

It was lost on none of these scholars that to revise the histories of Christianity and Spanish to concur with the lead books was also to reimagine the place of Granada in Spain's past and present alike. Regional pride played a central role in shaping these Sacromonte debates. Granadan historians Francisco Bermúdez de Pedraza and Luis de la Cueva included in their well-known texts *Antigvedad y excelencias de Granada* and *Diálogos de las cosas notables de Granada, y lengua española, y algunas cosas curiosas*, respectively, what in retrospect looks like a harebrained theory on the ancient origins of the Spanish language. Mirroring the views of López de Madera and others before him, Bermúdez de Pedraza and Cueva argued that the Spanish language was brought to the peninsula by a Chaldean colonizer and descendent of Noah named Tubal.[56] Signaling the extent to which this line of defense for primitive Spanish was simultaneously an apology for the lead books' authenticity and a celebration of local religious and linguistic exemplarity, Bermúdez de Pedraza integrated his chapters on the history of the Spanish language into the fourth book of *Antigvedad y excelencias*, which is largely concerned with the Sacromonte discoveries. Needless to say, the Sacromonte episode kindled a contest over regional precedence in matters of Christian orthodoxy and linguistic history, one that by the time of the Morisco expulsions had grown into a conflagration of antagonism over regional political and military policy as well.

Although the Morisco question was settled by expulsion just two short decades after the discovery of the lead books, the philological debate about the history of the Spanish language and theological disagreements about the orthodoxy of the lead books were not resolved until the late seventeenth-century papal rejection. In the end, institutional modes for demarcating the blurry lines between different types of narrative and spheres of knowledge performed their task of conservation. Paradoxically reaffirming both the conventional boundaries of Christianity and the power of humanist method, Rome found unconvincing the skeptical invocation of the miraculous. For all their scholastic and philological formalism, defenders of the lead books could neither convince their most crucial interlocutors of their position nor force the texts themselves into the canon. Their failure echoed the failure of the forgers, whose attempt to imagine a shared space of understanding among New and Old Christians was a last-ditch effort to reimagine the history along with the future of Granada. The Sacromonte episode raised opportune concerns about the conventions of scholarship and the boundaries of orthodoxy at the turn of the seventeenth century. But it also forced commentators to look anew at Granada's recent history of Morisco uprising. Just as scholars of law and language employed debates about New Christian assimilation to transform the conditions of their disciplines, so too did historians from diverse corners exploit the multidimensional story of Granada to stake their claim to legitimacy and reimagine their craft. With the fall of Nasrid Granada, the expulsion and conversion of the Jews, and the initial forays into the New World receding into the past, the Sacromonte episode became a new leaden touchstone of Spanish history.

CHAPTER FIVE

War Stories

Cobbled together by fledgling Arabists and earnest antiquarians, the many codices containing manuscript and print materials related to the Sacromonte discoveries display the porousness of the early modern period's disciplinary boundaries. Tentative translations, marginal notes, and Arabic and Hebrew word lists and alphabet charts jostle for attention with the historical and theological treatises composed by the discoveries' defenders and opponents. Like late sixteenth- and early seventeenth-century commentators and collectors, archivists of future generations had to renegotiate the boundaries of authenticity in their approach to this corpus of texts and images. To group Sacromonte documents with other forgeries, such the Jesuit Jerónimo Román de Higuera's "false chronicles," for instance, was implicitly to dismiss the lead books and Turpiana manuscript as inventions.[1] At once erudite entertainment and scholarly admonition, these volumes were anthologies of peninsular deception and naiveté. In contrast, to group treatises in defense of the Spanish language's antiquity or the Virgin Mary's immaculate conception alongside the political and military history of the moment was to stake a claim for the veracity of the Sacromonte martyrs and their writings. In this subtle and sometimes insidious way, the hundred-year effort to transcribe, translate, interpret, and judge the lead books and Turpiana manuscript entailed revisiting not only conventional accounts of Granada's ancient founding, but also the history of the region's Moriscos, whom the historian Luis de Mármol Carvajal and others identified in the 1590s as possible sources for the Sacromonte falsifications.[2]

A volume now held in Spain's national library, which contains a copy of the early seventeenth-century cultural theorist Juan Herreros de Almansa's

Invención del Sacro Monte de Granada sandwiched between two manuscript versions of the soldier-humanist Diego Hurtado de Mendoza's *Guerra de Granada*, offers an apt material record of how the Sacromonte discoveries renewed interest in Granadan and Morisco history.[3] Though both authors portrayed their texts as reliable chronicles, their two works served opposite historiographical ends. Herreros de Almansa's *Invención* was an attempt to establish a consensus on the truthfulness of Saint Cecilius's version of Granada's pre-Islamic past. As Herreros de Almansa explained in a prologue to readers, though no such consensus yet existed at the time of his writing, he nevertheless was confident that some or all of the discoveries would eventually "prove to be truthful."[4] Like Gregorio López de Madera's *Discurso de la certidumbre*, Herreros de Almansa's *Invención* was a work of apologetic history. Hurtado de Mendoza's *Guerra de Granada*, on the other hand, recounted the Morisco uprising that began almost three decades before the Sacromonte episode. The revolt exploded in Granada and the surrounding Alpujarras Mountains in 1568, and it ended only three years later, after Felipe II's half brother Juan de Austria arrived with imperial reinforcements. This Second Alpujarras War, as the conflict became known, was devastating for the defeated Moriscos.[5] But as Hurtado de Mendoza, Luis de Mármol Carvajal, Ginés Pérez de Hita, and the event's other early chroniclers recalled, disobedient Old Christian soldiers and their incompetent or rapacious leaders left the entire Kingdom of Granada in shambles as well. Unlike most sixteenth-century Spanish accounts of imperial affairs, Hurtado de Mendoza's *Guerra de Granada* was stridently critical rather than triumphalist. Herreros de Almansa's and Hurtado de Mendoza's texts consequently represented divergent approaches to Granada's past in particular and to the practice of history more generally. Their appearance side by side in one volume highlights the elastic bibliographic and analytical conditions of early modern history, which are the subject of this chapter.

My argument is that to grapple with the failure of Morisco integration was also to interrogate the craft of history, by which I mean the selection and citation of sources, methods of narrative framing, modes of interpretation, and rhetorical tactics that early modern authors employed in their reconstruction of the past. The late sixteenth- and early seventeenth-century accounts of the Alpujarras conflict were the terrain upon which this disciplinary reflection occurred, and, as I show, the political and moral stakes of such reflection were high. My goal is not to circumscribe what counted as history writing or to adjudicate who was or was not a historian, but rather to examine the blurriness of these very categories in the late sixteenth century.

The latter half of this chapter looks at the Second Alpujarras War through the lens of its first chroniclers, whose accounts, in addition to documenting the action itself, also underscore the relationship between the craft of history and the politics of religious difference. By demonstrating that historians of the Alpujarras conflict presented their own methodologies and presuppositions in order to distinguish themselves both from each other and from other historians of their day, the first half of the chapter introduces readers to early modern debates about history writing. The chapter ends by showing how the representation of the conclusion of the Alpujarras war anticipated and even aimed to shape the Morisco expulsions of 1609–14.

Because gaps of many years separate the composition from the publication of Hurtado de Mendoza's, Luis de Mármol Carvajal's, and Ginés Pérez de Hita's accounts of the Alpujarras revolt, the production and early reception of these works reflect multiple historical moments. The historian Mármol Carvajal's *Historia del rebelión y castigo de los Moriscos de este reino de Granada*, for example, was composed in the late 1570s and approved for publication as early as 1580, but it did not first appear in print until 1600.[6] Published as debates about Morisco forgery, apostasy, and expulsion began to intensify, *Historia del rebelión* offered a trove of archival materials and a point of historical reference for interpreting the events that followed its composition and preceded its publication. Similarly, the soldier, poet, and historian Ginés Pérez de Hita's *Segunda parte de las guerras civiles de Granada* was penned in the early 1590s and granted publishing rights in 1610, but the earliest of more than twenty extant editions was published only in 1619. Pérez de Hita's text, which did not circulate in manuscript copy, thus remained unknown for three decades despite great anticipation surrounding its release, the product of the success of the first volume of *Guerras civiles*, a 1595 fictionalization of the civil wars that had wracked the final years of Nasrid Granada, *Historia de los bandos de los Zegríes y Abencerrajes*.[7] Among the probable reasons for the publication delays of Mármol Carvajal's and Pérez de Hita's texts was concern about the unflattering shadow that accounts of the Alpujarras conflict might cast on Felipe II, who died in 1598. Hurtado de Mendoza specified another reason for delaying the publication of his *Guerra de Granada*, composed in the early 1570s but never published during his lifetime. As Luis de Tribaldos, the editor of the first edition of 1627, explained in his prologue, Hurtado de Mendoza argued that given the contemptuous nature of his account, it was preferable to wait until the generation of soldiers that participated in the Second Alpujarras War had died rather than to offend them directly in print.[8] As we have already seen, though, manuscript versions of Hurtado de Mendoza's account circulated widely around the turn of the seventeenth century, often in conjunction with Sacromonte or other Granada-focused material. Scholars interested in the Sacromonte debates evidently turned to manuscript copies of Hurtado de Mendoza *Guerra de Granada* and printed editions of Mármol Carvajal's *Historia del rebelión* to understand Granada and its Moriscos. That printing delays characterized the production and circulation histories of other early modern historical texts does not render the circumstances surrounding these first accounts of the Alpujarras war any less significant. As I have shown elsewhere, hidden beneath the veneer of shared material conditions are often rich microhistories of local rivalry and shrewd marketing.[9] Taken together, the details of these convoluted composition and publication histories of the Second Alpujarras War highlight the period's deep-seated uncertainty about how, when, and even whether to craft a Morisco history of the present.

This uncertainty was understandable. "To write about the events of one's own time is dangerous and difficult," explained the historian Luis Cabrera de Córdoba in *De historia para entenderla y escriverla*, a compendium of early modern views on the understanding and writing of history published in 1611. It was risky to study "new material," as Cabrera de Córdoba called accounts of contemporary affairs like those by Hurtado de Mendoza, Mármol Carvajal, and Pérez de Hita, because the emotions of the participants in such recent events remained raw.[10] Despite the hurdles posed by the "love of one's own" and the "hatred of enemies," however, Cabrera de Córdoba, like Cicero, believed that it was the historian's obligation to try to formulate a "neutral" record of imperial history, and to do so as quickly as possible.[11] Having failed to secure the elite position of royal chronicler, Cabrera de Córdoba nevertheless thought it most effective to produce such a record by writing from a position of proximity to the court. On the one hand, this was pragmatic advice, for the diplomats, advisors, and soldiers with privileged knowledge of imperial goings-on flowed through court with information and intrigue. In the king's company, an adroit chronicler could surely examine correspondence and other relevant materials before they were sent to Simancas, founded in 1540, for safeguarding. Moreover, the Escorial, built in the latter half of the sixteenth century by Felipe II and his team of learned bibliophiles, which included Benito Arias Montano and the humanist historian Juan Páez de Castro, was relatively near Madrid. Geographical convenience facilitated consultation of the Escorial's concentration of learned manuscripts and printed book collections that Cabrera de Córdoba and others understood to compose the building blocks of history. On the other hand, Cabrera de Córdoba acknowledged the scholarly costs that intimacy with the perceived actors of history entailed. A biographer of Felipe II writing during the tendentious reign of Felipe III, Cabrera de Córdoba nevertheless cautioned court historians not to "accommodate" their accounts to the whims of their princes, as the ancient Greek historian Pausanius and others feared they might.[12] Cabrera de Córdoba knew that the slope from tact to censorship was slippery, particularly when formulating history from within the chambers of power. Even so, he saw an account of one's own day, composed in dialogue with those influential men who operated the recondite levers of government, as the core of imperial chronicle.

Students of Cabrera de Córdoba's model of history would later paint the Second Alpujarras War as a deathblow to a hobbled pastoral project, as an example of the Moriscos' intractable refusal to assimilate. Yet Mármol Carvajal and Pérez de Hita in different ways followed Hurtado de Mendoza in eschewing such a triumphalist narrative of indignity. In an effort to avoid the mistakes committed by the subjects of their histories, Hurtado de Mendoza and Mármol Carvajal traced disagreement within the Morisco community and dissention among their opponents through the private manuscript collections, first-person interviews, and published material that constituted their respective archives. They strained against both the moral and the methodological limitations of "official history," to use Richard Kagan's phrase, by tracking down sources from outside the confines of court, by reconstructing a story that might instruct as well as celebrate.[13] Pérez de Hita and the epic poet Juan Rufo, whose *La Austriada*, first published in 1584, celebrated Juan de Austria's role in subduing the Alpujarras uprising and subsequently defeating the Ottoman Turks at the naval battle of Lepanto, took a different approach. They trafficked in contrasting economies of sentimentality, Pérez de Hita by painting the Morisco uprising and Old Christian response in the language of late medieval romance and Rufo by mimicking a Virgilian heroic register. These authors used accounts of Granada's Morisco revolt to reformulate and reimagine a conventional historical method that had already for several decades been in flux. Through the effort to reconstruct the origins, action, and consequences of the Alpujarras conflict, the longstanding crisis over how to recognize and forcibly eliminate New Christian dissimulation grew into a concern about historical evidence and reasoning, even as the disciplinary crisis about how and why to write history informed late sixteenth-century accounts of the Moriscos. Debate about Morisco assimilation and expulsion ran together with the peninsular practice of history and the early modern politics of nostalgia.

THE MORISCOS AND HISTORICAL METHOD

Diego Hurtado de Mendoza opened *Guerra de Granada* with a statement on historical method. As he explained in the text's prologue, his account of the war was not a chronicle of great sieges and noble intrigue, of captive kings and storied lineages. Though he acknowledged that such material provided the grist for most historians' mills, particularly those court historians who chronicled the *res gestae* of the imperial realm, Hurtado de Mendoza was uninterested in this sort of celebratory narrative. Following both Tacitus's ancient example of critical history and Leonardo Bruni, Lorenzo Valla, and Niccolò Machiavelli's modern Italian obsession with rhetoric and style, his goal instead was to recount "humble beginnings, a bandit's rebellion," one that was defined by "hatreds, ambitions, and pretensions" and waged crudely by nobles and slaves alike. Hurtado de Mendoza's was a forceful and carefully wrought story of decline. Consider the polemical rhetoric of his oft-cited introductory passage:

> My goal is to write the history of the war that the Catholic king of Spain Felipe II, son of the never defeated emperor Don Carlos, had in the Kingdom of Granada against the newly converted rebels . . . I know well enough that in comparison to the great things written about Spain, many of the things that I describe will seem to some too light and slight for history: long wars of various events, the capture and desolation of populous cities, kings defeated and imprisoned, discord among fathers and sons, brothers and sisters, parents and sons-in-law, dispossessions and restitutions, and dispossessions once again, and deaths by the sword; lineages ended, royal successions altered—these offer a free and extended field, a wide outlet for writers. I chose the more narrow, laborious, and sterile path, without glory but beneficial and generative for those who will come later: humble beginnings, a bandit's rebellion, groups of slaves, tumult of ruffians, competitions, hatreds, ambitions and pretensions; the misallocation of provisions, lack of money, inconveniences either not believed or little valued; remission and looseness in minds accustomed to understanding, providing, and dissimulating greater things; and yet, it will not be considered a wasteful endeavor to consider how, from such light beginnings and particular causes, come the utmost of difficult labors and public injuries, almost without remedy.[14]

In telling the story of the Alpujarras conflict from below, so to speak, Hurtado de Mendoza knew that he risked producing a text that his early modern audience might scarcely consider history at all. Contemporary theorists of historical writing, such as the Jesuit humanist Juan Páez de Castro, mentioned above, and the philosopher Sebastián Fox Morcillo, had come to see history as the record of deeds from which a king might learn to govern with wisdom and prudence.[15] These and later scholars, such as Cabrera de Córdoba, believed that kings became great by consulting catalogues of past greatness. By maintaining the memory of valiant action, historians helped to cultivate the heroism of the future. In Hurtado de Mendoza's view, however, this model of historical writing was incongruent with the details of both the Alpujarras conflict and the Morisco experience.

Hurtado de Mendoza's objections to the sort of history practiced and advised by Fox Morcillo, Páez de Castro, and Cabrera de Córdoba ran deeper than his sense that the local lessons of the Second Alpujarras War belied the Crown's imperial rhetoric. He was interested not only in finding an appropriately critical register to recount the story of the war, but also in unsettling the expectations of readers too accustomed to the stale presumptions of history as an arm of the state. *Guerra de Granada* presented a case for reimagining the production of knowledge about the past, for testing established conventions of scholarship by thinking diachronically about history as a discipline. Hurtado de Mendoza himself took care to underscore these methodological stakes while facilitating the circulation of his still-unpublished work in the years before his death. According to Luis de Tribaldos, when Hurtado de Mendoza gave a personally transcribed copy of *Guerra de Granada* to an unnamed friend near the end of his life, he (like Isaac Casaubon or Benito Arias Montano) included in the top margin an aphorism from Seneca's letter to Lucius on the rewards of scientific discovery.[16] In the cited passage, Seneca explained that the true virtue of a scholar often remained hidden during that individual's own time. "Suppressed by the spite of contemporaries," the insights of the wisest and most creative thinkers come to be appreciated only by subsequent generations, Seneca warned. "It is to these that you should have regard."[17] In Tribaldos's telling, Hurtado de Mendoza believed that his contemporaries would be unable or unwilling to appreciate his effort to revive in Spain an ancient model of critical history. Boldly likening himself not only to Tacitus, but also to Socrates, Cato, Epicurus, and other ancient thinkers whose innovative approaches were ignored or misunderstood in their own day, Hurtado de Mendoza saw his writing about the Alpujarras conflict as a reflection on the limitations of imperial history as a genre and the shortsightedness of many historians as scholarly interlocutors.

Unlike the universal histories produced both within and beyond court by varied late sixteenth- and early seventeenth-century chroniclers, *Guerra de Granada* was what we might now call local history. It was a story of Morisco estrangement in Granada framed as an account of imperial mismanagement; it was a cautionary tale delivered from the periphery by a decorated warrior and noble ambassador who was once a vital cog in Felipe II's administrative machinery but who, after drawing his sword on a fellow courtier in the royal palace in Madrid, found himself relegated to the margins of power. This was why in 1569, during the height of the Alpujarras conflict, Hurtado de Mendoza retired to Granada, where three generations of Mendozas had helped to govern the restive city.[18] Already banished from court, Hurtado de Mendoza produced *Guerra de Granada* as a frank depiction of martial negligence and a defense of Granada's local autonomy. The text was a reproach to Felipe II, whom he largely excluded from his account, even as he lavished nostalgic praise upon Carlos V. What is more, the narrowness of Hurtado de Mendoza's focus on the Alpujarras uprising and its Morisco rebels was another, more subtle form of political criticism, for this internal unrest among a minority population of dubious Christianity was as embarrassing to Felipe II in the 1570s as it had been to Carlos V in the 1520s. In Hurtado de Mendoza's version of the events, the eventual defeat of the Morisco revolt by Juan de Austria was a fortunate conclusion to a conflict whose prolonged and costly existence was nonetheless a humiliation. *Guerra de Granada* made it difficult to see the triumph through the disgrace.

In his *Historia general del mundo,* by contrast, royal chronicler to Felipe II, Felipe III, and Felipe IV Antonio de Herrera y Tordesillas weaved a brief account of the Second Alpujarras War into a broader celebration of Felipe II's exploits. He then folded this grand story, published between 1601 and 1612, into a narrative of natural, social, and religious history as well. The sprawling empire's rivers and mountains, the dress and rituals of its diverse subjects, the monuments and wonders of its cities, and the genealogical record and deeds of its royal family all shared space on Herrera y Tordesillas's pages. This was history as an echo chamber of transatlantic preeminence. To write official history during and after Felipe II's lengthy reign, in other words, was to write synthetic history. In turning away from biographies of particular kings and resurrecting a patriotic goal of comprehensiveness, epitomized by Alfonso X's mid-thirteenth-century *General estoria,* early modern historians such as Ambrosio de Morales and Juan de Mariana expressed their truth claims in the language of universality; they composed or extended "general" histories for a new era.[19] Appointed in 1569 as royal chronicler, a post established around the turn of the fifteenth century by many European monarchs eager to burnish their image and protect their claims to privilege and territory, Ambrosio de Morales in particular led Felipe II's effort to tell the history of the world as Habsburg history. Over the course of the 1570s and 1580s, he extended Florián de Ocampo's *Coronica general de España* up through the beginning of the eleventh century and published an archeological and geographic treatise entitled *Antiguedades de las ciudades de España*. These texts were a product of Felipe II's mania for the documentary evidence of political history as well as the profane counterpart to apologetic *historia sacra*.[20] This effort to compile and collate peninsular evidence of royal authority took the form of a historical inquiry that inched toward the present, as Mariana's later *Historiae de rebus Hispaniae*, published in several revised and expanded editions in the 1590s, eventually covered events up to the death of King Fernando in 1516.[21] Even some regional histories, however, such as the Granadan historian Francisco Bermúdez de Pedraza's early seventeenth-century *Antigvedad y excelencias de Granada* and *Historia ecclesiastica de Granada*, echoed the encyclopedic and accumulative style, if not the universal scale, of both Mariana's history, which in 1601 he translated into Spanish as *Historia general de Espana*, and Herrera y Tordesillas's *Historia general del mundo*. In sum, these texts sought to legitimize rulers' claims to power, appeal to the pride of Spanish audiences, and create a sense of continuity between the peninsula's ancient past and early modern present.

Focusing on a local event rather than on an imperial or regional synthesis, Hurtado de Mendoza cautioned readers that his narrative would eschew this sort of "wide terrain" of royal chronology and gallant action in order to tread instead on an inglorious and "narrow path." Although Morales dedicated part of his *Coronica general* to Hurtado de Mendoza, when the Granadan scholar fashioned his own history, he did not follow Morales's example. With the polemical aim of writing a historical narrative that seemed, precisely, "too light and slight for history," Hurtado de Mendoza instead cast the Alpujarras conflict differently. In celebrating the lightness of history, that is, Hurtado de Mendoza thumbed his nose at both historical convention and his scholarly interlocutors. *Guerra de Granada* was a blunt answer to the likes of Juan Páez de Castro, an occasional advisor to Hurtado de Mendoza who had also served as Carlos V's royal chronicler and, as mentioned above, Felipe II's first point man on the Escorial archive and library projects. Páez de Castro had argued that history was weighty and difficult: "To write history is not so easy and light a thing as the people think," he maintained.[22] Historians needed the eloquence of the poet to render their texts accessible and comprehensible, the scientific mind of the natural philosopher to gauge the relationship among causes for important events, and the discretion of the courtier to acquire and organize letters, treatises, and other sources compiled from inside and outside the court.

Hurtado de Mendoza too recognized the need for historians to be well-rounded intellectuals and careful writers, but he took issue with Páez de Castro's smugness. Unlike the professional historian, who worked to eliminate uncertainty, Hurtado de Mendoza aimed to make uncertainty a vital feature of his work. In *Guerra de Granada* he told the history of the Alpujarras conflict and the conditions of Morisco life out of which the war emerged as a tale unfolding in real time; it was unclear until the conclusion of the war "whether it was we or our enemies whom God wanted to punish," explained Hurtado de Mendoza at the beginning of his text. "Only at the end of it all was it discovered that we were the threatened ones, and they the punished ones."[23] In recounting the Alpujarras conflict as a popular rebellion whose denouement remained undecided for years rather than as an overdetermined repetition of the *reconquista,* Hurtado de Mendoza ridiculed the court historian's familiar tropes and plot lines. In their place he did not insert some easy fiction of first-person experience, a narrative strategy that he irreverently attacked in his personal correspondence; instead, he emphasized the confusion and uncertainty that characterized the experience of the war even for its participants and witnesses.[24]

To depict the conflict in this way entailed consulting Arabic texts and Arabic-speaking combatants as well as more traditional Romance or Latin informants and written sources. Aware that the historian's "toolbox," to borrow an idea from Anthony Grafton and Suzanne Marchand, contained "implements of discovery as well as of persuasion," Hurtado de Mendoza, Mármol Carvajal, and Pérez de Hita all underscored the importance of such Arabic sources, though they employed them to different ends.[25] Deepening his narrative with interviews with the vanquished, Hurtado de Mendoza recalled pressing Moriscos from the region of Granada about the details of the violence and the suffering it produced. However crucial such oral evidence actually may have been to Hurtado de Mendoza's project, in recounting stories of its collection he also sought to authorize his text in a new way. Similarly, in the course of briefly narrating Granada's ancient history, Hurtado de Mendoza boasted that he had consulted Arabic books found both in Granada and in the library of the king of Tunis, Muley Zidan. Whatever his capacity to read or understand Arabic—and given the state of peninsular comparative Semitic philology described in chapter 3, there is reason to be skeptical—Hurtado de Mendoza was at least an avid buyer of Arabic manuscripts, which, like Juan Páez de Castro's and others' collections of Arabic materials, eventually became part of the holdings of the Escorial library. In *Guerra de Granada,* the integration of these sorts of Arabic sources, many of which, Hurtado de Mendoza practically boasted, "will not be in agreement with the opinion" of his readers, was part of the project's polemical thrust.[26] He argued that more familiar ancient sources had long misled Old Christian readers about their own past. Toponymy served Hurtado de Mendoza as the emblematic case in this regard: "While the Arabs and the Asians talk about their sites as they write about them," Hurtado de Mendoza explained, "the complete opposite is the case for the peoples of Europe."[27] In Hurtado de Mendoza's view, historians and informants who communicated in Arabic constituted a transparent historical lens, while the ancient Romance and Latin sources—even those collected from across the peninsula by Páez de Castro, Morales, and other court historians charged by Felipe II with buttressing Spain's political and religious history in this way—were unreliable or misleading. Hurtado de Mendoza employed contemporary Arabic sources to depict more accurately the violent details of the Alpujarras conflict and medieval Arabic sources, however inapt to the rebellion itself, to reformulate the conventions of historical accuracy.

Mármol Carvajal was more circumspect than Hurtado de Mendoza about the trustworthiness of medieval Arabic sources, even as he too insisted upon the need to consult them. As a rejoinder to Hurtado de Mendoza's *Guerra de Granada*, upon which he nevertheless drew deeply and without attribution, Mármol Carvajal presented his own account of Granada's unstable ancient name. However, he underscored the Arabic language's troubling variability rather than its reliability: Granada used to be known as either "'Iliberia' or 'Eliberia'—the 'e' is easily taken for the 'i,' and the 'o' for the 'u,'" Mármol Carvajal expounded, "because there is little difference among the characters where such markers are placed."[28] Arabic place names were ambiguous because of variation in the pronunciation of short vowels. The flexibility of the language itself, celebrated by Ignacio de Las Casas in his defense of pastoral work with the Moriscos, was cause for concern when it came to writing history or documenting heresy. It was this confusion that the Granadan Franciscan Diego de Guadix sought to remedy with his encyclopedic toponymical study of 1593, *Recopilación de algunos nombres arábigos*.[29] But the epistemological quandary signaled by Guadix's text would not be so easily resolved. For early modern peninsular scholars interested in the Morisco question or writing about Andalusian regional history, Arabic sources were at once alluring and frightening, just as real or invented medieval Celtic and ancient Etruscan sources were for historians in early modern England and Italy, respectively. From one perspective, these peninsular Arabic texts offered a bridge that connected the medieval history of peninsular Islam to the contemporary Morisco reality. To see how the Moriscos read, translated, and circulated their own Arabic materials was to judge this community through its engagement with its Islamic past. And to examine those medieval Arabic codices that had survived nearly a century of inquisitorial purges was to access the points of intellectual exchange and conflict that had defined peninsular scientific, literary, and religious history in the thirteenth and fourteenth centuries. But from another perspective, these Arabic sources were a barrier to knowledge. Their difficulty separated New and Old Christians from their shared origins and bred an abiding sense of mutual suspicion. More than Hurtado de Mendoza, Mármol Carvajal was mindful of the fact that Arabic was a necessary but dangerous tool in the recounting of peninsular history.

Despite these worries about Arabic's unreliability, Mármol Carvajal echoed Hurtado de Mendoza in claiming to have consulted an array of Arabic evidence. His sources ranged from old Moriscos' stories to Arab writings and epitaphs on ancient stones scattered among Granada's ruins.[30] Importantly, Mármol Carvajal also included in his *Historia del rebelión* actual Spanish translations of Arabic war correspondence, such as missives written by the rebel leaders Farax Aben Farax and Aben Daud to rouse their compatriots in the Alpujarras Mountains and to appeal for help to allies in North Africa. According to Mármol Carvajal's account of this correspondence's history, local guardsmen in the coastal city of Adra seized some of the letters when one of Aben Daud's fellow Moriscos double-crossed him during a meeting with nearby insurgents. In their hurry to escape, the fighters lost "a silk sack, which held a large book in Arabic script, in which were found a letter and a lamentation, and which by the tenor of both seemed to be dictated by Daud himself."[31] Whatever his concerns about Arabic's unreliability, Mármol Carvajal was dedicated to providing his readers with privileged access to notable Arabic language primary evidence. The details of this episode also capture Mármol Carvajal's effort to present such evidence to his Old Christian readers with caution. Unlike Hurtado de Mendoza, who was eager to challenge if not offend readers by upending their expectations, Mármol Carvajal sought to confirm his readers' prejudices about the Moriscos by emphasizing specific aspects of the texts' capture. The "silk sack" in this episode, for example, recalled the Moriscos' longstanding role as craftsmen in the peninsular silk industry, a connection underscored by the Arabic etymology of Mármol Carvajal's word choice for "bag," *talega*.[32] Despite their technical expertise, however, Mármol Carvajal also suggested that Moriscos were untrustworthy collaborators. The betrayal of Daud by his compatriot was, in Mármol

Carvajal's words, "a very ordinary thing among the Moors."[33] And the large Arabic book, whose use in this case was to conceal pressing war communication rather than to protect medieval wisdom, highlights Old Christian unease about the possible deceptive uses of Arabic writing and manuscript culture. Here Mármol Carvajal's methodological point oddly echoed Daud's written warning to his co-religionists: "You must know, gentlemen," argued Daud, referring to the proclamation of the *nueva pragmática* in 1567, "that the Christians have ordered us to give up the Arabic language, but he who loses the Arabic language loses his law."[34] For Mármol Carvajal, of course, weak Arabic knowledge threatened historical accuracy rather than religious orthodoxy. Interweaving metahistorical commentary with a familiar discourse of "maurophobia," Mármol Carvajal argued that however unreliable these and other Arabic documents might be, it was impossible to write an account of the Alpujarras conflict without consulting them.

In the second volume of his *Guerras civiles de Granada*, Ginés Pérez de Hita fictionalized Hurtado de Mendoza's and Mármol Carvajal's preoccupation with Arabic sources. Feigning translation of sentimental poetry, letters, orations, and histories originally composed in Arabic, Pérez de Hita chronicled the Alpujarras conflict in a linguistic and generic register reminiscent of late medieval romance. Like the anonymous novella *El Abencerraje*, or story of Ozmín y Daraja, included in the first part of Mateo Alemán's picaresque tale *Guzmán de Alfarache*, the first volume of Pérez de Hita's *Guerras civiles de Granada* presented peninsular Muslims as worthy and honorable foes who largely abided by the rules of chivalric conduct. By framing his relation of the Alpujarras war as an extension of this strain of "maurophilia," as some scholars have called this body of literature, Pérez de Hita raised the relationship among literary genre, historical method, and contemporary politics as an epistemological problem.[35]

Pérez de Hita's account of the Alpujarras uprising in the second volume of his history opened with a series of fretful letters between Morisco rebels and a potential Algerian ally named Ochalí. In this correspondence, the undermanned and out-armed Moriscos hoped to extract a commitment of Turkish or Berber reinforcements. Pérez de Hita used this imagined correspondence to depict the realpolitik driving both the Moriscos' appeal to a shared sense of Islamic identity and other Mediterranean Muslims' wariness of involvement in peninsular affairs. Many other invented invocations of Arabic lyric and martial prose punctuated the rest of the text, as if it were an anthology of Morisco writing rather than a work of political and military history. Echoing Mármol Carvajal's skeptical employment of Arabic sources,

Pérez de Hita pretended to take only partial responsibility for this corpus of poetry, speeches, and letters. "These verses," Pérez de Hita explained in a typical comment about an interpolated poem, "were sung in Arabic with a Morisco trumpet, and because they are rendered exactly as they were in Arabic, which is no easy task, they have not turned out as well as they could have."[36] Whereas Hurtado de Mendoza and Mármol Carvajal's disagreement about the reliability of Arabic sources reflected an intimate engagement with the conventions and limitations of scholarly inquiry, Pérez de Hita's poetic haughtiness and rhetoric of exactitude marked the line separating fiction from history. Publishing decades after Hurtado de Mendoza's *Guerra de Granada* had begun to circulate widely and several years after the publication of Mármol Carvajal *Historia del rebelión*, in other words, Pérez de Hita was not aiming to outdo his predecessors in archival source collection. For him, the Alpujarras conflict was rather a storytelling opportunity, one that had the potential, as María Soledad Carrasco Urgoiti and Francisco Márquez Villanueva have argued, to influence real debate about the future of the Moriscos on the peninsula.[37] The uprising served Pérez de Hita as a textual showcase of lyrical range and political allegory. In fictionalizing both the conflict and Hurtado de Mendoza's and Mármol Carvajal's modes of representing that conflict, Pérez de Hita drew attention to the methodological challenges of producing Morisco history.

Despite the reality of the Alpujarras violence and the truth claim of Hurtado de Mendoza's and Mármol Carvajal's accounts, the second part of *Guerras civiles* was also a reminder that to draw on Arabic sources in early modern Spain was a literary trope as well as a historiographical obsession. The Granadan Morisco and lead books translator Miguel de Luna, for instance, had gone so far as to insist that his sympathetic account of the eighth-century Muslim invasions of the Iberian peninsula, *La verdadera historia del Rey Don Rodrigo*, was but a translation of an archival discovery. Like Pérez de Hita after him, Luna hinted at this original fiction by exaggerating the difficulty of translating between Arabic and Spanish, which are "so repugnant to each other."[38] Discerning sixteenth-century readers of classical prose surely would have recognized that the "true history" of Luna's title alluded to Lucian of Samosota's *True Histories*, which were anything but. Mimicking this trope of the Arabic source text in the first part of *Don Quijote*, Miguel de Cervantes presented the entirety of his narrative as an archival Arabic manuscript fortuitously picked up on the cheap in the marketplace of Toledo. But the open secret of Luna's fib or the shadow of Cervantes's satirical experimentalism must not obscure the real epistemological challenges faced both by early modern historians eager to weave Arabic sources into their histories and, as chapter 4 explained, by learned readers as committed to distinguishing between the archival and the imaginary as between the orthodox and the heterodox. As historians from the second-century Greek scholar Polybius to Hayden White have noted, to seal history off from rhetoric is an impossible task. Styles of expression and forms of narration have always traveled across disciplines and genres, providing opportunities for invention and deception as well as truth or instruction. Even so, as Arnaldo Momigliano put it in a response to White, "historians (it seems necessary to state) do research, as the word *historia* has implied since the days of Herodotus," and this marshaling of evidence is compulsory for the historian and optional for the poet, novelist, or playwright.[39] Despite dramatizing their own search for and interpretation of unusual sources, Hurtado de Mendoza and Mármol Carvajal combined research and rhetoric in a way distinct from that of Luna and Cervantes.

The difficulty of cleaving historical truth from fiction or allegory underscores the extent to which the first accounts of the Alpujarras conflict, however historically imprecise or generically flexible, were deeply engaged with problems of scholarly method. New angst over the role of the historian, the relationship between apologetic and critical history, and the reliability of Arabic sources grew in the peninsular context out of the struggle to construct an authoritative account of the Morisco uprising. This struggle entailed revisiting both the immediate origins of the conflict and the social and religious circumstances of Granada's Morisco community over the course of previous decades. To recount the multiple ends of Islamic Iberia at the dawn of the seventeenth century was to begin to consolidate the sources for Morisco history. The first accounts of the Alpujarras uprising constituted initial attempts at this consolidation, even as they also served as an experiment in historical argumentation.

RECONSTRUCTING THE WAR'S ORIGINS

Hurtado de Mendoza, Mármol Carvajal, Pérez de Hita, and Juan Rufo all detailed two principal causes for the explosion of hostilities in late 1568. The first and most obvious impetus for war was the pronouncement of the *nueva pragmática* at the beginning of 1567. The restrictions, which signaled the end of a forty-year royal policy of dispensation, angered the Granadan Morisco community. Though the elderly Morisco Francisco Núñez Muley pleaded his countrymen's case with the president of the Chancellery of Granada,

Pedro de Deza, he was unable to convince either Deza or the Crown to delay once again the implementation of these restrictions. In Hurtado de Mendoza's and Mármol Carvajal's views, the second major cause for the Alpujarras uprising was the Moriscos' belief in a series of false prophecies that foretold the imminent end of Christian rule in Granada. These divinations, which were likely invented by Islamic jurists in the years after the fall of Nasrid Granada and then revised and recorded by learned members of the Morisco community some decades later, predicted that the reversal of the *reconquista* would begin with a Granadan rebellion. To examine the origins of the Alpujarras uprising was thus to study both the war's immediate legal context and a deeper history of Morisco piety, class hierarchy, and political antagonism.

As you will recall from chapter 1, Núñez Muley submitted his petition nearly two years before the start of the uprising, but Hurtado de Mendoza's and Mármol Carvajal's accounts of his confrontation with Deza in different ways conflated the petition's failure and the subsequent armed conflict. Imitating Thucydides's penchant for oratorical set pieces in his *History of the Peloponnesian War*, both Hurtado de Mendoza and Mármol Carvajal fictionalized Núñez Muley's petition as a speech.[40] In *Guerra de Granada*, Hurtado de Mendoza presented Núñez Muley's words in the mouth of the rebel leader, Fernando de Valor el-Zaguer. Though Valor el-Zaguer's speech was a much-condensed version of Núñez Muley's text, Hurtado de Mendoza did convey the petition's fundamental point, which was that a misunderstanding between Old and New Christians threatened to produce a civil war of "Spaniards against Spaniards."[41] By warning against the dangers of Christianity's expansion into the cultural sphere, Núñez Muley had attempted to avoid such violent confrontation, and he framed his defense of Morisco cultural autonomy as a protection of Christian orthodoxy. By focusing on the martial rhetoric rather than the religious and cultural arguments articulated by Núñez Muley, however, Hurtado de Mendoza's version of Núñez Muley's words was nothing less than a call to arms: "Such was the speech that Fernando de Valor el Zaguer gave them," Hurtado de Mendoza related, that his countrymen "ended up energized, indignant, and generally resolved immediately to rebel."[42] In Hurtado de Mendoza's view, the Moriscos were neither religious heretics seeking to undermine Christian orthodoxy nor well-intentioned subjects hoping to protect the integrity of the Crown and the unity of peninsular Christianity. They were rebels whose actions were disloyal but whose complaints were comprehensible.

Hurtado de Mendoza's depiction of Morisco reactions to the *nueva pragmática* was important because it established a paradigm for later authors, such as Juan Rufo and Ginés Pérez de Hita, both of whom relied on manuscript editions of *Guerra de Granada* in the composition of their works. Like Hurtado de Mendoza, Rufo largely dismissed religion as an explanatory tool for the war, and he focused on the relationship between Morisco autonomy and imperial military strategy. But unlike Hurtado de Mendoza, who described the martial consequences of the *nueva pragmática,* Rufo examined the military logic driving its passage and implementation. The restrictions, Rufo argued, rightly punished the Moriscos for their unwillingness to serve as soldiers in the forces of the Crown. While Old Christians risked life and limb on boats bound for Italy and the New World, and while they engaged in battles in Asia, Africa, and elsewhere, the Moriscos remained on the peninsula, free, at least in Rufo's selective vision of the Morisco experience, to build their wealth and grow their families. "While their estates and lineage expanded," explained Rufo in *La Austriada,* "so too did our wars and wanderings."[43] Ignoring the fact that a series of regulations had excluded Moriscos from imperial service and global travel, Rufo depicted the Moriscos' homebound reality as a shirking of imperial duty. In Rufo's view, the Moriscos were guilty not only of treason or apostasy, but also of ingratitude to the "common fatherland" (*patria comun*) that hosted them and the "common army" (*comun ejercicio*) that protected them.[44] Such freeloading constituted an insult to those men who sacrificed for the good of the empire. To allow the Morisco community to multiply in numbers and affluence, Rufo argued, was to permit a cancer at the heart of the body politic. For those who doubted that Felipe II had acted prudently to confront this threat to peace and security, Rufo pointed to the fervor with which the Moriscos countered the *nueva pragmática* as evidence of its necessity. Turning Hurtado de Mendoza's focus on the political and economic origins of the Alpujarras conflict to apologetic rather than critical ends, Rufo helped to establish a narrative linking the defeat of the Morisco rebels in Granada to the victory over the Ottoman Turks at the Battle of Lepanto.

In Pérez de Hita's double-edged recapitulation of Hurtado de Mendoza's account, on the other hand, Felipe II's intentions were pastoral rather than martial, and his aims were justifiable on both religious and political grounds. Nevertheless, in underestimating the swiftness and scope of the Moriscos' reaction, Pérez de Hita argued that Felipe II had gravely erred. The *nueva pragmática* was "rightly agreed upon and commanded, because the heart of the king is in the hand of God," Pérez de Hita explained, but "it is also true that from this action resulted great loss and spillage of Christian blood, great diminution of the rents of Your Majesty, and the ruin of many towns in the Kingdom of Granada, which have fallen and been lost forever."[45] Despite the laudatory rhetoric, Pérez de Hita's critical lesson was that action in the name of religious orthodoxy was sometimes not worth the cost. As Francisco de Vitoria had recognized in his discussion of compulsory conversion in both the New and the Old Worlds, even those with the most pious intentions cannot anticipate all of the consequences of religious coercion.

Hurtado de Mendoza's *Guerra de Granada* served Rufo, Pérez de Hita, and even Mármol Carvajal as a point of departure. But on the question of the Alpujarras conflict's origins, Mármol Carvajal's *Historia del rebelión* offered a more detailed explanation, replete with primary sources. Until the mid-twentieth century, when an autograph copy of Núñez Muley's petition was discovered in the Biblioteca Nacional de España, for example, *Historia del rebelión* was the main source of information about both Núñez Muley and his petition to Deza at the Chancellery of Granada. Mármol Carvajal presented the specifics of the 1567 decrees, described the Moriscos' initial reaction to the news of their curtailed freedom, reproduced Núñez Muley's text in slightly condensed format, and, like Hurtado de Mendoza, fictionalized the petition as a speech. In Mármol Carvajal's telling, though, Núñez Muley's petition emerged out of the initial chaos caused by the publication of the new decrees, which Deza ordered solemnly read aloud in Granada's public plazas. The reaction in the Albaicín neighborhood, which remained the center of Morisco life even in the second half of the sixteenth century, was fierce: "Such was their upheaval," related Mármol Carvajal, "that no sane person could help but recognize the damage to their freedoms."[46] Before deciding to take up arms, however, the Moriscos extensively debated, both in public and in secret, other possible plans of action. Rather than move directly to violence, the community chose instead the path of "false humility" (*fingida humildad*) and calmly asked Deza to suspend the *nueva pragmática.*[47] Mármol Carvajal's language here is significant. Like Núñez Muley himself, Mármol Carvajal deemphasized the issue of apostasy. False humility is different from religious dissimulation. According to Mármol Carvajal, the Moriscos were careful legal and political tacticians rather than unrepentant and wily heretics intent upon deceiving their Old Christian counterparts or zealous fighters eager for vengeance. In representing the encounter between Núñez Muley and Deza in this way, Mármol Carvajal brought to life the legal and theological debate upon which the future of the Morisco community hung, even as he made a historical judgment about that community's agenda. The Moriscos were duplicitous toward their Old Christian counterparts, Mármol Carvajal argued, but primarily in a political rather than a religious sense.

In Mármol Carvajal's charitable account of the origins of the Alpujarras conflict, moreover, it was the Moriscos themselves who suffered the harshest consequences of their own dissimulation. The rebel, largely rural masses overestimated their prospects in armed conflict because their upper-class counterparts, based in Granada's Albaicín and eager to retain their privilege, had cultivated a desperate fantasy of salvation. "Some dissimulated," related Mármol Carvajal, "while others, who had less to lose, were more bold and began to advocate revolt."[48] A tool of such political dissimulation and thus a "principal cause" of the Alpujarras war was a series of Morisco prophecies forecasting the end of Christian rule and the restoration of Islamic independence on the Iberian Peninsula.[49] Employing an elusive allegorical language that for historians of the medieval Mediterranean might recall the apocalyptic rhetoric of the First Crusade, recently studied by Jay Rubenstein, these prophecies depicted an imminent rebellion, organized by local zealots and aided by Ottoman intervention.[50] As Mármol Carvajal explained, Granada's religious leaders had invented previous versions of similar "divinations or prophecies, or better said, fictions" at the end of the fifteenth century as a way to foment unrest and disrupt the new Christian leadership of the city. Though the sturdiness of the new Christian order soon became clear, the "Arab grammarians" who penned the prophecies continued to circulate them, "for the consolation of their audiences when our Christians had finished conquering that kingdom."[51] The language and history of these prophecies were a philological nightmare. At least according to Alonso de Castillo, who had discovered the Arabic texts in the Granadan archives of the Holy Office and passed selections of his Spanish translations along to Mármol Carvajal, Morisco copyists had imprecisely reproduced the predictions in a tangle of fragmentary prose and disordered script. Castillo's criticisms foreshadowed the interpretive hedging that would characterize his early translations of the Sacromonte discoveries. Lest he be held responsible for mistranslating or misinterpreting tricky Morisco documents, that is, Castillo asserted that the paleographic features of the prophecies made it difficult for him to read the texts. And he argued, as Mármol Carvajal did about the ancient name of Granada, that the very Arabic letters and words of the prophecies, which all except the most learned of Morisco *alfaquíes* would have known only in oral form, were opaque: "The Arabic language is so equivocal that many times the very same thing written with an accent long or short means two contrary things."[52] Although Mármol Carvajal was here again concerned about the reliability and transparency of the Arabic language, he was convinced that these decades-old prophecies had come to serve their original, provocative role in the lead-up to the Alpujarras uprising.

Mármol Carvajal thus argued that the learned colluded with the opacity of the Arabic language in order to foment local unrest. Deliberate grammar errors and polyvalent roots amplified the already powerful allegorical quality of these divinations, which, according to Castillo, their cunning propagators had "bent to the will of the inconsolable and battered Moors."[53] While the divinations' elite authors hid behind this linguistic and literary impenetrability, the vulnerable Morisco masses, most of whom, as the biography of Ignacio de Las Casas underscores, grew up learning only the local dialectical Arabic, settled on a wishful interpretation of the documents. "It is no wonder," explained Mármol Carvajal, that the Moriscos "understood one thing for another," growing hopeful both for victory against their Old Christian adversaries and for a return to their former independence and wealth.[54] But just as no Ottoman Turks came to the defeated Muslims' rescue at the dawn of the sixteenth century, few came to the Moriscos' aid eighty years later, when the Second Alpujarras War began to turn against the insurgents. The Moriscos' "jofores o pronósticos," as Mármol Carvajal called the prophecies, proved to be false. The war was disaster for the Morisco communities in and around Granada, which imperial foot soldiers and knights on horseback thoroughly pillaged. Paleographic impenetrability, linguistic difficulty, and eschatological allegory had turned out to be instruments of Morisco self-deception. Their insurrectionary resolve rested upon a duplicitous set of fictions whose misreading was calamitous. All the same, this was a misreading that proved popular among Moriscos even at the beginning of the seventeenth century, when, according to Ignacio de Las Casas, they hurried to purchase both Mármol Carvajal's *Historia del rebelión* and Miguel de Luna's *La verdadera historia* as soon as they appeared in print. In Las Casas's estimation, this was neither a uniquely Morisco historical sensibility nor a benign nostalgia, because they "took the prophecies contained there to be true," and their reading "caused them completely to cool off to the faith and to light and inflame them in their own things."[55] This reception of the prophecies both before the Alpujarras conflict and after the appearance of *Historia del rebelión* proved Mármol Carvajal's methodological insight correct: in both the writing and the making of history, it was necessary to interpret primary texts like a skeptical literary critic.

Mármol Carvajal cribbed entire passages from Hurtado de Mendoza's *Guerra de Granada*, but his account of these prophecies was the result of his own analysis and his close relationship with Castillo. Although Hurtado de

Mendoza concurred with Mármol Carvajal that the Morisco community had forgotten reason and succumbed to the lure of the prognostications, he only briefly described their content and impact. In *Guerra de Granada*, they served as an interlude between Fernando de Valor el-Zaguer's call to arms and the beginning of actual hostilities. Conflating the elderly Núñez Muley with the prophecies' inventors, Hurtado de Mendoza described an aging Granadan rising to address his Morisco compatriots in support of the war: "He did not neglect to remind them," Hurtado de Mendoza recounted of this gentleman, that "many years ago, in the mouths of important and learned men, through the movements and shadows of the stars, and via the prophets of their law, it was declared that they would rise up and reclaim what was their own . . . and the predicted time corresponded exactly with this rebellion."[56] This old man then described the animal births, visions of armed men hovering in the air above the mountains outside of Granada, and other marvels that together suggested that the moment for the anticipated struggle was nigh. Like Mármol Carvajal, Hurtado de Mendoza emphasized a materialist logic of the war's origins, in which some Moriscos were naive while others were cynical and self-interested. But unlike Mármol Carvajal, who excavated layers of Morisco belief as evidence for the construction of Granadan political and military history, Hurtado de Mendoza found the rebels' credulity to be risible. He failed to see the explanatory power of comparative close reading.

Only in retrospect did Mármol Carvajal recognize the full payoff of consulting Morisco primary sources like this corpus of prophecies. As he argued in a letter to Archbishop of Granada Pedro de Castro in 1593, these texts provided the thematic and structural building blocks for the Sacromonte lead books and Turpiana manuscript. This perhaps explains why Mármol Carvajal chose to integrate selections of Castillo's translations into his *Historia del rebelión*, which was not published until after the Sacromonte debates were in full swing. To select and gloss the prophecies was to make an old story, composed in the 1570s, current for a turn of the seventeenth century audience keenly interested in the Sacromonte discoveries. Given this previous research, Mármol Carvajal came to the Sacromonte episode primed to historicize, which is likely why, along with Benito Arias Montano, he was one of the first scholars to doubt openly the discoveries' authenticity. While Montano's letter to Archbishop Pedro de Castro, signed with his customary "talmīd" moniker and also sent in 1593, focused on the historical and philological inconsistences, Mármol Carvajal advised the archbishop to follow a different sort of interpretive approach. He maintained that it was necessary to compare the Turpiana manuscript's language with the "letter" of those old prophecies translated by Castillo, in order to see if the similarity of style, the phrasings, and the meanings conformed to each other.[57] A year later, Mármol Carvajal wrote again to say that he was convinced that the texts emerged from shared Morisco sources. "It is well understood," he declared to Pedro de Castro, "that they deal with one and the same material."[58] To understand the origins of the Alpujarras conflict and the Sacromonte discoveries, Mármol Carvajal maintained, it was necessary to examine the primary sources of Morisco social history.

I do not mean to reduce all early modern Spanish reflection on history writing to disagreement over how to recount the Second Alpujarras War. Disagreement over how to write the history of the Alpujarras conflict intensified a historiographical crisis that had already begun in the previous decades. What I do want to insist on, however, is that in reconstructing the origins of the war, its first historians began to establish the outlines of a specifically Morisco history. And once established, this Morisco history became a new and potent tool in the further transformation of history as a discipline. With early seventeenth-century hindsight, moreover, the stakes of conflicting narratives about the Alpujarras conflict loomed even larger, for the uncertain future of the entire peninsular Morisco community came to be read through that uprising from the late 1560s and early 1570s. In negotiating a story about the social and religious conditions out of which the war emerged, Hurtado de Mendoza, Mármol Carvajal, Pérez de Hita, and Juan Rufo were in fact engaging in a much broader debate about the diminishing prospects of Morisco assimilation and the overlapping conventions of historical inquiry and political decision making. What was true about the war's origins also held true for the conflict's other main episodes.

MORISCO UPRISING, CIVIL WAR

Concerned about the security of the Andalusian coast and discord between the third marquis of Mondéjar, Iñigo López de Mendoza (Hurtado de Mendoza's nephew), and Marquis of Vélez Luis Fajardo, two leaders of the splintered Old Christian forces that initially waged the Alpujarras war, Felipe II decided in 1570 to send his half brother Juan de Austria to take charge of the counterrevolutionary effort. Don Juan's arrival offered the first chroniclers of the conflict a built-in narrative turning point. Late sixteenth- and early seventeenth-century readers would have known of Don Juan's success not only in subduing the Morisco uprising, but also in subsequently leading a Christian alliance called the Holy League to victory against an imposing Ottoman naval fleet at the Battle of Lepanto. Participating in the same economy of eastern Mediterranean exemplarity that Juan Ginés de Sepúlveda had in another context, Juan Rufo in his treatment of both these conflicts in *La Austriada* employed Don Juan as a link between triumphs over Islamic foes. The failure of local troops to bring the Alpujarras conflict to a swift conclusion was, in Rufo's account, simply a prelude to Don Juan's momentous entry into the war and poem alike. Recounting Felipe II's choice of Don Juan in the elaborate style characteristic of Virgilian epic and its many early modern imitators, Rufo described God's thundering approval of the decision, and he took advantage of the narrative moment to offer a comprehensive biography of the young prince. Victory in both the western and the eastern Mediterranean was possible only with Don Juan at the head of the imperial forces. Nothing less than an instrument of fate, Rufo's Don Juan both reflected and shaped a late sixteenth-century Iberian triumphalism that has to this day clouded histories of Spanish-Ottoman relations.[59]

Against Rufo's celebratory treatment of Don Juan's arrival on the military stage, the causticity of Hurtado de Mendoza's account and nuance of Mármol Carvajal's depiction stand out. In Hurtado de Mendoza's telling, Don Juan did not resolve the tensions between López de Mendoza and Luis Fajardo or transform the course of the conflict. The circumstances surrounding Don Juan's entrance instead slowed military decision making and upended the regular functioning of Granada's local government. Although Don Juan's authority over a specially formed war council seemed to be total, in fact Felipe II kept their man in the south on a short leash: "His commission was without any limitation," explained Hurtado de Mendoza, "but his freedom was so bound that no thing, great or small, could be arranged without communication and consultation with advisors and the command of the king, except to negate and delay."[60] Don Juan was an emblem of peninsular power struggles rather than a sign of divine favor. Whatever the politics of Don Juan's appointment, moreover, Hurtado de Mendoza harped on the ambitious general's personal failure to exert authority even over his own troops. Don Juan's admirable if clumsy attempt at military reform was not, in other words, the turning point in the war effort that readers familiar with Rufo's celebratory rhetoric might have expected. It was rather an opportunity for Hurtado de Mendoza to inventory unchanging imperial mismanagement, as enlisted men continued their unruliness and captains persisted in exaggerating costs even after Don Juan's arrival.[61] In Hurtado de Mendoza's view, fault for this miscarriage of reform did not rest with Don Juan alone, however. Accustomed to the profligacy of Spain's military ventures elsewhere in Europe, Don Juan's attaché and longtime tutor Luis Quijada exacerbated the already extant lack of discipline, and neither López de Mendoza nor any other local strongman possessed the combination of leadership experience and determination to respond. Hurtado de Mendoza recalled the direness of the situation in staccato: "There were few bureaucrats, the solders lost all respect, vice became customary, and the good name and reputation of the military was degraded." Only with the arrival of further reinforcements from as far afield as Castile and Extremadura, Hurtado de Mendoza halfheartedly conceded, did this strategic and organizational deficiency finally "seem to resolve itself."[62]

In his account of this same period in the war, Mármol Carvajal also emphasized the disagreement and disorder driving Felipe II's decision to include Juan de Austria in the Alpujarras conflict. Some advocates at court, such as the powerful Morisco Alonso de Granada Venegas, believed that if Felipe II simply traveled to Granada in a personal display of power, all the disturbances would end.[63] Granada Venegas hoped for as peaceful a resolution to the conflict as possible. But members of the king's court were more concerned about the geopolitical optics of a royal visit to Granada, which risked legitimizing the Morisco uprising and thus undermining the authority of the Crown. "The crimes of those unfortunates did not deserve" such a visit, argued Felipe II's advisors, who also fretted that the king might find himself marooned in Granada unable to tend to the "great matters that might occur elsewhere."[64] Sending Juan de Austria to Granada with the king's authority to form a war council was a compromise solution. Echoing Hurtado de Mendoza's *Guerra de Granada*, Mármol Carvajal pointed out that although such a council was an important addition to the war's organization, it delayed the resolution of issues requiring brevity. Because news of the leadership shakeup reached Granada before Don Juan himself, undisciplined soldiers eager both to take advantage of their final opportunity for rapacity and to impress the approaching prince with a show of force went on an illicit pillaging spree. What is more, Mármol Carvajal explained, "the very men in charge were those who engaged in the greatest disturbances."[65] Conceived as a way to resolve the chaos resulting from tensions between "the two Marquises," as Mármol Carvajal somewhat discourteously called López de Mendoza and Fajardo, Juan de Austria's entry into the conflict instead produced more disorder.

Mármol Carvajal's depiction of the actual ceremonies honoring Juan de Austria's arrival in Granada reflected his ongoing interest in how different groups sought, even as the war's outcome remained in doubt, to shape its meaning and history. Local church and city officials exited Granada's walls to greet Don Juan in what Mármol Carvajal described as a sincere and fitting expression of welcome, but others were more interested in shaping the new arrival's first impressions of the conflict. In a "pious spectacle worthy of compassion, though industriously accomplished in order to provoke his anger against the Moriscos," more than four hundred Christian women held captive in the Alpujarras Mountains by Morisco rebels went out of the city to receive the prince with a "shower of tears" and "dolorous laments." Inside the city, Mármol Carvajal dryly remarked in continuation, Juan de Austria "saw less tears and more regalia and festivity," but this was only "because the street-facing windows along his route had been decorated with fabrics of gold and silk, and a great number of richly adorned ladies and maidens had crowded the city's streets to see him."[66] By establishing this contrast between the howling mourners beyond the city gates and the luxurious women inside them, Mármol Carvajal presented the Alpujarras war as a contest of performance and perception as well as bloody battles. Juan de Austria's interpretive challenge upon arriving in Granada, in other words, paralleled the historian's effort at reconstructing the events after the fact: it was necessary to parse competing agendas, displays of emotion, and rhetorical techniques in order to understand the causes and recognize the lessons of the conflict.

After the initial celebrations in honor of Don Juan had subsided, subsequent rituals of welcome took an even more cynical turn. Continuing to explore class divisions within the Morisco community, Mármol Carvajal described how the "richest and most important" Moriscos from the Albaicín went to kiss the hand of the prince in an effort to convince him of their loyalty to the Crown and their belief in God. Keen to distinguish themselves from the "authors of this evil" uprising, these elite Moriscos also complained about robberies and other ill treatment suffered at the hands of Old Christian soldiers garrisoned in Granada. Though they were likely involved in fomenting the uprising, they nevertheless presented themselves to Don Juan as victims of Morisco disloyalty and Old Christian vengeance. Echoing Hurtado de Mendoza's account, Mármol Carvajal employed Don Juan's appearance as an opportunity to depict tensions within as well as between the Morisco and the Old Christian camps. In this way, Hurtado de Mendoza and Mármol Carvajal refused the sort of celebratory rhetoric of imperial and religious essentialism visible in Rufo's *La Austriada* and later imperial chronicles by Antonio de Herrera y Tordesillas and Luis Cabrera de Córdoba.

THE WAR'S CONCLUSION AND THE COMING EXPULSION

The first chroniclers of the Second Alpujarras War were engaged in an experiment in how to formulate and frame Morisco history. Divergent paradigms for understanding the motivations and identities of the Morisco rebels produced a crisis of historical method. To examine the political and religious circumstances out of which the Alpujarras conflict emerged and to reconstruct its immediate consequences were to consult unusual archival sources, engage in political and economic intrigue, and, most importantly, negotiate a tension between the apologetic and the critical uses of history writing. In depicting the end of the Morisco uprising in particular, however, Hurtado de Mendoza, Mármol Carvajal, Pérez de Hita, and Rufo looked forward as well as backward. As chapter 6 demonstrates, their representations of the Moriscos' expulsion from the Kingdom of Granada at the end of the war established the terms in which opponents of Morisco expulsion later argued. By narrating the failure of assimilation in starkly violent imagery, these first chroniclers of the Alpujarras uprising seized the mantle of scholarly legitimacy from the canon lawyers and philologists who had previously overdetermined the nature of debate about Morisco assimilation and New Christian history more broadly. Turning away from the theological problems posed by dissimulation and apostasy, they framed the Morisco question as a political and economic issue. In this way, to describe the conclusion of the Alpujarras war at the end of the sixteenth century was also to lay the groundwork for seventeenth-century debates among *arbitristas*, or economic advisors to the Crown, about the costs and benefits of expulsion.

Hurtado de Mendoza concluded *Guerra de Granada* in the Tacitan language with which he opened it. The text culminated in a succession of gory details: Abenabó, the final leader of the Morisco rebellion, died at the hands of his fellow fighters; the brothers Francisco and Alonso Barredo discovered, eviscerated, and preserved Abenabó's corpse in order to ceremoniously carry it to the gates of Granada, where the decapitated head was impaled and displayed on a pole; and in the text's final sentence, Francisco Barredo, whom Felipe II liberally rewarded for his troubles with money and seized property, was murdered at a banquet. Juan de Austria's imperial forces may have defeated the Morisco uprising, but Hurtado de Mendoza's closing imagery emphasized the terrible cost and dubious legitimacy of the counterrevolutionary effort. The worst of these costs were borne by the Morisco rebels themselves. "Among the Moors who remained, some peacefully surrendered, others left for North Africa, and death squads, mountain cold, and illness finished off the rest; that was how the war and uprising concluded," explained Hurtado de Mendoza.[67] But it was also true that the Kingdom of Granada, the very region that the war was supposed to protect, "ended up depopulated and destroyed."[68] Three years of battles had obliterated the region's infrastructure and farmland, displaced several hundred thousand of its most productive workers, and frayed its social and religious fabric. The Crown was able to lure new inhabitants only with the sort of rewards enjoyed by Barredo. Free housing and a small yearly tribute eventually attracted the adventurous and desperate from all over Spain. Yet Barredo's sudden and unexplained murder punctured any easy sense of the victors' righteousness, which such a detente might otherwise have engendered. Like a judgment day punishment, Barredo's death served Hurtado de Mendoza as a disapproving epilogue. The Alpujarras triumph was an empty one.

In addition to his attention to the material costs of the war and his ambivalence about the conflict's meaning, Hurtado de Mendoza was also upset that the revolt had upended Granada's traditional hierarchy, atop which his family had sat for decades. Diego himself was born in the Alhambra. He was the son of the count of Tendilla and first mayor of Granada, Iñigo López de Mendoza, and the grandson of the fifteenth-century poet and bibliophile the Marquis of Santillana.[69] Although *Guerra de Granada* chronicled in less than splendid terms the exploits of Diego Hurtado de Mendoza's nephew, also named Iñigo López de Mendoza, its author nevertheless did not agree with the diminution of the noble Mendoza family's local power in the aftermath of the war. Hurtado de Mendoza's antipathy toward the Crown was evident in another of his text's concluding episodes—one not mentioned by Mármol Carvajal or any other contemporary account—in which Don Juan's final order before departing Granada to join the Holy League and prepare for the Battle of Lepanto was to appoint in his absence Pedro de Deza as captain general. A theologian and imperial bureaucrat previously limited to the Chancellery of Granada, Deza represented the same encroachment of royal authority as Juan de Austria's arrival in Granada. Don Juan's appointment of Deza was salt in the wound for the Mendozas, which is perhaps why Hurtado de Mendoza was quick to point out that Deza and the other men left in control upon Don Juan's departure were unable to restrain the bands of marauding soldiers under their chain of command. Along with the subsequent, ominous concluding passages of *Guerra de Granada*, this episode highlights Hurtado de Mendoza's criticism of the war's violence and mismanagement, as well as his condemnation of the shifting power relations produced by the conflict. And by finishing on a negative note, he offered a decisive reproach to the apologetic rhetoric defining the imperial chronicles of the period.

Despite Hurtado de Mendoza's critical approach, when Antonio de Herrera y Tordesillas and Luis Cabrera de Córdoba set out to distill extant accounts of the Second Alpujarras War in subsequent decades, they paradoxically relied on *Guerra de Granada*. In *Felipe II, Rey de España*, for instance, Cabrera de Córdoba went so far as to copy without acknowledgment Hurtado de Mendoza's important comment concerning uncertainty among the Alpujarras war's participants over who would be "punished" and who simply "threatened." In their original context, Hurtado de Mendoza's words were part of a larger introductory statement on historical method. For Cabrera de Córdoba, though, this passage served as a bit of easy pathos tacked on in italics after the conclusion of several chapters on the Alpujarras uprising.[70] By nestling Hurtado de Mendoza's moving statement on the war's violence and the uncertainty of its outcome between Don Juan's deft departure for Madrid and a discussion of the Holy League's formation, Cabrera de Córdoba defanged the passage of its methodological bite. Because it was italicized, casual readers may have recognized the passage as a citation, though only astute historians and Morisco specialists would have known in 1619, the year that *Felipe II, Rey de España* was published, that Cabrera de Córdoba was copying directly from manuscript versions of Hurtado de Mendoza's *Guerra de Granada* in particular, for the text had not yet appeared in print.

While Mármol Carvajal followed closely Hurtado de Mendoza's account of the action at the end of the Alpujarras war, his final statement was far from a scathing condemnation of the war's violence and mismanagement. It was, rather, flattery that collapsed the entirety of the Morisco period into one sentimental passage. "Oh how happy an hour was it for you, celebrated city of Granada, when those Catholic Monarchs Fernando and Isabel removed you from the demon's oppression," crooned Mármol Carvajal. "They ennobled you with sumptuous buildings, they expanded and advanced you in both divine religion and temporal affairs, making your ceremonial mosques, in which you venerated the false Muhammad, into holy temples." Mármol Carvajal then added that Granada owed even more to subsequent princes, such as Felipe II, who at great price stamped out the "heresy that had remained in the Moriscos' hearts" (*herejía, que había quedado en los corazones de los nuevamente convertidos de moros*) and left to his son, Felipe III, a Granada "free and clear of that nation" (*libre y desembarazada de aquella nación*).[71] This was one of the few moments in *Historia del rebelión* where religion served as an explanatory mechanism of history. In Mármol Carvajal's depiction, the hundred-year-long effort to eliminate Islam from the Kingdom of Granada was the noble and pious aim of four generations of Spanish monarchs. Christian princes joined the battle on many fronts, reconstructing Granada's buildings and its inhabitants' hearts alike. But the unusually lyrical nature of this concluding passage differs from Mármol Carvajal's tenor in the rest of his text. You can hear him exaggerating the stock story so evident in Rufo's *La Austriada* as a way of covering for his evenhanded tone throughout the rest of the text. And note the fiction of the Morisco question's resolution by Felipe II, when at the time of this text's publication Felipe III's advisors were hotly contesting the possibility of expulsion.

Pérez de Hita imitated Mármol Carvajal's lyricism at the end of his *Guerras civiles,* but to different ends. Rather than addressing Granada in a fit of apostrophic emotion, he instead depicted the defeated Moriscos as they lamented their expulsion from Granada at the war's conclusion, just as the Trojans wept while fleeing a burning Troy: "'Oh, my God! Oh my lands, which we do not anticipate ever seeing again!' Many pronounced those exact words that Aeneas spoke upon leaving Troy: 'Oh three and four times lucky are those who died fighting at the foot of their walls, for in the end they remained, though dead, in their own lands.' Thus lamented the Moriscos, piously crying."[72] Pérez de Hita's stylized representation of the end of the Alpujarras conflict both echoed popular poetry about the sorrowful departure of the last Nasrid king, Boabdil, from Granada in 1492 and anticipated the expulsion of the Moriscos, not just from the Kingdom of Granada, but also from the entire peninsula. Drawing on the Virgilian tradition in a different way than Rufo, Pérez de Hita painted the Moriscos like so many "pious" Aeneases forced to leave their homelands in a wave of suffering, and if we follow the allusion to its logical end, he moreover hinted at the possibility that this departure might eventually lead to a new Morisco nation elsewhere in the Mediterranean. The Moriscos' piety was not some heretical and dangerous Islamic piety, but rather an admirable, civic attachment tempered by respect for the unknowable workings of fate and buoyed, as readers of Paulus Orosius's *Historiae adversus paganus* and later medieval chronicles knew, by the cyclical nature of universal history. Despite this rhetoric of piety, moreover, Pérez de Hita depicted the end of the war in strikingly nonessentialist religious terms. Like Virgil, who asked his readers to see the lines of filiation running from the defeated Trojans to the triumphant Emperor Augustus, Pérez de Hita urged his Christian readers to identify with the defeated Moriscos rather than to remain remote from them. He stopped well short of celebrating the Berber and Islamic origins of early modern Spanish culture and identity, but by giving the Moriscos the final word on the Second Alpujarras War, Pérez de Hita at the very least inserted their voices into early seventeenth-century debates about expulsion.

The end of the Alpujarras war thus marked the beginning of a protracted debate about Morisco expulsion. If Juan Rufo provided Archbishop of Valencia Juan de Ribera, the Dominican historian Jaime Bleda, and other proponents of Morisco expulsion a vocabulary of exclusion and set of essentialist religious tropes, Hurtado de Mendoza, Mármol Carvajal, and Pérez de Hita pointed toward ways of reframing the Morisco question in civic and even secular terms. Pedro de Valencia and Ignacio de Las Casas integrated this critical strand of early Alpujarras historiography into a recognizable and powerful inquisitorial and scholastic language of coercion, particularly when reframing the early decades of the Morisco period for a turn of the seventeenth century audience. But it was apologists for rather than opponents of Morisco expulsion who most effectively consolidated the archive of Morisco history that came to shape the scholarship of subsequent centuries. Not surprisingly, the Second Alpujarras War is an ambivalent presence in these two groups of texts, serving sometimes as evidence of continued Morisco perfidy and other times as a disturbing example of royal maladroitness. As *arbitristas* concerned about Spain's imperial decline, depopulation, industrial woes, and rampant poverty argued, however, the century-long failure of the Crown to find a resolution to the Morisco question perhaps did less harm than expulsion itself. In debating the conditions and meaning of the end of the Morisco period, competing communities of regional, Church, and economic historians wielded both an old language of religious polemic and a nascent vocabulary of capital. It is to this contested Morisco archive and its legacy that we now turn.

CHAPTER SIX

Archives of Failure

"Retract the memory of that thing that we saw in Granada," Archbishop of Valencia Juan de Ribera advised King Felipe III in a 1602 letter advocating the expulsion of Spain's Moriscos.[1] Ribera was eager to resolve a century-old challenge, one that particularly had troubled his own diocese. He also hoped that a definitive answer to the Morisco question in Valencia might hasten the forgetting of the Second Alpujarras War in Granada, which he could not bring himself even to name in his letter to Felipe III. Along with the Aragonese priest Pedro Aznar Cardona and the Dominican historian and inquisitorial censor Jaime Bleda, Ribera sought to employ the Moriscos' departure from Valencia to seize from Granada the mantle of reconquest exemplarity. Early seventeenth-century opponents of Morisco expulsion like Ignacio de Las Casas, however, saw in another light the didactic potential of a Valencian resolution to the Morisco question. "The conversion of all the descendants of Moors that there are in Spain depends, in my judgment (and I am not deceived)," wrote a confident Las Casas to Pope Clement VIII in his *Información acerca de los moriscos de España*, "only on converting those of the Kingdom of Valencia, and the reason for this is that the others understand that these people listen to and see all the rituals and ceremonies of their sect, and they know the entire Qur'an exactly." Before the regulations of the *nueva pragmática* and the resettlements that followed the Alpujarras uprising, Granada's Moriscos used to hold this place of preeminence, continued Las Casas in the same passage, but by the composition of the *Información* in 1605, they had "lost this honor and credit to those of Valencia."[2] In Las Casas's hopeful view, because Valencia's Moriscos were paradigmatic in their apostasy, their reform might become a model for the peninsula's other imperfect Christians. Granada had been a test case for the compulsory assimilation policy of the mid-sixteenth century, and at the end of the century it became a workshop for retooling the early modern craft of history. But treatises and early chronicles about the Morisco expulsion from Valencia established the definitive material and narrative conditions for future Spanish histories of sixteenth-century conversion and assimilation.

However notable Valencia's Muslim and Morisco past, it was no accident of geography or demography that the expulsions began there. Some *arbitristas*, such as Martín González de Cellorigo and Cristóbal Pérez de Herrera, and two of Spain's notable archbishops, Pedro Guerrero and Juan Bautista Pérez, joined Ignacio de Las Casas and Pedro de Valencia in begging Felipe III to dissimulate with the Moriscos. In opposition to expulsion, these men advocated turning a blind eye to Morisco apostasy in the short term with the expectation that the pastoral process might yet run its course in the long term. Conversely, Aznar Cardona, Bleda, and the Aragonese Franciscan Damián Fonseca mounted in Rome a failed effort to convince the pope to support expulsion, while Archbishop Ribera more successfully lobbied Felipe III in Madrid.[3] The first *bando de la expulsión*, or expulsion decree, finally announced in Valencia on September 22, 1609, contains a record of this longstanding disagreement between expulsion opponents and proponents. The document recalls the hasty organization by the Crown of a final learned council "to justify the removal" of Valencia's Moriscos, a candid instrumentalism that suggests continuing discord rather than agreement.[4] In a response to expulsion foes like Valencia and Las Casas, the decree advocated a quick resolution to the Morisco question, especially "given the danger and irreparable harm that dissimulating with them [*disimular con ellos*] might occasion."[5] Though Ribera worried that it might be wise to begin the expulsions with the smaller and perhaps more compliant Morisco communities of Castile before turning to those of Valencia, Bleda for years had urged beginning in his hometown. As the expulsion decree demonstrates, Ribera and Felipe III eventually came to embrace Bleda's call for Valencia to be a leader in the expulsion project, whatever the strategic risks.

Despite decades of disagreement over the prospect of expulsion, once the Crown publicized its decision, action was swift. Less than two weeks after the September proclamation, seventeen Neapolitan galley ships and an array of additional vessels transported nearly seven thousand Moriscos from Denia, a port city south of Valencia, to the then Spanish-controlled North African city of Orán. From there, this first group of exiled Moriscos headed to Tlemcen, where the local Islamic governor received what he mistakenly imagined would be a well-to-do group of peninsular refugees. No sooner had the five-year process of removal commenced, however, than dispute over whether and how to rid Spain of its nearly three hundred thousand Moriscos morphed into a conversation about the meaning and legacy of the expulsions. Aznar Cardona, for instance, painted the "miraculous smoothness" of the departure of this first group of Moriscos from Denia as a sign of God's approval of the expulsion project as a whole. In a pivotal chapter of his *Expvlsion ivstificada de los moriscos españoles* of 1612, Aznar Cardona argued that it was nothing less than marvelous that a few unarmed men managed, "without any scandal, sedition, chaos, or death of any Christian," to guide thousands of Moriscos to their departure. "Who would believe it?" he asked with a half-feigned incredulity that was also, I believe, an underhanded reference to the violence of the Alpujarras uprising and subsequent Morisco resettlements.[6] Although Aznar Cardona admitted later in the same chapter that some violence did eventually erupt, like Ribera he painted the successful Valencian expulsions as an eclipse of Granadan failure. The intellectual and print history of this transition from policy deliberation to historical inquiry and propagandistic description is the subject of this chapter.

I argue that both enemies and advocates of expulsion employed debate about the Morisco period's endgame to counter a pervasive narrative of imperial decline and to stake their respective claims on contemporary public affairs. Though Diego Hurtado de Mendoza's Tacitan account of the Alpujarras uprising had given form to a lachrymose peninsular narrative, years of plague, agricultural underproduction, and population collapse provided the content. González de Cellorigo captured the period's common sentiment in his *Memorial de la politica necesaria, y vtil restauracion à la Republica de España* of 1600, in which he claimed that Granada's reconquest in 1492 had been a high point: "it is impossible now to have that time's perfect monarchy in our Spain . . . for afterward it began to decline to these days."[7] Dispute over the legitimacy and logistics of expulsion compelled González de Cellorigo, Valencia, and Las Casas to reimagine the relationship between Spanish religious and civic identity. They formulated linked solutions, however controversial, to political anxiety and economic woe. Like Augustine and his inquisitorial admirers examined at the beginning of this book, moreover, Valencia and Las Casas aimed to manage the juridical conditions of New Christian faith. They insisted upon the efficacy of the early sixteenth century's mass baptisms even though they were performed under coercive circumstances. The first part of this chapter explores how scholastic debate about ritual efficacy and the boundaries of orthodoxy led to an innovative peninsular model of Christian charity, one that relied upon the underlying logic and authoritative language of inquisition even while seeking to limit the reach of the Holy Office.

By collecting apologies for expulsion and publishing them alongside accounts of the events as they unfolded, in contrast, Ribera and his successors presented Valencia as an example of how to resolve Spain's imperial problems. "Thus from the evil that has occurred in this event," wrote the epic poet Gaspar de Aguilar of the Valencian expulsions in 1610, "emerges a universal good."[8] Like their opponents, these scholars underscored the moral as well as the political and material dimensions of expulsion. By coopting an agrarian imagery of tolerance found in the Gospel of Matthew and favored by northern European religious reformers, Ribera in particular attempted to turn peninsular population decline and agricultural underproduction into a story of Christian triumph. Largely based in Valencia and Aragon but also publishing in Pamplona, Rome, and elsewhere, Ribera and his successors recognized more quickly than their adversaries the importance of print in establishing the intellectual and political significance of the expulsion. The rest of this chapter studies the substance of these scholars' arguments and the publication and reception of their texts, particularly within the context of late sixteenth- and early seventeenth-century debate among *arbitristas* over agricultural policy. Quickly shifting from theological advocacy to ex post facto justification, Juan de Ribera, Pedro Aznar Cardona, Damián Fonseca, Jaime Bleda, and Marco de Guadalajara y Xavier, among others, composed their accounts of expulsion in order to establish a Morisco history of the present.

Rival camps on Morisco expulsion compiled disparate archives of arguments and episodes to explain the failure of Morisco assimilation. These archives—by which I mean both the primary sources included in early printed texts about the expulsions and the corpus of manuscript treatises and published works that constitute the frames for those primary sources—offer distinct models of regional exemplarity, scriptural exegesis, and textual production. Writing about the challenges facing modern scholars of peninsular cryptoreligion, one specialist has astutely noted that "the Morisco problem is above all an historical problem," one whose solution demands both an attention to these multilayered documents and a willingness to read Spanish history against the grain.[9] Yet as I demonstrate in this chapter, already in the early seventeenth century the opposite was also true: Spanish history itself was a product of the Morisco question and its contentious resolution.

IN DEFENSE OF INDIFFERENCE

According to Pedro de Valencia, it was sometimes necessary to pretend as if Morisco crimes against the Church were offenses against the Crown. In his *Tratado acerca de los moriscos de España*, Valencia proposed adjudicating irregular religious practices through a "secular tribunal" (*tribunal seglar*) rather than an ecclesiastical court.[10] As a result of this jurisdictional "dissimulation or dispensation" (*disimulación o dispensación*), punishments for the guilty would include fines instead of public penitence or *autos de fe*.[11] In Valencia's schema, which obscured the contentious history of the *patronato real* beneath a fiction of separation between Church and State, the stigmatization associated with inquisitorial interrogation and imprisonment would play an ever-shrinking punitive role. Valencia was one of a few scholars who thought at the beginning of the seventeenth century that it was still possible to integrate these converts and their progeny into Christian society.[12] But like the elderly Morisco Francisco Núñez Muley, whose petition in the Chancellery of Granada he likely knew from Hurtado de Mendoza's and Luis de Mármol Carvajal's accounts of the Alpujarras uprising, Valencia believed that the Moriscos would cease acting like treasonous heretics only when Old Christians stopped treating them as such. At least in the short term, Valencia argued, it was neither necessary nor prudent to trust the Moriscos' Christian sincerity or imperial allegiance—to dissimulate doing so would suffice.

A classicist and Hebraist who studied with Benito Arias Montano and Francisco Sánchez de Las Brozas, Valencia became royal chronicler to Felipe III in 1607 and chronicler of the Indies in 1609. He was part of a new breed of intellectuals who sat astride traditional disciplinary divisions. A philologist and historian, he was also conversant in both civil law and scholastic theology. Valencia wrote the *Tratado* in late 1605 or early 1606 at the request of Felipe III's chaplain, Fray Diego de Mardones. Though it fell on deaf ears in its own day, the text is important because it demonstrates that although Valencia and fellow critics of expulsion were by and large political moderates and religious reformers, they were not, as some scholars have suggested, part of a dissident strand in Iberian intellectual culture.[13] In fact, Valencia and his allies shared the pastoral agenda and disciplinary presuppositions of Ribera, Bleda, and other churchmen who favored expulsion. Valencia argued against certain forms of popular violence and learned bigotry for which early modern Spain is justly infamous while also crafting an apology for other kinds of religious instruction and social control that drew directly upon the principles of inquisition. Along with a more open path for Morisco professional advancement, for example, compulsory intermarriage and resettlement were part of Valencia's proposed program of assimilation.[14] In Valencia's view, based on readings of Seneca, Pythagoras, and Virgil, these courses of action were integral features of "permistión," a Latinism that he defined as "total mixture, such that it is impossible to distinguish or discern who is of this or that nation."[15] Valencia saw religion as an effect rather than a cause of lived local conditions, which is why he thought that fostering Christian orthodoxy and republican unity required this kind of mixing.

In the *Tratado*, Valencia's clever response to conflict among competing models of assimilation was to replace Old Christian anxiety about Morisco *taqīyya*, which he unequivocally dubbed a "diabolic design," with a dissimulation based in Christian pedagogy.[16] You will recall from chapter 1 that Antonio de Guevara recognized the strategic importance of Christian dissimulation, especially in those first decades after the mass conversions over which he and Francisco Jiménez de Cisneros had presided in Valencia and Granada. "It was sometimes better to dissimulate than to castigate," Guevara had argued in a letter from the 1520s, which later was published in his *Epistolas familiares*.[17] Anticipating the concerns of Francisco de Vitoria in the context of the New World conversions, Guevara had worried that the public punishment of Morisco apostasy might anger the Morisco community and encourage Berber or Ottoman intervention in peninsular affairs. Valencia's defense of dissimulation echoed Guevara's pragmatism, but to broader civic ends. He agreed with Guevara and Cisneros, not to mention the casuist Martin Azpilcueta and his imitators, that Christian dissimulation was an irreplaceable tool for countering Morisco *taqīyya*, but he turned this defense of mendacity against its most vocal proponents. Valencia's was a charitable rather than a coercive deception.

In his commentary on Acts and Galatians, *Para declaracion de vna gran parte dela Eystoria Apostolica en los Actos y enla epistola ad Galatas advertencias*, Valencia pieced together the biblical and patristic sources for dissimulation as pastoral method. In so doing, he came to agree with Jerome's defense of Peter's actions at Antioch, related by Paul in Galatians, as explained above in chapter 1. Unequivocally describing Peter as "without any blame" and "not himself guilty in any way," Valencia chose Jerome's humanist faith in the reader over Augustine's insistence upon scripture's unambiguousness.[18] For Valencia and Guevara, Jerome's reasoning offered the principal legal precedent for pastoral mendacity. In his *Tratado* on the Moriscos, written two or three years before the 1608 commentary on Galatians, Valencia amplified and generalized this defense of dissimulation, always with an eye toward the contemporary circumstances: "The Holy Apostles by divine dispensation and economy of the Holy Spirit dissimulated for a long time in the Church with the frail converts from Judaism, who along with the light wanted to engage and conserve the shadows of the law, and still kept its ceremonies after baptism."[19] The parallel would have been self-evident to early seventeenth-century readers, especially those familiar with Guevara's account of evangelization in the 1520s or the Jesuits' practices of accommodation in subsequent decades: Valencia was advising King Felipe III, along with charitable Old Christians throughout the Iberian Peninsula, to dissimulate with the Moriscos just as Peter had with the Jews. In Valencia's opinion, it was necessary to pretend as if the Moriscos' continued participation in Islamic rituals were irrelevant to their status as Christians. In this way, he also followed Augustine in implying that their heterodox beliefs were beside the theological point, not least because they were sometimes unknowable, as the inquisitor Francisco Peña previously had acknowledged as well. Given these epistemological limitations, Valencia argued that Peter's virtuous deception and Jerome's charitable reading were beyond reproach not only in the Church's early and patristic periods. They were also necessary components of a contemporary pastoral policy that might respond thoughtfully to such limitations. In Valencia's view, inquisitors did not hold a monopoly on holy deception.

Nor did the inquisitors hold a monopoly on coercion. Acknowledging that it was not always possible to ignore or rebrand inexact practices or heterodox beliefs, Valencia presented civil law as an instrument in his program of charitable dissimulation. While fines and other minor penalties might sometimes suffice, it was occasionally necessary to punish more seriously the flouting of orthodox norms. In this sense, Valencia agreed with the underlying disciplinary premise of the *nueva pragmática* and, indeed, with longstanding modes of inquisitorial discipline. Though Erasmus's moderate Catholicism and critical insights influenced Valencia along with many other peninsular intellectuals of the period, Valencia's program for reform was by no means thoroughly *erasmista* in emphasis or design. Unlike Erasmus, the Spanish theologian and scientist Michael Servetus, the French Calvinist Sebastian Castellio, or other reformers now seen as pioneers of modern religious tolerance, Valencia did not cite the Gospel of Matthew's "parable of the tares" in his argument for patience with the Moriscos. Ribera and his ilk were, as we will see below, ready with aggressive if disingenuous counterarguments to such readings of the gospels. Valencia instead constructed his argument by using as precedent the 1525 Council of Madrid, which declared binding the forced baptisms of the previous decades. In other words, even Valencia's proposed punishments implied a misconduct born of binding baptism, although he envisioned secular rather than ecclesiastical authorities meting out the sentences. This judicial reform was a way to maintain Morisco discipline while transforming Old Christian identity. Citing both Plato's advice for fashioning republican unity and, again, Jerome's gloss on Galatians, Valencia argued in the *Tratado* that Morisco integration required persuading Old Christians—"even through deception" (*aunque sea con mentira*)—that Old and New Christians were all part of one political entity. We must realize, Valencia continued in the same passage, that we are all "citizens of a single republic, brothers of one blood and lineage, and native to that same land."[20] Although he championed peaceful assimilation against Juan de Ribera and other proponents of expulsion, Valencia's case hinged upon representing religious coercion as civic brotherhood. Recalling the first-century BC Greek philosopher and historian Strabo, Valencia insisted that untruthfulness was the only way to "do away with the Jews and the Moors, joining them together in the new body and name of republic."[21]

Valencia, Las Casas, and González de Cellorigo all agreed that in order to preserve the plausibility of this mixing, it was necessary to regulate Old and New Christians alike. In a short pamphlet on the Morisco question printed in Valladolid in 1597, for instance, González de Cellorigo suggested protecting Moriscos against slander by fining Old Christian defamers, and like Valencia he insisted upon social integration through mixed neighborhoods and intermarriage.[22] Opponents of expulsion maintained that carefully orchestrated facts on the ground would eventually turn Morisco apostates into true Christians, even if it was difficult if not impossible to gauge effectively the truth of any individual's Christianity. As a general rule, wrote Valencia, false faiths undermined unity, commerce, and peace, but if the Greeks and Romans, with their vast and diverse empires, "tolerated them all [*todas las toleraron*] as long as they did not impede public peace," then perhaps Spain could abide a bit of heresy in the near term too.[23] This was a coercive and bigoted tolerance of the sort examined in a different context by the political theorist Wendy Brown, but filtered through a uniquely Spanish lens: Valencia asked the state to assume some of the power previously monopolized by the Holy Office of the Inquisition, but he did so by employing an inquisitorial logic and vocabulary.[24]

To be clear, Valencia did not simply defend the inquisitors' "relaxing" of unrepentant heretics to civil authorities for capital punishment. Nor did he advocate an intensification of Morisco control as an alternative to expulsion. Instead, he hoped to limit the instances of punitive action while cutting the Holy Office out of the judicial loop completely. Individual and communal discipline was the essence of Christian orthodoxy, but Rome should not retain control over the implementation, operation, and improvement of this discipline. According to Valencia, the noble end of New Christian assimilation justified the deceptive means necessary to accomplish such jurisdictional reconfiguration. Furthermore, it did not matter whether the Moriscos and their representatives were duplicitous. Morisco dissimulation and assimilation both depended upon a shifting sense of collective Spanish political identity and imperial history rather than on Morisco insincerity or sincerity. Because duplicity and earnestness were products of social and political conditions, those interested in New Christian orthodoxy should focus on changing these conditions. Valencia's pretense that Morisco dissimulation was either nonexistent or unproblematic served as an apology for a wide-ranging regime of secular discipline.

There is a resonance here with Hurtado de Mendoza's depiction of the Moriscos as political adversaries and military foes rather than unrepentant heretics. In reframing the Morisco problem as a general issue of Christian reform and imperial history rather than one of inquisitorial control, Valencia aimed to secularize the crime of heresy in the same terms that his predecessors had used to sacralize Morisco cultural practice. For Valencia, the political realm offered a more flexible set of instruments for resolving the issues raised by New Christian apostasy than did the ecclesiastical realm. Even in his extensive writings about Mexico, Peru, and New Granada, Valencia the chronicler of the Indies remained consistent in this regard. For instance, he divided his compilations of information about those remote parts of the Spanish empire into three discrete sections treating natural, moral and political, and military information, only occasionally adding a fourth section on ecclesiastical matters.[25] Steeped in humanistic education and, unlike Hurtado de Mendoza, working as an official historian at court, Valencia saw government as an instrument of public good, even though he agreed with his more strident predecessor that religion was sometimes an inapt explanatory category for the determination of state affairs.

Like Valencia, Ignacio de Las Casas opposed expulsion by recasting Morisco *taqīyya* as part of an ongoing and dynamic process of conversion and assimilation. Arguing that the Moriscos were imperfect Christians in need of reform, Las Casas acknowledged that their Islam-tinged beliefs were heterodox, but in describing them for Pope Clement VIII, he was profoundly, even provocatively, blasé. He called these beliefs "doubts rather than certifiable, adjudicated errors," and he described the Moriscos as "neither absolutely Moor nor Christian, but rather like atheists, trusting in salvation only through natural law without believing anything of written law or grace."[26] Las Casas drew on both the Salamanca scholastics and his immediate predecessor, Martín González de Cellorigo, who in the same pamphlet cited above insisted that if the Moriscos had been properly instructed, their "natural reason would have removed them from the blindness of their false sect."[27] Even so, Las Casas was quick to point out that these "atheists" had it wrong. Salvation was inaccessible to them because they believed that Jesus was not the son of God, the teachings of the Church were corrupted versions of Jesus's evangelical doctrine, and the Qur'an contained the final, sealed truth of all earlier scriptures. Las Casas's forbearance in outlining these heretical "doubts," to say nothing of his attentiveness to Islamic creed, is striking. These Islamic stances had been subjects of derision by European Christian writers at least since the mid-twelfth century, when the theologian and philologist Robert of Ketton had first translated sections of the Qur'an into Latin. Although their opinions of Christian dogma reflected the conventional religious points of contention, the Moriscos, Las Casas argued, did not speak for Islam. Neither absolutely Moor nor Christian, they subscribed only to the "natural law" regulating all rational beings. As chapter 2 argued, in order to stake a public claim to scholasticism's moral and political authority, Francisco de Vitoria and Domingo de Soto had employed the example of peninsular Muslims and Jews to hone this line of reasoning in their discussions of indigenous faith in the New World. Valencia, González de Cellorigo, and Las Casas then turned debate about the New World back upon the Morisco expulsions. I want to emphasize that negotiating the boundaries of New Christianity involved following these transatlantic routes of precedent in both directions.[28]

In Las Casas's and Valencia's view, the Moriscos preferred a shared religious terrain determined only by the affirmation of God's omnipotence and omniscience. By admitting the Islamic doctrinal points raised by the Moriscos as innocuous doubts rather than attacks on the doctrinal core of Christianity, they attempted to redefine both belief and its role in religious identity. Like English and French Deism, or the natural religion that emerged in the middle decades of the seventeenth century and remained popular during the Enlightenment, natural law established this suitably common religious experience. While proponents of expulsion invoked New Christian dissimulation as a seemingly intractable problem, Valencia and Las Casas proposed a reading of the Morisco conversions so charitable that it was a kind of dissimulation itself. Their approach evoked Ignacio de Loyola's advice to spiritual guides in the *Exercises*, a text that the Jesuit Las Casas undoubtedly knew well: "To assure better cooperation between the one who is giving the Exercises and the exercitant, and more beneficial results for both, it is necessary to suppose that every good Christian is more ready to put a good interpretation on another's statement than to condemn it as false."[29] While Loyola recommended giving exercitants the benefit of the doubt in order to lead them into a new community of Christians, Las Casas's and Valencia's objectives were juridical and historical as well as pastoral. Their goal was to redefine the history of Morisco heresy.

JUAN DE RIBERA'S PALIMPSEST

On September 27, 1609, the venerable Archbishop Juan de Ribera stood before his flock at the Cathedral of Valencia to deliver what would become a famous sermon in defense of the Morisco expulsions, news of which had been promulgated publicly for the first time five days before. As Damián Fonseca crowed in the fourth book of his 1611 defense of expulsion, *Del givsto scacciamento de moreschi da Spagna*, which included an Italian translation of the archbishop's sermon, Ribera spoke with grace and power despite his advanced age.[30] During the address, Ribera argued, as he had in several missives sent over the course of the previous decade to King Felipe III and the duke of Lerma, Francisco Gómez de Sandoval, that Morisco intransigence had long constituted a threat to the spiritual health of the peninsula's Christian community. As if to overwrite the arguments of Valencia and Las Casas, Ribera chose Galatians 5:12 as his sermon's point of departure. Glossing Paul, Ribera justified the Crown's momentous decision to expel the Moriscos after more than a century of negotiation, evangelization, and violence:

> In order to treat this issue, it has occurred to me to consider the words of the apostle Saint Paul, written to the Galatians: Vtinam abscindantur qui vos conturbant. The holy apostle managed to subjugate the Greek gentiles of that city to the faith of the Gospel, and many had given signs of their conversion; but on account of the evil company of the gentiles that were among them, they had grown uneasy, such that the commotion in the city was great. Hoping to avoid

> these inconveniences, the apostle wrote to them, and the first remedy that he suggested in order to conserve the peace and cease the disturbance was to beg our Lord that the unbelievers and disturbers be cut off [*cortados*] (not pollarded, but cut off).[31]

Thus opened Ribera's shrewd but misleading interpretation of Paul, whose main concern in this and nearby verses of Galatians was not the realpolitik of apostasy, as Ribera suggested, but the role of circumcision in the early Christian community. In Galatians 5:6, Paul had stated that circumcision, like the Jewish dietary laws discussed elsewhere in the text, was immaterial to salvation in Jesus. "Neither circumcision nor uncircumcision counts for anything; the only thing that counts is faith working through love," was Paul's turn of phrase.[32] The source of confusion for Paul's Galatian interlocutors, however, was that as local neophytes began to recognize the importance of faith over law, some naysayers argued, as the Jews did, for instance, that circumcision remained a condition of salvation even after the appearance of Jesus. These and other opponents also pointed out that Paul himself seemed to express contradictory views on circumcision depending upon whom he was addressing, just as Peter had hedged his bets in Antioch. In these verses, Paul defended his own interpretive authority and reassured the beleaguered Galatian converts. He insisted that neither circumcision nor special diets were necessary for salvation, and he ended his argument with the caustic line cited above in Latin by Ribera, which in the New Revised Standard Version of the Bible reads, "I wish those who unsettle you would castrate themselves." In Paul's voice, the Latin word *abscindantur* was a mordant pun. Paul desired the circumcision defenders and their bothersome allies to leave the Galatian converts to Christianity alone. He wished that these adversaries would "cut themselves off" from dispute with the still shaky believers, and he expressed this desire for social and religious separation through the stark corporal metaphor of castration.

Not surprisingly, Ribera obscured Paul's corporal vocabulary and its relationship to early Christian debates about circumcision, which implied the apt though infelicitous image of the Crown castrating its own political body. Despite Ribera's selective gloss, this image did become part of the Morisco apologists' arsenal, for Damián Fonseca dubbed Jaime Bleda, the most resolute of hardliners on expulsion, the "sole knife of the Morisco nation."[33] As some early seventeenth-century economic and political advisors pointed out, there was perhaps some truth in representing expulsion as castration. To expel the Moriscos was to banish some of the realm's most able laborers and skilled craftsmen. As I demonstrate below, this was an issue debated by *arbitristas* Sancho de Moncada and Cristóbal Pérez de Herrera. For his part, Ribera employed the *arbitristas'* language of statecraft while quarantining the anxiety that ran through much of their writing. Similarly, he aimed to contain Paul's allegorical meaning and sarcastic double entendre within his own commentary. In Ribera's sanitized reading of Paul, the Morisco expulsions were nothing more than a bit of efficient urban policing. Conservation of peace and cessation of disturbances were the reasonable objectives of removing local agitators, as if they were teenage hooligans bent on rabble-rousing rather than religious adversaries contesting salvation. In a letter praising Ribera's sermon "on the expulsion *and affairs of state*" (emphasis mine), the duke of Lerma, an architect of the Crown's Morisco policy, evidently appreciated the archbishop's use of Galatians to interlace the pastoral and the political.[34]

In censoring Paul's castration pun, Ribera exaggerated an orthodox precedent. "*Utinam abscindantur* is not understood carnally," reads the medieval collection of biblical commentary the *Glossa ordinaria*, "but instead it means that the agitators might lose their power of generation in you or in others."[35] Despite the neat contrast between "generation" in its reproductive sense and sterility caused by castration, medieval commentators chose to emphasize the tropological rather than the literal meaning of the passage. In their separation from adherents to the new Christian sect, the dissenters attacked by Paul lost their ability to cause confusion and discord. Ribera and his skittish predecessors robbed Paul of his humor, even as their selective reading confirmed Paul's primary argument, which was that the niceties of the circumcision debates were a distraction. No less than the circumcision status of the new Christian adherents, the integrity of the agitators' members was irrelevant. Ribera followed medieval models in presenting Galatians as a general statement on power and community rather than as a particular claim about circumcision.

Instead of simply reiterating the *Glossa ordinaria*'s interpretation, however, Ribera filled the exegetical vacuum with an agricultural language that might at first glance seem strange: *Abscindantur* does not mean "desmochado," or pollarded, added Ribera in a concise parenthetical aside. But, a skeptical reader might rightly wonder, did anyone suggest that it did? And what does it mean to pollard, anyhow? In addition to appearing as a character's nickname in Miguel de Cervantes's exemplary novel *Rinconete y Cortadillo*, the word *desmochado* refers to something whose top has been cut off, sometimes a bull's horns, but usually a tree. To pollard in the agricultural sense is to remove a tree's upper branches in order to facilitate dense growth while at the same time limiting the plant's height. Often mentioned in the *Obra de agricultura* of 1513, a compendium of agricultural knowledge funded by Francisco Jiménez de Cisneros and composed by Gabriel Alonso de Herrera, pollarding was a common pruning method in the sixteenth century, and it remains so in many places today. In the context of debate about the Moriscos, it is easy to see why Ribera wanted to distinguish between this type of pruning for the promotion of growth and the complete cutting away of invasive or parasitic plants. Yet it is puzzling that Ribera would go out of his way to introduce the word *desmochado* only in order to dismiss it as an imprecise translation of *abscindantur*. This addition was not simply an issue of intertextual, exegetical anxiety, for when Matthew recalls Jesus's use of the Latin word *abscide* to demand that sinners "cut off" their sinning extremities (hands and feet in these cases, rather than the genitals suggested by Paul), there is no implicit agricultural meaning that Ribera might as a result feel the need to address in the word's Pauline context as well.[36] Of course, the language of agricultural production offers a ready collection of metaphors for depicting human reproduction as well as Christian eschatology. But the passage cited by Ribera does not exactly beg for an explanation of why agricultural imagery is inappropriate or absent. Ribera protests too much with his "desmochado" interposition. Why?

By introducing and then dismissing the pollarding image, Ribera guided his audience to see the Morisco question in agricultural terms. To quibble with the relevancy of specific arborist lingo was to refer to a broader set of agricultural tropes that appeared often in Ribera's writing. In a previous 1609 letter to Felipe III about the Moriscos, composed just months before his sermon in Valencia, for example, Ribera urged the Crown "to pluck them out by the roots, so that they will neither do harm nor sprout new seedlings that shortly grow into trees."[37] Seeming to cite divine authority, though without mentioning any particular book or verse, Ribera continued in this agricultural vein: "God told his people through a prophet (to teach them how they should govern their affairs), do not sow in fields that have evil herbs, but rather first pluck them out and then sow."[38] He then repeated the point, insisting that scripture "advised and commanded" those confronted with "evil people" to "pull them out by the root from our company."[39] It was the Crown's responsibility to rid the kingdom of the Moriscos, represented along with other apostates and heretics as dangerous weeds. Slipping from "evil herbs" and "evil people" in this letter to "evil company" in his later sermon, Ribera painted the Moriscos as invasive overgrowth encroaching upon the garden of the faithful. And just a paragraph later, Ribera introduced Paul's now familiar line from Galatians, begging the Crown to be "motivated by the desires that the Apostle Paul harbored when he said: If only they would remove themselves [*se arrancassen*] from you, those who disturb you."[40] By framing this citation from Galatians with an extended agricultural allegory of royal responsibility, Ribera left the mistaken impression that Paul himself employed the imagery of cultivation rather than castration in order to demarcate the limits of early Christianity. In this letter, Ribera even translated Paul differently than he did in his subsequent sermon, rendering Paul's Latin *abscindantur* with a reflexive form of the Spanish verb *arrancar*, which means to remove or pluck, rather than with *cortar*, to cut. Ribera's pollarding reference in his 1609 sermon on the Morisco expulsions was thus anything but flippant. He argued that the time for the mere pruning of apostasy had passed, that biblical parables of cultivation taught an ardent rather than a laid-back approach to spiritual cultivation.

With this talk of roots, sowing, pruning, and harvesting, Ribera both reframed contemporary anxiety around agricultural underproduction and destabilized the power of his intellectual adversaries' own scriptural sources, the most important of which were Jesus's "parable of the tares" and "parable of the sower," both included in Matthew 13. By invoking the language of these parables to support expulsion, Ribera sought to undercut Erasmus's, Luther's, Servetus's, and Castellio's scriptural language of tolerance. In so doing, he imitated the approach of the late fifteenth-century canon of Toledo Alonso de Ortiz, whose answer to inquisition critic Juan de Lucena hinged on these gospel episodes as well. As in so many other cases in debates about the Moriscos, previous disagreements about peninsular Jews and *conversos* offered a ready model.[41]

Consider the two parables in detail: In the parable of the tares an elusive planter sowed weeds by night in an unknowing farmer's wheat field. When the weeds and grain appeared side by side, the farmer's slaves asked him whether they should go and gather up the weeds, to which the farmer responded, "No, for in gathering the weeds you would uproot [*eradicetis*] the wheat along with them. Let both of them grow until the harvest; and at harvest time I will tell the reapers, 'Collect the weeds first and bind them in bundles to be burned, but gather the wheat into my barn.'"[42] As Jesus explained a few verses later, the guerrilla sower represented the devil, the weeds stood for the devil's children, the wheat farm exemplified the Kingdom of Heaven, and the coming harvest signified an end-of-days judgment. The lesson taught by this parable was not, as Ribera implied through his confusion of this passage with Paul's line in Galatians, that zealous cultivators of Christian faith should pull out the weeds of heresy and apostasy by their roots, but rather, as even Augustine noted, that such weeds should be left alone.[43] Similarly, Ribera misrepresented Jesus's subsequent parable of the sower, which warned Christian evangelizers not to plant their metaphorical seeds either in dry and rocky land or in plots already occupied by those thorny bushes that represented enemies of Christianity. Jesus taught the importance of cultivating new Christian communities where there were few natural, social, and political obstacles. Though he employed the paratactic style of scripture and placed the admonition in the mouth of God, Ribera's comment about the importance of removing inhospitable native plants before planting the seeds of Christianity was inventive annotation rather than citation. Although Jesus employed agricultural imagery to theorize Christian charity and pastoral practice in Matthew, Ribera insured that no audience of his would imagine agriculture in such irenic terms. In Ribera's view, the responsible Christian gardener was a decidedly interventionist one.

Ribera harped on this agricultural imagery because he knew that it cut to the heart of the expulsion opponents' arguments. "They say that these people are new plants," wrote Ribera of the Moriscos and their allies' allegorical presentation. "They are not, your Catholic Majesty, new plants, but rather prematurely old and feeble trees, full of knots of heresy and treason."[44] Ribera insisted that the Moriscos should not be considered vulnerable seedlings in need of special nourishment. The plantlets struggling to survive unfavorable conditions in the parable of the sower were, in Ribera's view, a false parallel of the Moriscos for two reasons. First, Ribera argued, Valencia's Moriscos had enjoyed decades of nourishment in the form of multilingual catechism and pastoral accommodation, but to little effect. As Ribera put it incredulously in his 1609 letter, "these plants were born more than eighty years ago, and we still call them new. Those of Avila, Valladolid, and other cities must remain from the times that Spain was lost, and yet we say that they are new?"[45] Second, despite the fact that the Moriscos had all been baptized, in Ribera's opinion it was inexact to consider even a subset of them actual Christians: "Speaking with precision," wrote Ribera in a turn of phrase that recalled Francisco de Vitoria's mocking words from the middle of the sixteenth century, "we should not call them Moriscos, but Moors."[46] According to Ribera, the plant metaphor from the parable of the sower was unsuitable because the Moriscos corresponded more closely to inhospitable thorns or invasive weeds than to young Christian plants in need of affectionate cultivation. Despite the passing of nearly a century, the crucial question addressed by the Council of Madrid in 1525 and debated in subsequent decades by Francisco de Vitoria, Bartolomé de Las Casas, Juan Ginés de Sepúlveda, José de Acosta, and others examined over the course of this book still remained: How should the boundary between Christian apostates and unbelievers be determined, named, and policed? The inability to answer this question was precisely what made debates about New Christianity such fertile ground for scholarly innovation.

Unlike the cautious Valencia, who articulated his opposition to Morisco expulsion in the language of inquisition and scrupulously avoided invoking Matthew's agricultural imagery, Ribera took a more aggressive approach. His selective paraphrasing and activist glossing drained the irenic vitality of the parables of the tares and the sower and obscured the period's real agricultural challenges. Also unlike Valencia, who penned his manuscripts for the restricted audience of royal advisors who shaped contemporary policy, Ribera wrote for a wider readership of the present and the future alike. If the language of his multiple letters to the Crown and his famous sermon in the Cathedral of Valencia seeped into the apologetic discourse of seventeenth- and eighteenth-century Spain, it is because Ribera's successors recognized the power of print. Perhaps even more than Ribera himself, it was they who marshaled Jesus's parables on Christian forbearance toward an exclusionary history of early modern Spain.

EXPULSION IN PRINT

Ribera cast an eye toward his own legacy when he offered his 1602 and 1609 letters to the Crown and his 1609 sermon to the Valencian faithful. These texts were not merely private correspondence or timely theological and political commentary. The publication history of his 1609 sermon is illustrative in this regard. As Ribera's longtime confessor and first autobiographer, the Jesuit Francisco de Escrivà, explained in his *Vida del illvstrissimo y excellentissimo Señor Don Ivan de Ribera,* published in 1612, just a year after Ribera's death, the famous sermon on the Morisco expulsions was at first printed only in a limited Spanish run. As mentioned above, Damián Fonseca published an Italian translation in Rome as part of his *Del givsto scacciamento,* and he noted there that local Moriscos both knew the archbishop's texts on expulsion and recognized the gravity of their situation in 1609.[47] But it was Escrivà who made the original sermon more widely available, including it, along with much of Ribera's other Morisco-related correspondence, in an extensive appendix to his patron's 1612 biography. In Escrivà's hagiographic retelling, Ribera was unhappy that the sermon circulated at all: "In no way did the Patriarch want this sermon to be printed, even though," as Escrivà discreetly noted, "it seemed expedient." Representing his subject as a humble author, Escrivà continued that although "the pleas and arguments of many" eventually convinced Ribera to publish his text, he refused to allow that "his name be associated with it, or that the print run extend beyond a hundred copies, which would be distributed and sent to diverse parts, to important individuals."[48] However, given the short time between Ribera's death and the appearance of Escrivà's biography, Ribera likely authorized and helped to shape the story of his life as part of an expedited effort at canonization.[49] The fictions of anonymity and privacy that Escrivà employed to frame Ribera's texts were features of an ambitious archival project. More than a flattering portrayal of a powerful patron and potential local saint, Escrivà's biographical account provided the primary sources necessary to justify the Morisco expulsions.

The Franciscan friar Marco de Guadalajara y Xavier did not hide the fact that nearly the entirety of his *Memorable expvlsion y ivstissimo destierro de los moriscos de España*, published by Nicolas Assiayn in Pamplona in 1613, was less a polished and original narrative than a collection of expulsion materials culled from elsewhere. In the text's prologue, Guadalajara y Xavier acknowledged his reliance on "other pens," including those of the Valencian historian Gaspar Escolano and the Jesuit hagiographer Pedro de Ribadeneira, as well as Ribera and Bleda.[50] Though he did not cite Escrivà by name, Guadalajara y Xavier clearly consulted the *Vida*, published a year before his own work. He included many of Escrivà's primary materials, and he even presented them in nearly the same order: chapters 4 through 7 of Guadalajara y Xavier's *Memorable expvlsion* reproduce the Valencian Dominican Luis Beltrán's opinion on the Moriscos, Ribera's 1602 letter to Felipe III, short texts by the king's confessor Fray Gaspar de Córdoba and the duke of Lerma, and Ribera's longer 1609 missive to Felipe III.[51] By presenting these sources together as if they composed a dialogue, Escrivà's and Guadalajara y Xavier's collections simplified and consolidated what in fact was a multifaceted debate over expulsion. Consequently, as early as 1613 there existed an archive of primary documents on Morisco expulsion.[52]

Despite (or because of) his conformity to Escrivà's model, Guadalajara y Xavier was anxious about his role as a writer. Explaining why he decided to publish *Memorable expvlsion* under his own name even though he composed little of the material, Guadalajara y Xavier invoked his rigor of attribution and defended his added interpretive value: "I cite authors by proper names, and I include their own original texts and arguments; gleaning [*entresacando*] from their extensive works that which suits my goals, from some more, from others less, forming a honeycomb in the manner of the industrious bees; and I do all this for the benefit of the poor, who do not have the possibility to buy their great and costly books." Justifying his work of textual selection and recombination with a mixture of agricultural and apiological metaphors, Guadalajara y Xavier argued in the same passage that he made Morisco expulsion materials accessible to a wider audience. His stated objective was not to reinvent Morisco polemics, but rather "to put this Expulsion in order."[53] This explains the absence of Escrivà from the otherwise comprehensive "abecedario," or index of relevant authors, included at the end of *Memorable expvlsion*. For Guadalajara y Xavier, to cite Escrivà was to acknowledge that he had tidied up an expulsion narrative that did not want for order.

Nicolas Assiayn, Guadalajara y Xavier's publisher in Pamplona, embraced his author's loose definition of authorship. Even before the 1610 expulsion decrees were announced in the Kingdom of Navarre proper, the city of Pamplona had become an important stopover for Aragonese and Castilian Moriscos departing the peninsula northward over the Pyrenees, and Assiayn took advantage of this local development to cultivate something like an expulsion "list."[54] In addition to *Memorable expvlsion*, for instance, Assiayn also published Guadalajara y Xavier's *Prodicion y destierro de los moriscos de Castilla*, which appeared in 1614. Combining the voice of third-person historical narrative together with a wide range of military instructions, expulsion decrees, and other primary materials, this text repeated for the Kingdom of Castile what had evidently been a profitable model for telling the story of Valencia's and Aragon's Moriscos in *Memorable expvlsion*. Assiayn also produced the royal scribe of Aragon Juan Ripol's *Dialogo de consvelo por la expvlsion de los moriscos de España*, which appeared in the same year as Guadalajara y Xavier's *Memorable expvlsion*. Despite the title of Ripol's work, however, it only tangentially treated the melancholy suffered by a fictional Morisco sympathizer named Serapion. The text was in fact a conventional humanist dialogue on the nature of greed, hope, and jealousy masquerading as an inquiry into the emotive consequences of Morisco expulsion. This was a bit of shrewd marketing on the part of Assiayn, who offered to unsuspecting readers Ripol's *Dialogo de consvelo* as a new installment in a growing list of expulsion texts, when in fact it was something else entirely. Nevertheless, book buyers and later collectors took Assiayn's cue, binding together Ripol's *Dialogo de consvelo* and Guadalajara y Xavier's *Memorable expvlsion* and *Prodicion y destierro* in an array of mix-matched constellations.[55] The lesson of this Pamplona print history is that the years of upheaval produced by the expulsions afforded local editors a legitimate claim on the events. Authors like Escrivà and Guadalajara y Xavier may have selected, framed, and defended their anthologies of apologetic expulsion material, but Assiayn's Morisco volumes display the important role of the printer in the construction of the Morisco archive.[56]

While Guadalajara y Xavier imitated and developed Escrivà's Valencian paradigm for texts on the Morisco expulsions, Assiayn looked to Escrivà's printer in Valencia, Pedro Patricio Mey, as a model. Escrivà's *Vida* was just one of many Morisco-focused texts that came hot off Mey's press as Moriscos from around the peninsula began to arrive at the Valencian coast on their way elsewhere in the Mediterranean. In 1610, Pedro Patricio Mey, who ran the family printing business after his mother's passing (his father, Juan Mey, died years earlier), published both Gaspar Escolano's *Decadas de la insigne y coronada ciudad y Reyno de Valencia*, a multivolume history of the region that, among other topics, recounted a history of the local Morisco community, and Gaspar de Aguilar's epic poem *Expulsión de los moros de España*, which was the first long-form literary text to represent the expulsions proper. Underscoring the regional specificity of this imperial event in linguistic terms, one of the printing licenses in the front matter of Aguilar's volume even presented the poem as a "loyal translation to Castilian from the Valencian original."[57] This was regional and linguistic specificity with a storied print history connecting the present of Morisco expulsion to the recent past of Morisco evangelization. The Mey family had printed Ribera's 1599 edition of Martín Pérez de Ayala's *Catechismo para instrvccion de los nveuamente conuertidos de moros* and his 1566 *Doctrina Christiana en lengua Arauiga y Castellana*, both of which I studied in chapter 3. Pedro Patricio Mey in particular worked closely both with Valencia's city council and with Ribera in a range of typographical capacities, printing announcements, summaries, and other short texts in addition to complete editions of literary prose (Miguel de Cervantes's *Don Quijote*) and Valencian history (Pero Anton Beuter's *Crónica general de España, y especialmente del Reyno de Valencia*).[58] Like Ribera, the Mey family helped to establish a Valencian story of Morisco evangelization and expulsion.

Pedro Patricio Mey's nephew, Francisco Felipe Mey, published Jaime Bleda's voluminous *Corónica de los moros* in 1618, which included as the eighth chapter a treatise dedicated to the Morisco expulsion, *De la justa y general expulsion de los moriscos de España.* This section of the text advertised that the web of authorial and editorial imitation reconstructed above was simply the visible surface of a deep network of Valencian apologists, who often exchanged (and plagiarized) each other's manuscripts before publication.[59] Not surprisingly, Bleda presented himself at the center of this network, though he duly acknowledged a debt to Archbishop Ribera, who had urged him as a young acolyte to pursue pastoral work in Morisco communities near Valencia. In Bleda's telling, Ribera had sent him, a native Valencian, to serve as rector in the nearby Morisco village of Corbera, and despite Bleda's vocal complaints about the perfidy of his flock, Ribera did not permit him a change of duty. Four years after the completion of the expulsions, Bleda conveniently recalled that after just a short time in Corbera, he already knew that the prospects for assimilation were grim.

Offering the apologetic point as personal history, Bleda then turned to several fascinating stories of prepublication consultation and self-censorship involving Ribera, Fonseca, and others. In framing his own work not only as a systematized and *longue durée* account of Islamic Spain from the conquests of 711 to the expulsions of 1609–14, but also as the local intellectual history of the expulsion apologists themselves, Bleda claimed the last word on the end of the Morisco period. This was no doubt important to him because he had missed the opportunity to have the first word. Having borrowed extensively from Bleda's unpublished manuscripts, Damián Fonseca preempted his colleague with his own *Del givsto scacciamento,* the first major published volume to justify the expulsions. The text appeared in Rome, where Fonseca and Bleda were pleading the dual case for Ribera's beautification and Morisco expulsion.[60] Like Escrivà and Guadalajara y Xavier, Fonseca compiled royal letters, papal sources, historical vignettes, and other ephemera related to the Morisco expulsions as they were unfolding. But from the historical distance of 1618, Bleda was able to cast himself as a pioneer in Morisco matters. Recounting the back story of textual consultations and revisions, Bleda did not simply deliver the evidence of Morisco disloyalty or defend the standard arguments for expulsion. He also integrated an intellectual and social history of Morisco apologetics into the story of Islamic Spain itself, coopting and redefining the many texts composed about the New Christians over the course of the previous decade. Underscoring the importance of shifting from a theological to a historical register, Bleda even integrated long sections of Hurtado de Mendoza's *Guerra de Granada* directly into the sixth book of the *Corónica,* as the historian Luis Cabrera de Córdoba would do the subsequent year in his *Felipe II, Rey de España.* Bleda took a debate about the Alpujarras uprising and historical method and turned it into a model of imperial legitimation.

Among Ribera, Fonseca, Guadalajara y Xavier, Bleda, and other proponents of Morisco expulsion, it is as if the mania for collecting and citing the same sources over and over again insulated the unsavory reality of dispossession. From Ribera's early texts on expulsion to Bleda's *Corónica* of 1618, these scholars' works offer the decision to expel as the inevitable consequence of history rather than the contingent product of local economic, social, and religious circumstances. Printers of these volumes capitalized on their geographical advantage and popular xenophobia to produce a stable corpus of texts about the Morisco expulsions. Only centuries later, when the archives of the inquisition were opened to study, did professional historians begin to see the extent to which these texts and the stories they told were but the first of many layers of primary sources. If later scholars for so long mistook the archival form of the texts examined thus far in this chapter for a true archive of Morisco experience, it is because these texts' authors and editors successfully employed the expulsions to manage the moral and material conditions of historical inquiry.

THE ECONOMICS OF EXPULSION

Even before the expulsions, "Spain was taken to be sterile, on account of its low population," reasoned Serapion, one of the two interlocutors in Juan Ripol's *Dialogo de consvelo*. "What will happen now?"[61] This concern about the effect of expelling three hundred thousand of the peninsula's residents, many of them laborers, was a familiar trope of the period. It represented a realist counterweight to the alarmist triumphalism of authors like Juan Rufo, who, as I mentioned in chapter 5, agonized in epic verse over the Moriscos' accumulation of wealth and children while Old Christians sacrificed themselves for religion and empire abroad. Morisco productivity and reproductivity were sources of fear for a peninsular community suffering from agricultural underproduction and demographic woe. Long before Enlightenment *philosophes* propagated them to their own ends, Spanish scholars recognized that these concerns were well founded. "Spain is at risk," warned the *arbitrista* Sancho de Moncada in his *Restauración política de España*, a 1619 treatise on the causes and remedies for Spain's early seventeenth-century economic stagnation.[62] Although "the Spanish monarchy, on account of its greatness, may seem eternal to many," Sancho de Moncada cautioned that there was truth in the recent decades' fretful chatter, "where much is said of its widespread peril."[63]

So desperate was the economic situation of the Crown of Castile in 1619, a result of more than two decades of deficient agricultural production, costly wars of conquest and colonization, and an episode of the plague in 1600, that the Crown called a council of experts to help resolve the deepening crisis. As Pedro Fernández de Navarrete underscored in his *Conservación de monarquías y discursos políticos sobre la gran consulta que el consejo hizo al señor rey don Felipe tercero*, a text composed in preparation for the council and subsequently published in 1626, the Morisco expulsions were recurrent in these debates: To what extent had the expulsions exacerbated the population decline? What was the relationship between a longstanding Old Christian aversion to agricultural work and industrial craft, on the one hand, and the Moriscos' famous status as laborers and artisans, on the other hand? Finally, were the expulsions the pious act of a prudent monarch or an ill-advised final nail in the coffin of Spain's economic disaster?[64] To answer these questions after 1614 was to grapple with the mutual contingency of Morisco expulsion and Spanish imperial history.

Fernández de Navarrete lamented the expulsion of the Moriscos on both pastoral and economic grounds, though he celebrated the smoothness of the enterprise's execution in practice. Staking a middle position in dispute over the consequences of the Moriscos' departure, he both attacked the peninsula's minority communities as "enemies of our holy Catholic faith" and noted that "the first cause of the depopulation of Spain has been the many and numerous expulsions of Muslims and Jews."[65] In his view, the expulsions had become necessary not because of any natural Morisco obstinacy, but rather because of Old Christian disdain, which the Moriscos had learned to repay in turn. Like Diego Hurtado de Mendoza and Pedro de Valencia before him, Fernández de Navarrete imagined an alternative Morisco history: "And I say again that I consider it certain that if at the beginning there had been some way not to mark the Moriscos with a trace of infamy, they all would have managed to adopt the Catholic religion; and if they viewed that religion with hatred and horror, it was because they saw themselves battered and despised, and without hope of being able to erase the trace of their low birth."[66] In Fernández de Navarrete's view, depopulation and economic strife were the costs of longstanding Old Christian mistreatment of Moriscos. Fernández de Navarrete repeated González de Cellorigo's point from his *Memorial de la politica necesaria*, which was that the failure of Morisco assimilation suggested flawed pastoral and political policy. "Since these people have been converted and they are open to being instructed in the faith, they can be perfected," explained González de Cellorigo. "And our most Christian Catholic king must undertake to conserve his people, and swell his realms, attracting everyone to the true knowledge of the faith."[67] In González de Cellorigo's view from the late sixteenth century, expulsion was a shirking of royal responsibility to "conserve" the realm; from Fernández de Navarrete's perspective at the beginning of the seventeenth century, it was possible to address but not avert the consequences of royal miscalculation.

In *Conservación de monarquías y discursos políticos*, Fernández de Navarrete attempted to toe an apologetic line without obscuring the expulsion's economic and political lessons. Although the myriad *arbitristas* who joined Fernández de Navarrete in seeking the ears of the powerful were famous for trading accuracy and integrity of analysis for professional aggrandizement, there was little to gain in attacking Felipe III and the duke of Lerma for past errors. Yet according to Sancho de Moncada, a principal member of the so-called "Toledo school" of *arbitristas*, whose forerunners included the eminent historian Juan de Mariana as well as the commentator and doctor Cristóbal Pérez de Herrera, there was legitimate scholarly disagreement over whether expulsion was really a "first cause" of depopulation and agricultural collapse. As the long title of his *En razón de muchas cosas tocantes al bien, prosperidad, riqueza, fertilidad de estos reinos y restauración de la gente que se ha echado de ello* suggests, Pérez de Herrera took for granted already in 1610 that expulsion, depopulation, and agricultural underproduction were related, a point that Fernández de Navarrete echoed in *Conservación de monarquías y discursos políticos*. Sancho de Moncada knew the claims of Pérez de Herrera and Fernández de Navarrete, but he did not think much of their analysis. Drawing on Church records, Sancho de Moncada argued that the years of greatest population decline did not coincide either with the Morisco expulsions or with the plague, another likely cause for stark demographic change. "In many cities that experienced these plagues and expulsions, all the houses remained," Sancho de Moncada reasoned, "and only in the last two or three years are many of them closed." And in any case, he continued in a rather more alarmist vein, Moriscos had been the "cause of many deaths (as your Majesty said in the royal expulsion decree), and so [the expulsions] actually increased the numbers of the Spanish nation."[68] This curious mixture of astute and jingoistic analysis, here judiciously ascribed in parenthesis to the Crown, is what makes the writings of Sancho de Moncada and his fellow *arbitristas* at once fascinating and opaque. Sancho de Moncada gathered and analyzed evidence like a modern economic historian, yet he also celebrated the actions of Felipe III like a royal propagandist. In Sancho de Moncada's view, the Crown had acted prudently to expel the Jews and later the Moriscos, and he even suggested that the feat should be repeated with the peninsula's Gypsies. This was a common sentiment. Having caught the expulsion fever despite his extended discourse about the dangers of expulsion, Fernández de Navarrete reprised Sancho de Moncada's Gypsy proposal in his *Conservación de monarquías*. In hindsight, this minority scapegoating is unsurprising. What is surprising, however, is that even after the Morisco expulsions, the figure of the Morisco remained a tool of imperial self-examination. It is no exaggeration to say that the apologetic rhetoric of Spanish economic and political history emerged through a consideration of the Morisco expulsions' legacy.

Though they published their most important texts after the expulsions, Fernández de Navarrete and Sancho de Moncada were answering arguments formulated during the late sixteenth- and early seventeenth-century debates about the advisability of expulsions, which for scholars like Pedro de Valencia and Martín González de Cellorigo was a cultural as well as a religious or economic issue. In his *Discurso sobre el acrecentamiento de la labor de la tierra,* for instance, Valencia pointed out that explorers preferred to travel to the Indies rather than to put in a hard day's work back home, a point that Pérez de Herrera also made in *En razón de muchas cosas tocantes al bien*. In his *Tratado*, as you will recall from chapter 1, Valencia mocked the tall tales told by evangelizers who returned from the far reaches of the globe, but in this text Valencia turned sharper, arguing that nothing but irresponsible adventuring had led Old Christians abroad in the first place. By rendering explicit the cultural gap between Old Christian indolence and Morisco productivity, Valencia even argued in his *Discurso* on agricultural labor, which circulated in manuscript form during the same years as his *Tratado* on the Moriscos, that in order to rebrand agricultural work as honorable, Moriscos should be prevented from working the fields. Consider Valencia's creative logic concerning the Moriscos' vocations:

> They should not be permitted to be laborers. This would make the profession more honorable, and the Moriscos would be seen as less practiced and intrepid; though neither should they be allowed to enter other similar professions that produce good soldiers. Rather they should only be shopkeepers and dealers in the cities and plazas. If they become rich as a result, it would not be problematic—they would pay more taxes and would become feminized and fearful and cowardly, because, as Euripides says, wealth produces this effect.[69]

Valencia knew that culture and religion marked the meaning of work in early modern Spain. In his view, labor reform and Morisco policy were mutually determined. The possibility that his program of vocational restructuring might increase agricultural production while also growing the Moriscos' wealth was not an unfortunate consequence of good social policy. On the contrary, Valencia insisted, such a chain of events heralded an increase in tax revenue. What is more, as the Moriscos came to be perceived, like the *conversos*, as dishonorable because of their newfound bourgeois wealth, Old Christians would flee their company in the urban markets and return in droves to abandoned farms and workshops. Unlike Pérez de Herrera and González de Cellorigo, who argued that the Moriscos should be compelled to be laborers in order to resolve the economic crisis, Valencia aimed at transforming the perception of work.[70] If Valencia framed his *Tratado acerca de los Moriscos* as a program for political and economic reform, he offered his *Discurso sobre el acrecentamiento de la labor de la tierra* as a reflection on the Morisco question's shaping of politics and economics as fields of knowledge.

The Moriscos hover as a spectral presence over early modern Spanish debate about economic decline. Their productivity and fertility made Old Christian laziness, or *ociosidad*, to use the term popular in the period, all the more noteworthy. This laziness was an abiding concern for authors like Valencia, who composed a manuscript treatise only recently published as *Discurso contra la ociosidad*, and Pérez de Herrera, who in his *Discvrsos del amparo de los legitimos pobres y redvccion de los fingidos*, published in multiple Latin and Spanish editions in the 1590s and early 1600s, attacked false beggars guilty of "great laziness in life."[71] It was also a concern for several generations of royal advisors, including both the duke of Lerma and Felipe IV's favorite, the Count Duke of Olivares Gaspar de Guzmán, who went so far as to consider readmitting *conversos* who had fled to Portugal in order stimulate Spanish mercantilism and counter population decline. Even if this official "philo-Hebraism" was a myth publicized by Gaspar de Guzmán's detractors, as the Spanish scholar Juan Ignacio Pulido Serrano has insisted, economic analysis, minority stereotypes, and the history and future of expulsion were tightly interwoven.[72] Debate about the Moriscos was thus not only a disagreement about apostasy or evangelization. It was also a conversation about the cultural origins of imperial decline, one that had at least as much to do with the representation of religious difference as with recurring squabbles between the Crown and regional nobles over tax policy and inflation. The learned discourses of what we now call demography and epidemiology could not obscure the pernicious cultural norms staring these writers in their faces. Many Old Christians wore their laziness as a badge of honor, as either a sign of or pretension to privilege, even as concerned scholars from across the political spectrum were nervous about the material consequences of idleness.

My argument in this chapter has been that early modern Spain's celebratory narrative of Christian unity was a product of astute archive management and editorial self-fashioning. The first Spanish histories of expulsion crisscrossed linguistic registers, snaking their way through holy exegesis, iconographic self-promotion, religious and social reform, and economic inquiry. Debate about Muslim and Jewish conversion to Christianity had laid bare the instrumental uses of canon law just as debate about New Christian assimilation had unveiled the professional stakes of comparative philology. By the turn of the seventeenth century, debate over Morisco expulsion had put the practices of history writing on full display as well. There were flesh-and-blood New Christians whose fates turned on these disputes, but for the scholars examined in the pages of this book, such disputes were never only about the converts. They concerned as well the shifting boundaries between neighboring disciplines and the reinvention of scholarly practices. The long struggle to eliminate the last traces of Judaism and Islam from Spain and to convert indigenous peoples in the Americas revolutionized canon law, language study, and history writing. This revolution entailed disingenuousness and brute force. It also produced religious reform, political criticism, and scholarly innovation.

CONCLUSION

Excavating Islamic Spain

Notwithstanding Archbishop Juan de Ribera's triumphalist rhetoric, imitated by subsequent generations of peninsular chroniclers, lyricists, and political and economic theorists, the Morisco expulsions did not mark the decisive end of Islamic Spain. Either protected by local nobility or charged by the Crown with maintaining the empty houses and agricultural infrastructure of their ghost-villages, some Moriscos never left. Others, like Ricote, Sancho Panza's friend and former neighbor from the second part of Miguel de Cervantes's *Don Quijote*, returned to Spain in search of opportunity or familiarity. Many of those who did come back ended up on galley ships as punishment for their violation, though a few, especially those with discreet contacts and bureaucratic good fortune, blended into a peninsular society in upheaval, just as so many *conversos* had during the previous century.[1] Muslim slaves, renegade Christian corsairs, and Magharibi diplomats encountered these scattered Moriscos in a considerably shrunken yet still discernable seventeenth-century Islamic minority. In the eighteenth and nineteenth centuries, peripatetic scholars and foreign ambassadors from around the Mediterranean joined New World diplomats in traversing the peninsular routes of their former co-religionists.[2] In the twentieth and twenty-first centuries, laborers, students, and tourists have followed their own circuitous courses back to a modern Spain that has, however ambivalently, begun excavating and promoting its Semitic past. I have argued over the course of this book that debates about the meaning, practices, and limits of religious coercion became an engine of scholarly innovation and religious reform over the course of the sixteenth and early seventeenth centuries. Along with biblical parables and patristic glosses, the figure of the Morisco was the fuel that kept this engine humming. Even with a downshift in the decades after the Morisco expulsions, this engine never sputtered to a complete stop. The cycle of false endings ceased, but Islamic Spain never really ended.

Memory of peninsular Islam in the centuries after the expulsions was more closely tied to texts, artifacts, and architecture than to fragile networks of Muslim or Morisco individuals, however. While the Alhambra still towers over Granada and the Great Mosque still lies at Cordoba's center, two among many tributes to Spain's multiconfessional medieval past, extant evidence of early modern cryptoreligion is more prosaic and opaque.[3] Like the Sacromonte lead books, troves of Morisco manuscripts, sometimes carefully packed with salt in linen bags to protect against insects and humidity, have been discovered in diverse locations at irregular intervals from the seventeenth century to the present. The secret compartments containing these texts have appeared during the replacement of floorboards or renovation of walls and columns in the aging edifices of Ribera de Ebro (1687), Ricla (1728), Almonacid de la Sierra (1876, 1884), Saviñán (1957), Ocaña (1969), and Calanda (1988), among other locales.[4] Departing Moriscos or their local allies hid from neighbors and inquisitors these legal commentaries, literary anthologies, and grammars, many of which were composed in *aljamiado*. The enterprising locals who unearthed and salvaged these materials then sold them to specialists able to decipher the Islamic content and Spanish language hidden beneath the Arabic script. José Antonio Conde, Pablo Gil y Gil, Eduardo Saavedra, Francisco Guillén Robles, Pascal de Gayangos, Miguel Asín Palacios, and the other nineteenth- and early twentieth-century Orientalists who did much of this interpretive work also collected and catalogued the findings.[5] Later scholars rediscovered these texts along with many other Morisco manuscripts in the Biblioteca Nacional, the Real Academia de la Historia, and other archives where the once private collections of these Orientalists eventually landed.[6] Politically engaged and historically sensitive models of literary studies recently have helped to initiate wider interest in these materials, which the early twenty-first century's anxiety surrounding globalization and religious fundamentalism has only intensified. An in-depth consideration of *aljamiado* literature and its associated scholarship is beyond the scope of my project, which has focused on the intellectual consequences of peninsular debates about coercion rather than on New Christian cultural history. I nevertheless raise here the postexpulsion challenge of Morisco textuality in order to highlight an intriguing if troubling parallel: The peninsular religious blurriness that so embarrassed Carlos V in the early part of the sixteenth century has become since Spain's nineteenth-century endeavors of colonial expansion in North Africa an element of nationalist promotion.[7] Replicating the reading practices of early modern inquisitors, today's politicians and scholars also seek to unveil a history of New Christian apostasy, though to celebratory rather than castigatory ends.

A 2010 exhibition at Madrid's Biblioteca Nacional entitled *Memoria de los moriscos: Escritos y relatos de una diáspora cultural* championed this Spain of the "three faiths." Along with scattered woodcuts related to the Moriscos, the show displayed more than fifty manuscripts, the majority composed in Arabic or *aljamiado*. Like other conferences and exhibitions from this time, the show coincided with the fourth centenary of the expulsions, and organizers characterized it as a "recuperation of the Islamic past."[8] The exhibit made available a wide swath of materials from multiple archives, much of which had never before been collected and displayed together in this way. Housed in a space meant to evoke the old edifices where Morisco materials were often discovered, *Memoria de los moriscos* aimed to recreate the social and linguistic coherency that the Moriscos had struggled to maintain at the moment of their departure.[9] Not surprisingly, many of the texts on display traced their provenance to the larger of the Almonacid de la Sierra hoards, which, given the bookbinding tools found with the manuscripts, probably composed the stock of a once thriving Morisco bookstore. Among the multiple manuscripts chosen from this collection for the Madrid exhibition was a late sixteenth-century Arabic copy of Ibn a-Jurrum's grammar, *Al-jurumiyya*, which included with the original Arabic text an interlineal commentary in *aljamiado*. As you will recall from chapter 3, Ibn a-Jurrum's teaching text was popular among Hebraists in Salamanca, and it was later published by the Typographia Medicea in Rome and reedited by the Danish Orientalist Thomas Erpenius. Like their Old Christian counterparts, the Moriscos also strived to read Arabic, and judging from their reliance on *aljamiado* in this and many other manuscripts, the majority did so with similarly limited success. Nevertheless, for the Moriscos of Almonacid no less than for Benito Arias Montano, Fray Luis de León, and others at the center of peninsular erudition, to display an imperfect Arabic knowledge was a marker of intellectual and religious identity. By displaying these Morisco manuscripts, the curators of the *Memoria de los moriscos* exhibit reproduced this process of self-definition. Their goal was not to revolutionize the conventions of scholarship or defend a minority community on the point of disintegration, of course. The curators sought rather to make the early modern Moriscos speak from a temporal and geographic diaspora on behalf of modern Spain's reimagined past.

As it was in the sixteenth and seventeenth centuries, Morisco memory is again today a locus of debate. The discourse of pluralism that runs through these debates remains strangely disconnected from xenophobia in Europe and the United States after the terrorist attacks of September 11, 2001, in New York and March 11, 2004, in Madrid. It has become easier to celebrate early modern Moriscos than to protect the rights of Muslim immigrants in Madrid's Lavapiés neighborhood or on Brooklyn's Atlantic Avenue. In the process of negotiating this tension, however, we must do our best to avoid enveloping Spain's multiconfessional and transatlantic history in today's secular multiculturalism, with all its attendant presuppositions about the meanings and ends of religion. This book on the relationship between religious coercion and scholarly innovation represents an effort to study the former, but my hope is that it will aid some readers to chart the pitfalls of the latter.

Unable either to ignore or to resolve these concerns about religion and secularism, we are in a situation like the one described by Pedro de Valencia, whose words opened this book: "We will find ourselves in great danger and confusion," explained Valencia in his early seventeenth-century treatise on the Morisco question, "much like that expressed by the ancient proverb: auribus lupum teneo [I have the wolf by the ears]. He who has the wolf by the ears does not have a firm and secure grasp; it is advisable for him neither to hold on nor to let go."[10] Valencia employed this citation from the Roman playwright Terence to acknowledge the gravity and highlight the paradigmatic status of the Morisco question in his own day, yet Morisco memory offers a parable of coercion in our secular age, too. As if clutching a wolf's ears, we remain unable either to recuperate coercion's ethical potential or to control its dangerous consequences.

Acknowledgments

My thinking about early modern Spain and the history of religion has taken shape through conversations with many people, and it is my pleasure to thank them here. With their insightful questions and guidance, Anthony Cascardi and José Rabasa first helped me to articulate the structure and stakes of this project. Jesús Rodríguez-Velasco has extended constructive criticism and encouragement from start to finish. Feedback from Vincent Barletta, Mercedes García-Arenal, and Timothy Hampton came at crucial moments of the writing and revision process. To each of them I offer my gratitude.

Since 2012, I have found a supportive and engaging group of colleagues and friends in the New York area. I thank Carlos Alonso, Joaquín Barriendos, Adam Beaver, Karen Benezra, Orlando Bentancor, Susan Boynton, Ronald Briggs, Marina Brownlee, Hernán Díaz, Patricia Grieve, Marc Hertzman, Robert Maryks, Alberto Medina, Graciela Montaldo, Karla Nielsen, Gustavo Pérez Firmat, Alessandra Russo, Alan Stewart, Gareth Williams, and Aurélie Vialette for help with this book and sage professional advice more generally. Regular exchange of writing with Stefano Gulizia, Daniel Hershenzon, and Pier Mattia Tommasino has been instructive and fun. Suggestions and in many cases ongoing dialogues with my friends and teachers from California have proved essential in writing and finishing this book. Thanks to Michael Allan, Lanier Anderson, Heather Bamford, Brian Catlos, Jonathan Combs-Schilling, J. P. Daughton, Ivonne Del Valle, Samuel England, Barbara Fuchs, Victor Goldgel-Carballo, Roland Greene, Paul Haacke, Katie Harris, Michelle Hamilton, Charles Hirschkind, Victoria Kahn, Sharon Kinoshita, Jamie Kreiner, Seth Lerer, Kate Marshall, Tom McEnany, Leah Middlebrook,

James Monroe, Anna More, Ignacio Navarrete, Daniel Nemser, Katrina Olds, Dwight Reynolds, Sylvia Sellers-García, Sarah Wells, and Nina Zhiri.

I am grateful to my colleagues in the Department of Latin American and Iberian Cultures at Columbia University for a dynamic and caring intellectual community in which to work. Thanks also to my graduate students at both Stanford and Columbia for pushing me to see the big picture, and to Luis Carlos Fernández, Kosmas Pissakos, and Eunice Rodríguez Ferguson at Columbia for precious logistical support. A special thanks is due to the University Seminars at Columbia University, which in addition to providing a venue for discussing this book also offered a publication subvention through the Schoff Fund. I likewise would like to express my appreciation to Stanford University's Renaissances working group and Abbasi Program in Islamic Studies, the Department of Romance Languages at the University of Michigan at Ann Arbor, and the Department of Literatures, Cultures, and Languages at the University of Connecticut at Storrs for opportunities to share parts of the manuscript. At these presentations, comments and questions by Shahzad Bashir, Ryan Calderwood, Enrique García Santo-Tomás, Mayte Green-Mercado, Gustavo Nanclares, Osvaldo Pardo, Ryan Szpiech, and others already mentioned above helped me to refine my thinking about the relationship between coercion and scholarship. Theodor Dunkelgrün, Javier Irigoyen-García, Guy Lazure, Nabil Matar, David Nirenberg, Stefania Pastore, Jesús de Prado Plumed, Fernando Rodríguez Mediano, Elvira Vilches, Alison Weber, and Gerard Wiegers have also pointed me toward key references and new ideas at conferences in recent years.

I thank the archivists and librarians at the Biblioteca Nacional de España, the Fundación Galdiano, the Fundación Zabálburu, the Palacio Real, and the Real Academia de la Historia, all in Madrid, as well as those at the Biblioteca Universitaria in Salamanca and the Abadía de Sacromonte in Granada. I owe gratitude to the Department of Comparative Literature and the Graduate Division of the University of California at Berkeley for doctoral funding, the University of California Humanities Research Institute in Irvine for a residential research fellowship on the medieval and early modern Mediterranean, the United States Department of Education for a Jacob K. Javits Fellowship and a Foreign Language and Areas Studies Fellowship in Arabic, and the Woodrow Wilson Foundation for a Charlotte W. Newcombe Doctoral Dissertation Fellowship. In addition, I thank Stanford University for a two-year membership in the Andrew W. Mellon Fellowship of Scholars in the Humanities, which provided a lively intellectual environment in which to develop this project.

Thanks to Duke University Press and Vanderbilt University Press for allowing me to include revised parts of two previously published essays in this book: "'In the Choir with the Clerics': Secularism in the Age of Inquisition" appeared in *Comparative Literature* 65, no. 3, in summer 2013, and "Writing Religion: Sacromonte and the Literary Conventions of Orthodoxy" was published in 2012 in *Poiesis and Modernity in the Old and New Worlds*, a volume of the Hispanic Issues book series. I am grateful in addition to Randy Petilos at the University of Chicago Press for marshaling this book through the review process with efficiency and compassion, to the Press's two anonymous readers for their many astute suggestions, and to Susan Tarcov for her careful copyediting.

Finally, I would like to thank my family members, who have helped me in the writing of this book, along with considerably more. Shirley Kimmel and Marcia Katrosar have awaited the book's arrival with greater confidence than I ever could muster. Bernard Kimmel and Sidney Katrosar were my advocates, too. Simeon Kimmel has rightfully demanded from me argumentative clarity and contemporary relevance, offering in return unrivaled enthusiasm. Hinda Kimmel taught me to write with precision and helps me to roll with the punches, and Elliot Kimmel always prepared and encouraged me to embark on adventures. More than anyone else, Rachel Bernard has helped me to weather the struggles and celebrate the successes of being a writer and teacher. Her editorial eye is the one I most trust, but it is her patience, kindheartedness, and perceptiveness that I love and admire.

Notes

INTRODUCTION

1. Valencia, *Tratado acerca de los moriscos*, 83: "nunca nos habemos de poder asegurar de su fé, por más que digan y desdigan." On Valencia and the Moriscos, see Gómez Canseco, *El humanismo*, 234–41; Magnier, *Pedro de Valencia*, 245–89. Unless otherwise noted, all translations are my own.

2. Ames, *Righteous Persecution*, 10–16.

3. Although the roots of this conversation lie in the nineteenth century, for more recent research on religion as a shifting category of analysis in the early modern period, see Masuzawa, *Invention of World Religions*, 37–71; Stroumsa, *New Science*, 1–13; C. Taylor, *Secular Age*, 25–158. For a Hispanist perspective on these issues, see Cascardi, *Subject of Modernity*, 125–78; Kimmel, "'In the Choir,'" 286–90, 301–2. Historians of early modern religion will recognize in my formulation of the problem echoes of debates about "confessionalization," which in the 1980s and 1990s represented a rethinking of the interrelated processes of Protestant and Catholic reform and the history of secularization. See Reinhard, "Reformation," 390; Schilling, "Confessional Europe," 644; Lotz-Heumann, "Confessionalization," 35–38.

4. Castro, *España en su historia*, 305–12. For new iterations of Castro's view, see Dodds, Menocal, and Balbale, *Arts of Intimacy*; Mann, Glick, and Dodds, *Convivencia*; Menocal, *Ornament of the World*. Terse responses to Castro and his allies include Asensio, *La España imaginada*; Brann, "Andalusi 'Exceptionalism.'" For two review essays on this historiography, see Novikoff, "Between Tolerance and Intolerance"; Soifer Irish, "Beyond Convivencia."

5. Nirenberg, *Communities of Violence*, 3–40.

6. Jesus explains in Luke 14:15–28 that the rich man instructed his servant to comb the alleys and roads to find whomever he can and "compel them to come in that my house may be filled." The Latin Vulgate reads, "compelle intrare ut impleatur domus mea." See *Bibliorum sacrorum iuxta vulgatam clementinam*, 993. My paraphrase follows the Douay-Rheims English translation of the Vulgate. Another version of this "parable of the banquet" appears in Matthew 22:1–14. On Augustine, Jerome, and the question of coercion, see Gaddis, *There Is No Crime*, 131–50; P. Brown, *Augustine of Hippo*, 233–44; P. Brown, "St. Augustine's Attitude"; Shaw, *Sacred Violence*, 4.

7. This inelegant phrasing allegedly coined by Peter of Poitiers in the twelfth century was then reformulated and popularized by Pope Innocent III around the turn of the thirteenth century. See Innocent III, *De missarum mysteriis*, bk. 3, chap. 5, in *Patrologia Latina* (hereafter *PL*), vol. 217, cols. 0843C–0845A; Kennedy, "Sacraments." The irony of this defense of ritual efficacy is that it echoed ritual-based models of Judaism, against which Jesus's followers first defined themselves, and of Islam, which served as a foil to early modern Christians. For more on this paradox, see my discussions about ritual and dissimulation in chapters 1 and 6.

8. See Augustine's writings on the Donatists, a heterodox Christian sect that gained considerable traction in fourth- and fifth-century North Africa: Augustine, *De baptismo libri VII*, in *PL*, vol. 43, col. 0107; Augustine, "Scripta contra donatistas." For English translations, see Augustine, *Works*. On the Donatists, see Chadwick, *Early Church*, 219–25, and for a wider perspective on Augustine's view of ritual efficacy, see Nightingale, *Once Out of Nature*, 179–84.

9. Kamen, "Strategies of Survival," 207.

10. Bynum, *Christian Materiality*, 15–36.

11. Grévin, *Le parchemin*, 189–258.

12. Kamen, *Spanish Inquisition*, 1–7; Moreno, *La invención de la inquisición*, 125–42.

13. Dawkins, *God Delusion*, 309–15. For a thoughtful and entertaining response to Dawkins, see Eagleton, *Reason, Faith, and Revolution*, 1–46.

14. Perry, *Handless Maiden*, 5–15; Márquez Villanueva, *El problema morisco*, 1–12. Contrast Perry's and Márquez Villanueva's approaches to the older but still influential taxonomy of peninsular religion, Menéndez y Pelayo, *Historia de los heterodoxos españoles*. Another important scholar is Álvaro Galmés de Fuentes, who in Mercedes García-Arenal's formulation sees "irreducible Muslims" in the Moriscos but not Perry's and Márquez Villanueva's political dissent. See Galmés de Fuentes, *Los Moriscos;* García-Arenal, "Religious Dissent and Minorities," 898. For a bibliographic review of scholarship on *conversos* and Moriscos, see Amelang, *Historias paralelas*, 183–347.

15. Silverblatt, *Modern Inquisitions*, 6.

16. Pulgar, *Crónica de los señores Reyes Católicos*, vol. 5, chap. 120: "Con dulces raçones y blandas amonestaciones . . . e no con aquella cruel pena del fuego." This is an often-cited passage. See Pastore, *Il vangelo e la spada*, 87; Moreno, *La invención de la inquisición*, 98.

17. The Latin Vulgate of Matthew 11:30 reads, "iugum enim meum suave est et onus meum leve." For this passage, the repetition from Luke, and the parable of the wheat and the tares, see *Bibliorum sacrorum iuxta vulgatam clementinam*, 938, 940, 948–49; Pastore, *Una herejía española*, 104–5.

18. Bataillon, *Erasmo y España*; Kamen, *Rise of Toleration*; Kamen, "Toleration and Dissent"; Nederman, *Worlds of Difference*. For an important response to Bataillon, see Asensio, *El erasmismo*, 32–36, 75–96. For a review essay of recent scholarship on the *alumbrados*, see García-Arenal and Pereda, "A propósito de los alumbrados."

19. Schwartz, *All Can Be Saved*, 17, 53; Kaplan, *Divided by Faith*, 1–14.

20. On the problem of periodization in the Hispanic context, see Grazia, "Modern Divide"; Fuchs, "1492 and the Cleaving of Hispanism."

21. Moore, *Formation of a Persecuting Society*. For a response to Moore's view, see Nederman, "Introduction." For a perceptive take on the early modern politics of intolerance, see Simpson, *Burning to Read*, 1–33. And for more conventional studies, see Creppell, *Toleration and Identity*, 1–38; Zagorin, *How the Idea of Religious Toleration Came to the West*, 1–92.

22. Nirenberg's recent study of the figure of the Jew and the "Judaism of thought" is similar in this regard. See Nirenberg, *Anti-Judaism*, 1–12.

23. Mandosio and Petrus, *Repertorivm inqvisitorvm*, 765. See also a partial translation by Sala-Moulins into French as *Le dictionnaire des inquisiteurs*, as well as Homza, *Religious Authority*, xiii–xxiii, 113–49. On the underside of tolerance, see MacEvitt, *Crusades and the Christian World*, 21–26; W. Brown, *Regulating Aversion*, 25–47; and Marcuse's pioneering essay "Repressive Tolerance."

24. The *Glossa ordinaria*, an influential medieval reading aid that often accompanied early modern editions of the Vulgate, depicted coercion as a precondition for accepting the rich man's "gift of understanding" (*donum intellectus*), as the parable of the banquet dubbed knowledge and experience of Christianity. Santa María underscored the peninsular relevance of this parable, which in his view offered nothing less than a vision for evangelizing "modern Saracenes and Jews" (*Saraceni et Iudei moderni*). See *Bibliorum sacrorum cum Glossa ordinaria*, vol. 5, cols. 899, 901. For a variant

citation, see also Strabus, *Glossa ordinaria*, in *PL*, vol. 114, col. 0309B, which reads "house of understanding" (*domum intellectus*) rather than "gift of understanding" (*donum intellectus*). On Santa María and his legacy, see Asensio, "Exégesis bíblica en España," 246.

25. Bourdieu, *Field of Cultural Production*, 1–141; Certeau, *Practice of Everyday Life*, 91–110; Foucault, *Discipline and Punish*, 135–228.

26. Vives, *De disciplinis*; Vives, *On Education*; Kallendorf, *Humanist Educational Treatises*. My formulation here is indebted to Edward Said's Foucauldian definition of Orientalism as a "systematic discipline." See Said, *Orientalism*, 3.

CHAPTER ONE

1. Rummel, *Jiménez de Cisneros*, 34–35.

2. Harvey, *Muslims in Spain*, 24–31; A. K. Harris, *From Muslim to Christian Granada*, 8–27; Lea, *Los moriscos españoles*, 91–114.

3. Coleman, *Creating Christian Granada*, 1–12.

4. Sigüenza, *Historia de la Orden*, 288–318; Garrad, "Original Memorial." The autograph manuscript of Núñez Muley's petition is in the Biblioteca Nacional de España (MS 6176). I cite throughout from Garrad's edition and have slightly altered Vincent Barletta's English translation, published as Núñez Muley, *Memorandum for the President*. Although Núñez Muley's petition was known through contemporary secondary sources, Rafael Contreras first confirmed its archival history when he discovered an eighteenth-century summary of the text in Granada's Alhambra archives. See Contreras, "Nuevos datos."

5. Caro Baroja, *Los moriscos*, 37–47; A. K. Harris, *From Muslim to Christian Granada*, 11.

6. Harvey, *Muslims in Spain*, 99.

7. Guevara, *Epistolas familiares*, 543–44; Ehlers, *Between Christians and Moriscos*, 10–22.

8. Bernabé Pons, *Los moriscos*, 45–66; Lea, *Los moriscos españoles*, 146–158.

9. Lea, *Los moriscos españoles*, 128–234; Redondo, *Antonio de Guevara*, 223–43.

10. Aquinas, *Summa theologica*, II-II, question 10, article 8: "Respondeo dicendum quod infideles sunt qui nunquam susceperunt fidem, sicut gentiles et iudaei; et tales nullo modo sunt ad fidem compellendi ut ipsi credant, quia creder voluntatis est" (I answer that, among unbelievers there are some who have never received the faith, such as the heathens and the Jews; and these are by no means to be compelled to the faith, in order that they may believe, because to believe depends on the will). This and future English translations are slightly altered from *The Summa Theologica of St. Thomas Aquinas*. See also Carro, *Teología y los teólogos*, 154.

11. Aquinas, *Summa theologica*, II-II, question 10, article 8: "Alii vero sunt infideles qui quandoque fidem susceperunt, et iam profitentur, sicut haeretici, et quicumque apostatae et tales sunt etiam corporaliter compellendi, ut impleant quod promiserunt, et teneant quod semel susceperunt" (On the other hand, there are unbelievers who at some time have accepted the faith, and professed it, such as heretics and all apostates: such should be submitted even to bodily compulsion, that they may fulfill what they have promised, and hold what they at one time received).

12. Thompson, *Goths in Spain*, 172–74.

13. Concilium Toletatum quartum, "De Iudeis," LVII: "Ergo non vi sed libera arbitrii facultate ut convertantur suadendi sunt non potius impellendi."

14. Ibid.: "Qui autem iam pridem ad christianitatem coacti sunt . . . et baptismi gratiam suscepisse, et chrismate unctos esse, et corporis domini et sanguinis extitisse [g] participes."

15. Gregory IX, *Liber Extra* (1234), "De baptismo & eius effectu," bk. 3, title 42, collected in *Corpus juris canonici*, 1381–82: "Si baptizatus es, non te baptizo sed si nondum baptizatus es, ego te baptizo, & cætera."

16. Pérez de Ayala, *Sínodo de la diócesis de Guadix y Beza*.

17. AHN, Inquisition, libro 247, f. 169r, cited in Redondo, *Antonio de Guevara*, 229: "fuerça ni violencia precisa ni absoluta."

18. Lea, *Los moriscos españoles*, 126–27. See especially n. 22.

19. Beltrán de Heredía, *Los manuscritos*, 197. For more on the history and translation of these terms, see Vitoria, *Political Writings*, 343.

20. Santa Cruz, *Crónica del Emperador Carlos V*, vol. 2, 119: "Los moros de aquel Reino no hicieron ninguna resistencia cuando los bautizaban por fuerza, que la fe que por fuerza les hicieron tomar, que quisiesen o no, la habían de guardar." On the *germanías* and the Moriscos, see Harvey, *Muslims in Spain*, 92–94.

21. Sandoval, *Historia de la vida y hechos*, 677. Although the medievalist Brian Stock is primarily concerned with a different period, his idea of "textual communities" is relevant here as well. See Stock, *Implications of Literacy*, 88–150.

22. One way to understand Manrique and his colleagues' arguments is as counteroffensive against peninsular civil lawyers, who had acquired greater power in the sixteenth century. According to Richard Kagan, this shift represented a "legal revolution." See Kagan, *Lawsuits and Litigants*, xx–xxi, 24–26. On the complex history of the relationship between Church and State, see Suberbiola Martínez, *Real Patronato de Granada*, and on the epistemological challenge posed by inquisitorial careerism, see Lynn, *Between Court and Confessional*, 1–12.

23. Alfonso X, *Las siete partidas*, part 7, title 26, law 2: "Los hereges pueden ser acusados de cada vno del pueblo delante de los obispos, o delos vicarios, que tienen sus logares." The relevant part of López de Madera's note reads, "Crimen haeresis est merè ecclesiasticum . . . et Inquisitores per sedem Apostolicam deputati" (The crime of heresy is ecclesiastical in nature . . . and inquisitors are granted their authority by the Holy See). On the manuscript and early print history of the *Siete partidas*, see Samuel Parsons Scott and Robert Ignatius Burns's introduction to their edition of the text, Alfonso X, *Las siete partidas*, xxiv–xxv. All citations are from Gregorio López de Madera's 1555 edition.

24. Homza, *Spanish Inquisition*, ix–xxxvii; Moreno, *La invención de la inquisición*, 29–59; Lea, *History of the Inquisition*; Kamen, *Spanish Inquisition*, 37–192.

25. Jiménez Monteserín, *Introducción a la inquisición española*; Asad "Medieval Heresy," 355.

26. Eimeric, *Directorivm inqvisitorvm*, 438: "Sane quia multum interest . . . cognoscere cuius sunt sequaces haeresis, siue sectae, quod ex eorum uita, seu moribus, et ritibus ac signis exterioribus patet clarè." See also Martín's modern Spanish translation, *El manual de los inquisidores*, 157.

27. Root, "Speaking Christian." On Cisneros and the early sixteenth-century origins of Catholic reform, see O'Malley, *Trent*, 40–42.

28. Sullivan, *Inner Lives*, 172–80. The translations of these terms are Sullivan's.

29. Jiménez Monteserín, *Introducción a la inquisición española*, 95: "simulado y fingido converso a la fe."

30. Augustine, *De correctione donatistarum*, *PL*, vol. 33, col. 0804; Augustine, *Works*, 499; *Bibliorum sacrorum iuxta vulgatam clementinam*, 1086. Of the many recent studies that have joined Augustine in employing Paul to chart the limits of universalism, see Agamben, *Time That Remains*; Badiou, *Saint Paul*; Boyarin, *Radical Jew*.

31. Peter Brown went so far as to suggest that "Augustine may be the first theorist of the Inquisition." See P. Brown, *Augustine of Hippo*, 240; Gaddis, *There Is No Crime*, 337.

32. Gregory the Great, *Moralium libri*, bk. 26, chap. 10, *PL*, vol. 76: "Humanae aures verba nostra talia judicant qualia foris sonant; divina vero judicia talia ea audiunt qualia ex intimis proferuntur." On Aquinas and other scholastic sources on lying, see Zagorin, *Ways of Lying*, 15–37; Zagorin, "Historical Significance"; Jay, *Virtues of Mendacity*, 52–58; Snyder, *Dissimulation and the Culture of Secrecy*, 1–26.

33. Eimeric, *Directorivm inqvisitorvm*, 443; Eimeric, *El manual de los inquisidores*, 161: "quare ex hoc solo non videtur omnino praesumendum de haresi vel apostasia."

34. Eimeric, *Directorivm inqvisitorvm*, 443; Eimeric, *El manual de los inquisidores*, 161: "nisi ex damnatae sectae reuerentia et approbatione."

35. *Bibliorum sacrorum iuxta vulgatam clementinam*, 1090: "si tu cum Iudaeus sis gentiliter et non iudaice vivis quomodo gentes cogis iudaizare." On this episode, see also Nirenberg, *Anti-Judaism*, 59–62.

36. Augustine, *Epistola XXVIII*, in *PL*, vol. 33, col. 0112: "Mihi enim videtur exitiosissime credi, aliquod in Libris sanctis haberi mendacium." English versions of Augustine and Jerome's correspondence about Galatians are in Augustine, *Letters*. For Jerome's commentary on Galatians, see *PL*, vol. 26, and for Augustine's related treatise on lying, *De mendacio*, see *PL*, vol. 40. On Erasmus's and Luther's glosses on Galatians, see Zagorin, "Historical Significance," 869–76.

37. Augustine, *Epistola XXVIII*, in *PL*, vol. 33, cols. 0112–0113: "Admisso enim semel in tantum auctoritatis fastigium officioso aliquo mendacio, nulla illorum librorum particula remanebit, quae non ut cuique videbitur vel ad mores difficilis vel ad fidem incredibilis, eadem perniciosissima regula ad mentientis auctoris consilium officiumque referatur."

38. Guevara, *Epistolas familiares*, 543–44: "hallo en los Christianos nueuos tantas cosas de emendar que tomo por mas sano consejo, corregirlas en secreto que no castigarlas en publico."

39. Ibid., 544: "me mando Cesar mi señor, que visitasse tambien este Reyno de Granada, obra porcierto assaz necessaria, aunque a mi muy enojosa . . . Los grandes pecados y facinorosos delictos, a la hora que son publicados, a las vezes es mejor dissimularlos que no castigarlos; lo vno porque los atreuidos no se auezen de aquella manera a pecar, y lo otro porque los simples no se escandalizen de ver tan enormes pecados cometer."

40. Bossy, *Christianity in the West*, 126–40; Prosperi, "Confessione e dissimulazione"; Prosperi, *Tribunali della coscienza*, 400–548.

41. Childers, "Hispanic Casuistry Studies"; Jonsen and Toulmin, *Abuse of Casuistry*, 139–75; O'Banion, *Sacrament of Penance*, 1–18.

42. El Alaoui, *Jésuites, morisques et indiens*, 370: "baptizáronlos a manadas en las iglesias echándoles agua con hisopos, y entendían tan bien lo que recebían que muchos dellos se metían debaxo de los bancos o se cubrían en otras suertes porque no les tocasse el agua del sancto baptismo." El Alaoui's text is an edition and study of Las Casas's *memoriales*, including the *Información* (BL MS Add 10.238). See also El Alaoui, "Ignacio de Las Casas"; Griffin, "'Un muro invisible.'" There is no relation between Ignacio de Las Casas and his more famous predecessor of the same name, Bartolomé de Las Casas, though it is plausible that the former took or was given the name "Las Casas" in the latter's honor, perhaps by the Jesuit evangelizers who were his teachers in Granada.

43. For introductions to *taqīyya*, see "takiyya," in *The Encyclopaedia of Islam*; Barletta, *Covert Gestures*, xxviii–xxix; Catlos, *Muslims*, 282; Monroe, "Curious Morisco Appeal."

44. El Alaoui, *Jésuites, morisques et indiens*, 370: "y no lo encareço yo porque assí me an certificado muchos testigos de vista que pasó y los mesmos baptizados me an dicho aver sido assí verdad." On the importance of "looking for the institutional conditions" of knowledge about Islam, see Asad, "Idea of an Anthropology," 5.

45. An *aljamiado* version of the Oran *fatwā* is housed in the Real Academia de la Historia (RAH MS 11-9410); in this and subsequent citations I follow the transcription in Galmés de Fuentes, *Los manuscritos*, 95–96. For an English version, see Harvey, *Muslims in Spain*, 61. For background and debate about the text's dating, see Cantineau, "Lettre du moufti d'Oran"; García-Arenal, *Los Moriscos*, 44–45. On disagreement about *taqīyya* among Islamic scholars, see Hendrickson, "Islamic Obligation."

46. Caro Baroja, *Los moriscos*, 149–74; Lea, *Los moriscos españoles*, 213–70; O'Banion, *Sacrament of Penance*, 142–67.

47. Garrad, "Original Memorial," 215: "la zambra estava en el coro con los clérigos." For readings of this episode, see Fuchs, "Virtual Spaniards," 14–19; Kimmel, "'In the Choir.'" A recently

discovered archival source suggests that Núñez Muley mounted his petition with financial support from the Mendoza family as well as the Morisco community. See Castillo Fernández, "Las estructuras sociales," 214. Thanks to Javier Irigoyen-García for this reference.

48. Garrad, "Original Memorial," 215: "Dezía en la misa algunas palabras en arábigo—en especial, quando dezía 'Dominus Bobispon' [*sic*], dezía 'Ybara figun'; esto me acuerdo de ello como si fuese ayer."

49. Núñez Muley, *Memorandum for the President*, 80.

50. Garrad, "Original Memorial," 219.

51. Ibid., 215: "como se puede dezir que es los trumentos y zambras de moros?"

52. On the "Indies of the interior," see Vincent, "Les Jésuites et les Indes," 275; García-Arenal, "Moriscos e indios"; Prosperi, "'Otras indias.'"

53. Reproduced in Janer, *Condición social de los moriscos*, 331: "es como si uno que tiene la casa llena de víboras y escorpiones no pusiera cuidado en limpiarla dellos, y dejando en tan evidente peligro a su mujer e hijos se fuere a cazar leones ó avestruces a Africa por tenerlo por caza mayor, más real o más cierta" (it is as if someone who has his house full of vipers and scorpions takes no care to rid it of them, and leaving such an obvious danger to his wife and children, goes to hunt lions or ostriches in Africa, taking it to be a greater pursuit, more real and more certain).

54. Valencia, *Tratado acerca de los moriscos*, 115: "Dícese un refrán antiguo: Hic Rhodus, hic saltus. Por este cuento jactábase uno de ligereza excesiva en saltar y en esta razón decía que había hecho en Rodas un salto de muchos pasos, mucho mayor de lo que era creíble. Contradecían los presentes y él porfiaba afirmándose en su cuento. Salió un hombre avisado y díjole las palabras del refrán: 'No hay para qué porfiar; haced cuenta que estáis en Rodas y dad aquí otro salto y creeros hemos.' Esto se nos puede decir a los españoles: Que demos aquí el salto que en la China y en el Japón y que hagamos las maravillas en nuestra patria que se cuentan que hacemos en provincias tan extrañas y lejanas."

CHAPTER TWO

1. Beltrán de Heredia, *Los manuscritos*, 200: "Ex quo sequitur quod rex juste posset expeller sarracenos a patria, si probabiliter timeretur ab illis periculum de subversione fidelium vel de perditione patrie. Posset etiam legitime facere, dato sciat quod propter hoc convertentur ad fidem, nec per hoc compelluntur." See also Pagden and Lawrence's English translation in Vitoria, *Political Writings*, 348.

2. Beltrán de Heredia, *Los manuscritos*, 198: "ita debet fieri"; Vitoria, *Political Writings*, 345.

3. Beltrán de Heredia, *Los manuscritos*, 198; Vitoria, *Political Writings*, 344.

4. Vitoria, *Relecciones*, 370, 356: "Saraceni inter Christianos" and "nec à Saracenis, nec à Iudeis uel aliis infidelibus"; Vitoria, *Political Writings*, 244, 263. On the interrelation between New and Old World in debates about religion, see Stroumsa, *New Science*, 14–38.

5. Vitoria, *Relecciones*, 293: "Officium, ac munus Theologitam latè patet, vt nullum argumentum, nulla disputatio, nullus locus alienus videatur, à theologica professione et instituto"; Vitoria, *Political Writings*, 3.

6. Lombard, *Sententiarum libri IV*, bk. 1, dist. l, chap. 1, in *PL*, vol. 192: "ad significandum aliquid adhibentur." For this and subsequent English translations, see Lombard, *Sentences*. For more on Lombard and this section of the *Sentences*, see Rosemann, *Peter Lombard*, 59–61.

7. Lombard, *Sententiarum libri IV*, bk. 1, dist. 47, chap. 5, in *PL*, vol. 192: "decimus, aliquam esse differentiam inter."

8. Boureau, *L'empire du livre*, 242: "dans l'histoire culturelle commune, la scholastique apparaît souvent comme une machine à produire des divisions."

9. On this shift from monastic to scholastic *lectio*, see Illich, *In the Vineyard*, 51–92. For introductions to scholasticism, see Dahan, *L'exégèse chrétienne*; Le Goff, *Les intellectuels au moyen âge*;

Rosier-Catach, *La parole efficace*. On the pedagogical and epistemological stakes of learning to "do *doctrina*" rather than to communicate its meaning, see C. Brown, *Contrary Things*, 9.

10. Aquinas, *Scriptum super libros*, question 1, article 2: "ipsa unica manens, non multiplicata, diversarum rerum considerationem habet." On division and distinction as part of scholastic method, see Charland, *Ars praedicandi*, 150–51.

11. Echoing the early modern criticisms of Erasmus and Luther, Le Goff calls late scholasticism "flamboyant" for its performative aspect. See Le Goff, *Les intellectuels au moyen âge*, 92.

12. Azevedo Alves and Manuel Moreira, *Salamanca School*, 3.

13. B. Hamilton, *Political Thought*, 1–10.

14. See Beltrán de Heredía's introduction to Vitoria, *Comentarios a la Secunda secundae*, xxiv, xxix.

15. Beltrán de Heredía, *Los manuscritos*, 112.

16. Lombard, *Sententiarum libri IV*, bk. 3, dist. 25, chap. 4, in *PL*, vol. 192: "De fide Cornelii."

17. Ibid., chap. 1, in *PL*, vol. 192; Lombard, *Sentences*, vol. 3, 106: "est autem quaedam fidei mensura, sine qua nunquam potuit esse salus . . . fides quippe magna dicitur, cognitione, et articulorum quantitate, vel constantia, et devotione."

18. For a discussion of "implicit" and "explicit" faith, see Boureau, *L'empire du livre*, 89–95. Aquinas treats this issue in *Summa theologica*, II-II, question 2, article 6; Urdáñoz, "La necesidad de la fe explícita para salvarse."

19. Aquinas, *Summa theologica*, II-II, question 2, article 6: "Videtur quod aequaliter omnes teneantur ad habendum fidem explicitam."

20. Ibid. "Revelatio autem divina ordine quodam ad inferiores pervenit per superiores . . . ita etiam superiores homines, ad quos pertinet alios erudire, tenentur habere pleniorem notitiam de credendis et magis explicite credere."

21. Vitoria, *Comentarios a la Secunda secundae*, 66. "Qui nihil audit de fide, potest esse in gratia Dei, et gratia sufficit ad salutem. Sed illam potest ille habere sine fide, id est sine eo quod credat. Ergo fides et credere non est necessarium ad salutem. Antecedens patet. Veniat ille ad usum rationis qui nihil novit nisi per lumen naturale; proponat bene vivere. Jam ille erit in gratia, quia facit totum quod potest ad esse bonum et ad bene vivendum; et tamen non habet fidem, id est non credit. Probo, quia ille nihil cognoscit de articulis fidei. Item, nec potest cognoscere. Ergo credere non est necessarium ad salutem." For an encyclopedic history of debate about the "virtuous pagan," see Vitto, "Virtuous Pagan," 1–49.

22. The passage is located in BUS MS 43, f. 26v: "errore dicere que ad consequendam gloriam non requiritem fides."

23. BUS MS 43, f. 16r. The text is bound and contains a title page explaining Trigo's role in the production of Vitoria's *Scholia Secunda secundae*.

24. Vitoria, *Comentarios a la Secunda secundae*, 66.

25. Ibid., 66: "quod sine fide potest iste venire ad gratium, sed non potest salvari."

26. Aristotle, *Nicomachean Ethics*, 33–37, 395.

27. De Soto, *Quartum Sententiarum*, vol. 1, 126: "cognoscendum de Deo quod est et quod remunerator est."

28. On the further distinctions, see Cano, *Relectio de Sacramentis in genere*, 371–441. Cano's *alumbrados* citation appears in Pastore, *Una herejía española*, 166.

29. Pagden, *Fall of Natural Man*, 107.

30. Cantor, *Verbum abbreviatum*, chap. 1, in *PL*, vol. 205, col. 25A.

31. Le Goff, *Les intellectuels au moyen âge*, 90–92.

32. For introductions to the Valladolid dispute, see Adorno, *Polemics of Possession*, 61–124; Bataillon, *Études sur Bartolomé de Las Casas*; Hanke, *All Mankind Is One*, 57–112; Todorov, *Conquest of America*, 146–67.

33. De Soto's summary was included as a prologue to Las Casas's printed response to several of Sepúlveda's objections to Las Casas initial criticisms presented in the second Valladolid meeting.

Las Casas's argument is outlined in his manuscript *Argumentum apologiae adversus Genesium Sepulvedam theologum cordubensem*, presented in the first meeting at Valladolid and now known as the *Apologia*. I have consulted as well a Spanish translation entitled *Apología, o declaración y defensa universal de los derechos del hombre y de los pueblos*. De Soto's prologue, Sepúlveda's objections, and Las Casas's reply were all published together in a treatise by Las Casas entitled, "Aquí se contiene una disputa o controversía." For the citation from De Soto's prologue, see Las Casas, "Aquí se contiene una disputa," 106: "refirió de palabra las cabezas de sus argumentos"; "fundó ... su sentencia brevemente"; "tanta justicia."

34. De Soto's prologue to Las Casas, *Aquí se contiene una disputa*, 106.

35. Sepúlveda, *Apologia*, 194. Other than the summary of Sepúlveda's objections contained in Las Casas's 1552 treatise, this is the only printed text that approximates Sepúlveda's Valladolid argument. His views, however, were known because *Democrates secundus* circulated widely in the early modern period. It is now available in Spanish as *Demócrates segundo*. However, Sepúlveda's *Apologia* was difficult to acquire, as Las Casas himself noted, because Carlos V ordered all copies in Spain confiscated. See also Hanke, *All Mankind Is One*, 63; Pagden, *Fall of Natural Man*, 109.

36. See Moreno Hérnandez's introduction to Sepúlveda, *Apologia*, cxxxvii–cxxxviii. The published edition of this text is based on BNE MS 5785.

37. Sepúlveda, *Apologia*, 194: "meum librum vel non legerunt, vel lectum propter characteris paulo cultioris insolentiam non intellexerunt" (they have not read my book, or, if they have read it, they have not understood it because they are unaccustomed to reading books even a bit cultured).

38. Las Casas, *Aquí se contiene una disputa*, 133. The reference is from Sepúlveda's second objection, in which he cites various letters of Augustine, including *ad Vincent*, *ad Bonifacium donatistam*, and *ad Donatum*. At stake was not just the Donatist question, however, but the stability of the taxonomy of nonbelievers in general. See Barreda, "*La Apología* en su contexto teológico," lxvi.

39. Las Casas, *Aquí se contiene una disputa*, 156; Mariscal, "Bartolomé de las Casas on Imperial Ethics," 271–72.

40. See De Soto's summary in Las Casas, *Aquí se contiene una disputa*, 110–11: "frívolo y falso."

41. Hanke, *All Mankind Is One*, 18, 22–34, 67–69.

42. Ibid., 61–62.

43. On the Turkish advance and European debate about it, see Bisaha, *Creating East and West*, 135–74; Meserve, *Empires of Islam*, 1–21.

44. Hanke, *All Mankind Is One*, 114. Of the fourteen judges of the dispute, only Doctor Anaya's statement exists. Chapter 1's Gregorio López de Madera, another judge at the meeting, offered some of his opinions in defense of Las Casas's position in his edition of and commentary on Alfonso X's *Siete partidas*.

45. Nederman, *Worlds of Difference*, 99–115.

46. Pagden, *Fall of Natural Man*, 109–18; Mariscal, "Bartolomé de las Casas on Imperial Ethics," 261.

47. Schmitt, *Nomos of the Earth*, 56. For the argument that Schmitt criticizes, see J. S. Brown, *Spanish Origins of International Law*.

48. On Las Casas, Vitoria, and a Whiggish history of human rights, see Beuchot, *Los fundamentos de los derechos humanos*; Urdáñoz, "Las Casas y Francisco de Vitoria," 235–304. On the anthropological element in Las Casas's work, see Mahn-Lot, *Bartolomé de Las Casas et le droit des Indiens*, 180–92; Shuger, *Renaissance Bible*, 81–82. José Rabasa criticizes Pagden's view of Las Casas's anthropological approach in "Utopian Ethnology in Las Casas's Apologética." For prominent examples of the argument that Las Casas prefigured contemporary critiques of Eurocentrism and imperialism, see Dussel, "Núcleo simbólico lascasiano"; Wallerstein, *European Universalism*. For the opposite view that Las Casas engaged in "ecclesiastical imperialism," see Castro, *Another Face of Empire*, 63–104. As the titles imply, Castro's book is also an attack on Ricard, *Spiritual Conquest of Mexico*.

49. Las Casas, *Del único modo*. The text was composed before the Valladolid debate in the 1530s and circulated in manuscript form throughout the latter half of the sixteenth century, but was not published in Las Casas's era. See Gutiérrez, *En busca de los pobres de Jesucristo*, 219–74; No, "Teaching De unico vocationis modo," 124–31.

50. Las Casas elsewhere invoked Islam and its founder as an example of violent conquest mimicked by Christian conquistadors. See Las Casas, *Historia de las Indias*, bk. 3, chap. 115; Las Casas, "Memorial de los remedios," 121; Pagden, "Ius et Factum," 94.

51. In his editor's notes, Millares Carlos argues that Las Casas's source text for this dialogue is Alfonso de Spina's *Fortalitium fidei*, which in turn employs Beauvais's *Speculum historiale*. For more on this dialogue and Peter the Venerable, see Castro, "Disputa entre un cristiano y un judío." On evangelization and the danger of mimesis, see Las Casas, *Del único modo*, 460: "Quicumque enim voluit inducere homines ad veritatem sive ad mendacium, no potuit hoc facere sine aliqua vel saltem verisimili praedicatione" (all who have wanted to induce others to truth or falsehood could not accomplish this but by, at the very least, a verisimilar predication).

52. Las Casas, *Del único modo*, 94–95: "consuetudo est habitus ex ipsa generatur habitus ex frequentatis actibus acquisitis, qui non est natura, sed est quasi natura, quia quasi ita faciles, promptas et expeditas facit consuetudo operationes consuetas, ac si essent illae operationes a natura principiatae." Klor de Alva, "Colonizing Souls," 3–23.

53. Acosta, *De procuranda indorum salute*, vol. 2, 24–25: "Præsente tantum sacerdote christianos se simulent, clanculum ubi datur facultas, avitas superstitiones studiosissime obeant." See also Pagden, *Fall of Natural Man*, 149; Walter Mignolo's introduction to Acosta, *Natural and Moral History of the Indies*, xxi.

54. Ivonne Del Valle sees in Acosta's text this sharp tension between "being and doing." See Del Valle, "Jesuit Baroque," 151; Mateos, "Personalidad y escritos del P. José de Acosta," xxiii–xxiv.

55. Acosta, *De procuranda indorum salute*, vol. 2, 24–25. In his notes, Luciano Pereña suggests that Acosta is referring to a letter that Bartolomé Hernández, the rector of the Colegio de Lima, wrote to Juan de Ovando, the president of the Consejo de Indias, in which he remarks that the New World Indians, like the "Moors of Granada," are only "Christian in name and exterior ceremony, while on the interior they have no concept of the things of our faith" (como los moros de Granada . . . tel nombre de christiano y las cerimonias exteriors, y interiormente no tiene concepto de las cosas de nuestra fe).

56. Ibid., 216: "nihil aliud est quam cum ratione insanire." In his biography of Acosta, Burgaleta points out that Acosta shunned the scholastic forms like the *questio* and commentary, preferring a more eclectic, humanist method, which Burgaleta calls "Jesuit theological humanism." See Burgaleta, *José de Acosta*, 73–116.

57. Acosta, *De procuranda indorum salute*, vol. 2, 200–202, 204: "sine cuius misterii fide iustificari neminem et olim Beatus Thomas et nuper sancta sinodus Tridentina decrevit."

58. Acosta, *De procuranda indorum salute*, vol. 2, 216: "Nam si quis Aeneida aut Odisseam tenere sese diceret, neque tamen Aeneum aut Ulissem unquam audisset, quis obsecro risum tenere posset?" For more on Acosta's relationship with Salamanca scholasticism, see Lopetegu, "Notas sobre la actividad teológica"; Coelle de la Rosa, "Más allá del Incario."

59. Azevedo Alves and Manuel Moreira, *Salamanca School*, 10; Pagden, *Fall of Natural Man*, 147.

CHAPTER THREE

1. Pérez de Ayala, *Catechismo para instrvccion*, 2–3: "Dime la verdad, si lo desseas de coraçon . . . Porque la religion Christiana, como sea cosa tan sancta y tan perfecta, y venir a ella sea venir a Dios; quiere el coraçon del que ella se allega senzillo, sin doblez, ni fiction alguna; y no sufre que

haya uno en el coraçon, y otro en la lengua, y en las obras de fuera." Ehlers, *Between Christians and Moriscos*, 19–20.

2. Ehlers, *Between Christians and Moriscos*, 119–25; García-Arenal, "Religious Identity," 506. On the question of dubious authorship and the possible influence of the Valencian anti-Muslim polemical tradition on the *Catechismo*, see García Cárcel, "Estudio crítico del catecismo Ribera-Ayala."

3. Pastore, *Una herejía española*, 43–71; Rummel, *Jiménez de Cisneros*, 58–59; García de Oro, *El Cardenal Cisneros*, 492–501; Homza, *Religious Authority*, 1–48, 77–112. On comparative Semitic philology, see Olender, *Languages of Paradise*, 16–17; Dubois, *Mythe et langage*, 27–51.

4. Bataillon, *Erasmo y España*, 10–43; Fernández Marcos, *Filología bíblica y humanismo*, 245–60.

5. Monroe, *Islam and the Arabs*, 1–20.

6. García-Arenal and Rodríguez Mediano, *Un Oriente español*, 381. For a recent summary of parallel debates in northern Europe, see Stroumsa, *New Science*, 124–44.

7. Sigüenza, *Historia de la Orden*, 305: "Era de ver vn Arçobispo varon y anciano, en tantas cosas ocupado yr à lecion, y aprender los nominatiuos y conjugaciones Arabigas, solo por aprouechar à aquellas almas." On Montano and Sigüenza, see Rekers, *Benito Arias Montano*, 109–13.

8. Alcalá's two texts have been published together as *Arte para ligeramente saber la lengua arauiga*; García-Arenal, "Religious Identity," 502; Drost, "El Arte de Pedro de Alcalá," 57–69.

9. Sigüenza, *Historia de la Orden*, 305: "el dezia muchas vezes que diera vn ojo de su cara de buena gana por saber bien esta lengua." See also García-Arenal, "Religious Identity," 500; Giménez-Eguibar and Wasserman Soler, "La Mala Algaraba."

10. Liere, "After Nebrija," 1006; Rico, *Nebrija frente a los bárbaros*, 39–42.

11. Nebrija, *Gramática de la lengua castellana*; Rojinksy, *Companion to Empire*, 94–136; Álvar, *Nebrija y estudios sobre la edad de oro*, 14.

12. Valdés, *Diálogo de la lengua*, 66; Bahner, *La linguística española*, 69.

13. Bataillon, *Erasmo y España*, 509–15; Firpo, *Entre alumbrados y "espirituales,"* 67–124; Pastore, *Una herejía española*, 257–80.

14. Valdés, *Diálogo de la lengua*, 43: "porque he aprendido la lengua latina por arte y libros, y la castellana por uso, de manera que de la latina podría dar cuenta por el arte y por los libros en que la aprendí, y de la castellana no, sino por el uso común de hablar."

15. Mignolo, *Darker Side of the Renaissance*, 29–67.

16. Pérez de Ayala, "Discurso de la vida," 213. Pérez de Ayala lamented the "grosería del bárbaro modo del enseñar que en España tenían de tomar mucho de memoria del arte de Nebrija, que fatigaban mucho los ingenios de los niños, de tal manera que hacía odiosa la sciencia ó doctrina, con gran perjuicio, y aun ahora lo usan, aunque no tanto" (ugliness of the barbarian method of teaching in Spain, which consisted primarily of memorizing Nebrija's *Arte*, which greatly tired the minds of the children, such that science and teaching became odious, doing great damage; and they still use it, though not so much). On the ill effects of Nebrija's approach combined with decades of poor teachers, see Fernández, *Panorama social del humanismo español*, 98–116. The poet and satirist Francisco de Quevedo took up this portrayal of Nebrija with satirical glee in the next century, ridiculing his contemporary Luis de Góngora's *cultista* poetry as "so airy in hyperboles and so Nebrija-like in words" (tan airosa de hipérboles y tan nebrijense de palabras). See Quevedo's short satire, "La culta latiniparla," or "The Latin-speaking sect," in Quevedo, *Obras completas en prosa*, 97.

17. Pérez de Ayala, "Discurso de la vida," 220: "Yo creía su Majestad había tenido respecto en aquel nombramiento á que yo era predicador, y que sabía la lengua y costumbres de los moriscos, desengañando á Su Majestad si lo estaba, porque yo no acostumbraba á predicar, y aunque había estado en Granada no sabía nada de la lengua ni costumbres de moriscos" (I believed that Your Majesty had considered in that appointment that I was a preacher, and that I knew the languages and customs of the Moriscos, but if that were the case, Your Majesty must be disillusioned, because I was not accustomed to preaching, and although I had been in Granada, I did not know the language or the customs of the Moriscos).

18. Pérez de Ayala, *Sínodo de la diócesis*; Giménez-Eguibar and Wasserman Soler, "La Mala Algaraba," 239; Szpiech, "Preaching Paul to the Moriscos."

19. Pérez de Ayala, *Doctrina Christiana*; García-Arenal, "Religious Identity," 505; Burman, *Reading the Qur'ān*, 60–87.

20. Álvar, *Nebrija y estudios sobre la edad de oro*, 14–85; Ricard, "Remarques sur l'Arte et le Vocabulista."

21. Pérez de Ayala, *Doctrina Christiana*, f. 22v: "se forma en la misma garganta, como quien gariza, o arranca flemas del pecho. Desta mesmia manera pronuncian los Hebreos su chet, y quasi los Griego su chi."

22. Ibid., ff. 23r–v: "Y aun que su pronunciacion se forma en la garganta, pero no es aspera como el ha, sino blandamente retumba en la garganta, y parece que tiene un tantico del sonido de la g. En fin para bien pronunciar, has menester oyr la a un Aravigo natural."

23. Pezzi Martínez, "El problema de la confesión de moriscos."

24. Pérez de Ayala, *Doctrina Christiana*, f. 21v: "Lo de mas de la doctrina, andando el tiempo lo sabran."

25. El Alaoui, *Jésuites, morisques et indiens*, 383. "Por decir Jesús, dizen Chichigi que quiere dezir gallinas y cuando en Valencia oyen dezir Señor ver Deu, que es Señor verdadero Dios, nombrando al sacramento de la eucharistía, se mofan con risa porque en su lengua, verdeu es el rocín o mulo y como por dezir sanctificado sea tu nombre dizen sancto peccado tú hombre, y por dezir verná a juzgar los vivos y los muertos, dizen verná a jugar los huevos y los güertos como otros muy peores, y si los reprehenden se escusan con que ni saben ni entienden lo que se dizen y hazen."

26. Aznar Cardona, *Expvlsion ivstificada*, part 2, f. 12v: "escandalos de lengua"

27. El Alaoui, *Jésuites, morisques et indiens*, 594: "No podré darme a entender facilmente con nuestra lengua si no es así. Esta palabra pan sabemos lo que es pues si oyésemos dezir a un forastero dame pen luego lo entederíamos y aunque dixese dame pin o dame pon o pun; lo mesmo es dame vin, ven o ven, etc." See also Vincent, "Reflexión documentada sobre el uso del árabe y de las lenguas románicas en la España de los Moriscos (ss. XVI–XVII)," in *El río morisco*, 111–12. On *conversos* and the Jesuits, see Maryks, *Jesuit Order*, 41–115.

28. El Alaoui, *Jésuites, morisques et indiens*, 594: "parecerá que la gramática es ociosa."

29. García-Arenal and Rodríguez Mediano, *Un Oriente español*, 343; *Diccionario histórico*, vol. 3, 2769.

30. In subsequent years, Eliano also translated part of the decrees of the Council of Trent into Arabic, produced a manuscript Arabic grammar and dictionary, and oversaw work on a set of Arabic stamps for printing. See the *Diccionario histórico*, vol. 1, 807, and vol. 3, 2360; Frazee, *Catholics and Sultans*, 137–38.

31. Kagan, *Students and Society*, 50–61; Schwickerath, *Jesuit Education*, 107–88.

32. See the Latin-English bilingual version of Ladislaus Lukác's critical edition in *Ratio Studiorum*, 61: "Dum sacros libros interpretatur, non tam in rebus ac sententiis expendendis laboret, quam in vi ac potestate verborum, ac propriis eius linguae idiotismis, et in grammaticae praeceptis iuxta germanum auctorum usum observandis."

33. On the series of editions and revisions (new editions of the *Ratio* appeared in 1586, 1591, 1599), see Farrell, *Jesuit Code*, 219–401.

34. BUS MS 169, f. 107v: "en la primitiva iglesia disimulaban y permitian los sagrados Apostoles muchas ceremonias Judaicas y gentilicas por no apartar de la ley de Christo a los Gentiles y Paganos." For an introduction to this "Chinese Rites Controversy," as these debates were called, see Standert, "Jesuits in China"; Buc, *Dangers of Ritual*, 159–202.

35. BUS MS 169, f. 57r. Roboredo specifically refers to the Jesuits' decision to emphasize a vision of "Christ in Glory" rather than "Christ in agony," hoping not to alarm potential or new converts.

36. *Ratio Studiorum*, 64: "Ubi enim nec fidei doctrina nec morum integritas in discrimen adducitur, prudens caritas exigit, ut nostri se illis accommodent, cum quibus versantur." For Roboredo's

formulation, see BUS MS 170, f. 182r: "acomodarse a las cortesias, ceremonias, y modo politico." See also Liu, "Intricacies of Accommodation"; Mungello, *Curious Land*, 13–73; O'Malley, *First Jesuits*, 342.

37. Blaise Pascal's attack on the empty ceremoniousness of the Jesuits is perhaps the best-known criticism. See Pascal, *Les lettres provinciales*, 44, 109.

38. Cited and translated in Maman, *Comparative Semitic Philology*, 13: "l'barīm ketzofīm v'rosh l'chanefīm." See also Wechter, *Ibn Barūn's Arabic Works on Hebrew*, 5; Ibn Ezra, *Maḥberet mishire*, 17.

39. Wechter, *Ibn Barūn's Arabic Works on Hebrew*, 15.

40. On David Kimhi, see Talmage, *David Kimhi*. Pedro de Palencia's 1611 treatise in defense of rabbinic commentary has recently been edited as Palencia, *Glosas rabínicas*. In addition to works by Kimhi and Münster, the *Index* permitted commentaries and translations by the Hebraists John Buxtorsius, Mordecai Nathan, and Elia Levita, as well as early medieval scholars on biblical pronunciation and grammar known as Massoretes. See Jiménez Monteserín, *Introducción a la inquisición española*, 594–95; Raz-Krakotzkin, *Censor, the Editor, and the Text*, 95–119.

41. E. Nelson, *Hebrew Republic*; Stroumsa, *New Science*, 39–61.

42. Dannenfeldt, "Renaissance Humanists," 96–100.

43. Clénard, *Correspondance*, 113–15; Bataillon, "L'Arabe à Salamanque."

44. On the history and effects of censorship, see Kamen, *Spanish Inquisition*, 108–31. In addition to Alcalá's and Postel's crude Arabic type, previous Arabic printing attempts included two polyglot texts, the prayer book of Fano, published for the Egyptian Jacobites in 1514, and the Genoa Psalter, produced by the Genoese Dominican Agostino Giustiniani in 1516. See Wilkinson, *Kabbalistic Scholars*, 2–3.

45. López Baralt and Iversen, *A zaga de tu huella*, 19–38.

46. Ibid., 39–60. See the "Gramatica enla Jorrumia" in BNE MS 7887. See also BNE MSS 8432 and 8434, both of which contain notes, scribbles, verb charts, word lists, and translations along with versions of the *Al-jurumiyya*.

47. Bataillon, *Erasmo y España*, 739.

48. Rekers, *Benito Arias Montano*, 45–69; Wilkinson, *Kabbalistic Scholars*, 49–92. For more on the Plantin Press, see the encyclopedic Voet, *Golden Compass*.

49. The word *talmīd* does not to my knowledge exist in Arabic. The corresponding Arabic word is the Hebrew loanword *talmīḍ*, or "disciple" (note the distinct final letters). Perhaps Montano is not just underscoring his Hebraist use of Arabic script, but also executing a Judeo-Arabic trick of the second order. See Dunkelgrün, "Multiplicity of Scripture," 211.

50. Bataillon, *Erasmo y España*, 739. Montano's interest in arcane readings in *Liber Ioseph sive de arcano sermone* and *Liber Ieremiae sive de actione* stirred particular controversy. See Fernández Marcos, *Filología bíblica y humanismo*, 283–303.

51. Macías Rosendo, *La Correspondencia*, 152, 175.

52. Ibid., 175n23; Rekers, *Benito Arias Montano*, 49–50.

53. *El proceso inquisitorial*, 376: "al cavo del dicho librico estan dos renglones escriptos en griego, y renglon y medio en aravigo."

54. A multilingual and multiscriptural text in the upper margin of one of Julius Conradus Otto's letters to the famous classicist and philologist Isaac Casaubon is reprinted in Grafton and Weinberg, *"I have always loved the holy tongue,"* 236–39. See as well A. Hamilton's appendix to the same text, "Long Apprenticeship," 293–306.

55. See Becerra Hiraldo's introduction to Luis de León, *El Cantar de los Cantares*, 14–20.

56. Ibid., 130.

57. RAH 20/994: Luis de León, *Et Diuinorum librorum primi*, 127: "Arabice Açucena."

58. Wehr, *Dictionary of Modern Written Arabic*, 515. Two variant pronunciations (*sūsān* and *sūsan*) appear in Hava's classical Arabic dictionary, *Al-farā'id al-durīyya*, 344. In his dictionary

of Andalusian Arabic, Federico Corriente includes three other possible pronunciations, none of which coincides with the "açucena" of Francisco Sánchez's note. See Corriente, *Dictionary of Andalusi Arabic*, 267.

59. Sánchez de las Brozas, *Minerva*, bk. 1, chap. 2, http://www.hathitrust.org/. I have also consulted Sánchez Salor and Chaparro Gómez's Spanish translation and Latin edition at http://iessapostol.juntaextremadura.net/latin/minerva/I_2es.html. When the chapter numbers of the Spanish text do not align with the Latin version at Hathi Digital Trust, I follow the latter.

60. Palencia, *Glosas rabínicas*, 100: "Hazen lo mismo aora los sabios rabinos solamente por este proverbio: leshon ha-qodesh mebulal, que quiere decir revuelto y mezclado con vocablos de otras lenguas."

61. Sánchez de las Brozas, *Minerva*, bk. 4, chap. 1: "Ellipsis est defectus dictionis vel dictionum ad legitimam constructionem; ut, *Paucis te volo*." For an excellent introduction to Francisco Sánchez's innovations, see Breva-Claramonte, *Sanctius's Theory of Language*, 7–81.

62. Sánchez de las Brozas, *Minerva*, bk. 4, chap. 4: "Fidem. Ter. Phorm. *Prô Deûm immortalium*. Ubi Donatus ellipsis esse, et *fidem*, vel simile aliquid, desiderari ait. Cicero in Œconomico, *Quid igitur, Prô Deûm immortalium, primum eam ducebas quæso?* Terent. *Prô Deûm immortalium, hominum fidem*." As far as I can tell, Sánchez Salor and Chaparro Gómez have not included the alphabetical list of absent words in their online edition.

63. Chomsky, *Cartesian Linguistics*, 78–92; Chomsky, *Language and Mind*, 16; Lancelot and Arnauld, *Grammaire générale et raisonnée*; Tsiapera and Wheeler, *Port-Royal Grammar*, 60–63. On Chomsky, his descriptivist predecessors, and his later critics, see R. Harris, *Linguistics Wars*, 100–134, 160–97.

CHAPTER FOUR

1. The Sacromonte bibliography is vast, but places to start include Alonso, *Los apócrifos del Sacromonte*; Kendrick, *St. James in Spain*, 69–115; A. K. Harris, *From Muslim to Christian Granada*. Hagerty published an early modern Spanish translation of the texts in his *Los libros plúmbeos*. See also recent research cited below and collected in two volumes edited by García-Arenal and Barrios Aguilera: *Los plomos des Sacromonte* and *¿La historia inventada?*

2. A. Katie Harris and others have suggested that this Turpiana manuscript was an experiment by the Sacromonte forgers to gauge possible reactions to the much larger project of the lead books themselves. See A. K. Harris, "Forging History," 947; Koningsveld and Wiegers, "Parchment"; Cabanelas Rodríguez, *El morisco granadino*, 244–48.

3. Stratton, *Immaculate Conception*, 35–87.

4. García-Arenal, "El entorno de los plomos"; Cabanelas Rodríguez, *El morisco granadino*, 251–53. On the changes in Oriental studies wrought by the Sacromonte debates, see García-Arenal and Rodríguez Mediano, *Un Oriente español*, 229–307.

5. On the forgery problem and for an extended citation of the papal rejection, see Godoy Alcántara, *Historia crítica*, 44–128, 126–27: "puras ficciones humanas, fabricadas para ruina de la fe católica." Caro Baroja, *Las falsificaciones*, 115–43.

6. BNE MS 6437 contains miscellaneous arguments that the lead books should remain in Granada. For dates of the books' transfer to Rome, see Hagerty, *Los libros plúmbeos*, 46.

7. Eden, *Poetic and Legal Fiction*, 119–21. Eden outlines Augustine's taxonomy of narrative trickery in his *Soliloquies*, which distinguished between "fallacious" (*fallax*) texts whose end was deception itself and "fabulous" (*mendax*) narrative whose deception was intended by authors as entertainment. Scripture was the stable counterweight to these kinds of worrisome writing. On a similar problem in Tasso, see Fuchs, *Mimesis and Empire*, 22–34; and on Cervantes and the relationship between history and fable, see Fuchs, "Don Quijote 1," 396–98.

8. Ife, *Reading and Fiction*, 24–48; Nelson, *Fact or Fiction*, 92–115; Ferguson, *Trials of Desire*, 1–17.

9. BNE MS 7187, f. 119v, Pedro de Valencia, "Carta al Inquisidor general D. Bernardo de Sandoval y Rojas sobre el pergamino y láminas de Granada" (early seventeenth-century copy): "ficciones de libros hechos por erejes y de otros engaños con que se fingen y venden." On the dating of Valencia's letter, see Magnier, "Dating." Magnier has also edited the text as Valencia, *Sobre el pergamino*.

10. Luna's Latin and Spanish translations are at the AASG, the BNE, and the ABFZ. ABFZ Altamira, 161, GD.5, D.117 is unique for its early date and royal audience. Copies or summaries of Pectorano's interlineal translation are at the British Library, the Biblioteca Universitaria de Salamanca, and the RAH. *Sol veritatis* is RAH MS 9/7088. As points of reference, I have consulted other Arabic transcriptions of the corpus, such as RAH MSS 11/9009 and 11/9010 (Luna and Castillo) and AFG MS 149 (Luna and Diego de Urrea). But here I cite from Pectorano's Arabic text. When citing other authors' transliterations I usually leave unchanged their diacritical notation, but I have slightly modified Hagerty's versions of the lead books' Arabic titles, whose spellings diverge from modern standard usage.

11. Márquez Villanueva, *El problema morisco*, 45–98; Fuchs, *Mimesis and Empire*, 111–13. The first and second parts of Luna's *La verdadera historia* appeared in 1592 and 1600, respectively. I cite from a facsimile of the combined edition of 1606.

12. Caro Baroja, *Las falsificaciones*, 140.

13. In addition to Pectorano's RAH *Sol veritatis*, there is another manuscript of similar size, color, and binding, also entitled *Sol veritatis*, in the AASG. This is a commentary and defense of the lead books without the interlineal transcription and translation of the RAH version.

14. Luna did not totally avoid suspicion. On his inquisition case, see Godoy Alcántara, *Historia crítica*, 104–15. The continuing importance of manuscript culture in the print age has been a topic of fruitful inquiry for Fernando Bouza Álvarez, Roger Chartier, D. F. McKenzie, and others, but the Sacromonte episode highlights the possibility that other writing surfaces might still have a place and a power. See in particular Bouza Álvarez, *Corre manuscrito*, 15–84. On the special problem of translation from Arabic in Christian circles, see Burman, *Reading the Qur'ān*, 12–35.

15. ABFZ Altamira, 161, GD.5, D. 133, Miguel de Luna to Felipe II, March 14, 1595.

16. Centurión also wrote an apologetic history of the Sacromonte episode: *Informacion para la historia del Sacro Monte*. On the other translators, see Harvey and Wiegers, "Translation from Arabic"; Rodríguez Mediano and García-Arenal, "De Diego de Urrea a Marcos Dobelio," 297–333.

17. ABFZ Altamira, 161, GD.5, D.117, f. 1: "palabra por palabra, uerbum ex uerbo fielmente."

18. Ibid., f. 5. Subtly emphasizing the first-person narrative voice, Luna added the word *quiero*, although the Arabic equivalent is absent at least from Pectorano's Arabic edition of the text. Also, Pectorano writes in Arabic *muthalātha* rather than *muthālatha*, and *tawhid* rather than *tawhīd*, two examples either of divergent early modern spellings or of copyist error. These words had, unsurprisingly, often been contentious. The Morisco Aḥmad Ibn Qāsim al-Ḥajarī noticed that previous readers of the Turpiana manuscript had seen a "venerable threefold essence" (*al-dhāt al-karīma al-muthallatha*) where in fact the word *threefold* was absent. See Ibn Qāsim al-Ḥajarī, *Kitāb nāṣir al-dīn*, 77 (English, with Arabic transliteration variant), 21 (Arabic); Bernabé Pons, "Los mecanismos," 392.

19. ABFZ Altamira, 161, GD.5, D.117, f. 5: "la diccion arabiga 'mutalata' id est trina y esta adiectiva da como en el arabe."

20. RAH MS 9/7088, 6.

21. Ibid., 880.

22. ABFZ Altamira, 161, GD.5, D.117, ff. 5–6: "el padre primera persona: el hijo la persona segunda: y el spiritu sancto terçera persona: tres personas: en essencia una y assi Maria fue el espejo."

23. Stevens-Arroyo, "Evolution of Marian Devotionalism"; W. B. Taylor, "Virgin of Guadalupe," 11.

24. Pereda, *Las imágenes de la discordia*, 249–373. See also Cervantes Augustiniano's *Parecer de S. Augustin en favor de la concepcion purissima*, a defense of the Immaculate Conception and celebration of both Saint Cecilius and the Mary of the lead books; it is also dedicated to Archbishop Pedro de Castro. See in addition Christodouleas and Matar, "Mary of Sacromonte."

25. RAH MS 9/7088, 262. The Arabic original in Pectorano's interlineal translation reads, "mujtamiʿ al-kibār," which literally translates as a "huge assemblage."

26. Hagerty, *Los libros plúmbeos*, 131, 133, 134.

27. Ibid., 156: "se multiplicare el modo de hablar con metáforas y el fisgar."

28. I consulted Gerónimo de la Cruz's text in a bound compilation of printed and manuscript material catalogued in the BNE as R/24033. See *Sacrarum virginum vindicatio*, f. 9r: "las mismas contradiciones que oy padecen los plomos, padecio y mayores la Religion Catolica, quando se descubrio al mundo." It is also worth noting in this regard that in the varied Sacromonte archival materials, active readers often underlined the sections of the text that defended the Immaculate Conception of the Virgin Mary. They were looking for evidence.

29. BNE MS 10503, f. 9v. On December 8, the annual feast of the Immaculate Conception, hundreds of worshipers participate in a holy parade, visit the Sacromonte caves, and gather in the abbey for mass. According to the abbey's official tour, the institution's raison d'être is tied to the relics, not the lead books, which the Vatican held inaccessible from the middle of the seventeenth century until 2000, when Pope John Paul II returned them to Granada. For more on the abbey and the lead books' return, see Sánchez Ocaña, *El Sacro Monte*, 153–277.

30. ABFZ Altamira, 161, GD.5, D.117, f. 5: "Nadie entiende a Dios sino Dios: y si entendieramos a Dios: no seria Dios: por que el hombre su entendimiento es flaco."

31. BNE MS 6637, ff. 169–211. This manuscript is an anonymous printed defense of the lead books from the early seventeenth century. See also Bernabé Pons, "Los mecanismos," 390.

32. Bernabé Pons, "Los mecanismos," 393. On a parallel set of abbreviations, see Sánchez-Blanco, "De Pablo a Saulo," 142–48.

33. ABFZ Altamira, 161, GD.5, D.117, f. 13: "no ay otro Dios sino Dios."

34. Ibid.: "el arabe dice 'gua rabune alah,' que quiere decir y nuestro criador dios i 'gue' es copulativa y 'rabune' es nombre quiere decir criador compuesto con pronombre plural 'ne' criador nuestro 'alah' dios que quiere decir y criador nuestro dios."

35. Hagerty, *Los libros plúmbeos*, 77. Hagerty bases his edition of Centurión's text on various AASG manuscripts and BNE MSS 205 and 10503, probably produced in the 1620s.

36. RAH MS 9/7088, f. 24.

37. The Latin Vulgate reads, "Itaque linguae in signum sunt non fidelibus sed infidelibus; prophetia autem non infidelibus sed fidelibus." See *Bibliorum sacrorum iuxta vulgatam clementinam*, 1078. For the English, I have consulted the Douay-Rheims translation of the Vulgate Bible, as well as the Revised Standard Version.

38. On Sacromonte "syncretism," see Hagerty, "Los apócrifos granadinos"; Bernabé Pons, "Los libros plúmbeos"; Bernabé Pons, "Los mecanismos," 385–402; Roisse, "La historia del sello"; Cabanelas Rodríguez, "Intento de supervivencia."

39. Gumbrecht, *Powers of Philology*, 29.

40. Ibid., 47; Nichols, "Introduction: Philology in a Manuscript Culture."

41. López de Madera, *Historia y discvrsos*, ff. 10v–13v. For more on the several editions of López de Madera's text, see Binotti, *La teoría del "Castellano Primitivo,"* 39.

42. On scholarship and forgery, see Grafton, *Forgers and Critics*, 3–35; Lerer, *Error and the Academic Self*, 1–14.

43. BNE 7187. Benito Arias Montano to Don Pedro de Castro y Quiñones, 1595: "Ne contra pro incertis habeamus ipse temere assentiamur."

44. López de Madera, *Historia y discvrsos*, f. 23r: "porque quien en ellos lo fingiera, buscara lo mas verosimil."

45. Ibid., f. 23r: "mas facilmente persuadirlo a imitacion."

46. Ife, *Reading and Fiction*, 33–36.

47. On the relationship between aesthetics and subject formation in early modern Spain, see Cascardi, *Ideologies of History*, 105–31; Gilman, "Introduction"; Maravall, *La cultura del Barroco*, 131–75.

48. López de Madera, *Historia y discvrsos*, ff. 32v–33v.

49. Ibid., ff. 116r, 117r.

50. Ibid., f. 62r.

51. Beaver, "From Jerusalem to Toledo," 86–87.

52. Aldrete, *Del origen y principio*, bk. 2, chap. 1. For an introduction to Aldrete and philology in the Spanish Golden Age, see Bahner, *La linguística española*, 124–43. On Aldrete and the Sacromonte episode specifically, see Woolard, "Bernardo de Aldrete."

53. Aldrete, *Varias antiguedades*, 269–71.

54. Droixhe, *La linguistique*, 100.

55. Mignolo, *Darker Side of the Renaissance*, 29–67.

56. Cueva, *Dialagos de las cosas notables*, ff. A3–B4; Bermúdez de Pedraza, *Antigvedad y excelencias de Granada*, 156–66. See also Nieto Jiménez, "La lengua primitiva," 139–48; Binotti, *La teoría del "Castellano Primitivo,"* 77–93.

CHAPTER FIVE

1. Godoy Alcántara, *Historia crítica*, 8–43; Caro Baroja, *Las falsificaciones*, 163–87; Olds, "'False Chronicles,'" 1–10.

2. Selections of Luis de Mármol Carvajal's letters on the lead books, discussed in greater length below, have been published in Cabaneles Rodríguez, *El morisco granadino*, 250–56.

3. BNE MS 1603. This 353-folio volume is a mixture of late sixteenth- and seventeenth-century copies, parts of which correspond exactly to the 1627 first published edition of *Guerra de Granada*. See Foulché-Delbosc, "Étude sur la Guerra de Granada."

4. BNE MS 1603, f. 147r: "se vera sera verdadero."

5. Domínguez Ortíz and Vincent, *Historia de los moriscos*, 35–56; Caro Baroja, *Los moriscos*, 149–203.

6. Mármol Carvajal, *Historia del rebelión*. See also Sánchez Ramos, "El mejor cronista," 245–47.

7. Some scholars believe that the *princeps* edition of the second volume of *Guerras civiles de Granada* was published earlier, in 1604 or 1610, though Carrasco Urgoiti makes a compelling case for the 1619 date. See Carrasco Urgoiti, *Moorish Novel*, 84–86. On the publishing history of part 1, see Blanchard-Demouge's introduction to Pérez de Hita, *Historia de los bandos*, xcvii–xcviii; References to both volumes of the text itself are from Pérez de Hita, *Guerras civiles de Granada*.

8. Hurtado de Mendoza, *Guerra de Granada*, 91–94. For more on the manuscripts and publishing history of *Guerra de Granada*, see González Palencia and Mele, *Vida y obras*, vol. 3, 192–97.

9. Kimmel, "Local Turks," 24–30. On the production and reception of early Morisco historiography, see Bunes Ibarra, *Los moriscos*, 9–55; Márquez Villanueva, "El problema historiográfico."

10. Cabrera de Córdoba, *De historia*, f. 45r: "material nueva." See also Montero Díaz, "La doctrina de la historia"; Cepeda Adán, "El barroco español"; Mignolo, "El metatexto historiográfico"; Kelley, "Humanism and History," 256.

11. Cabrera de Córdoba, *De historia*, f. 47r: "El escriuir las cosas de su tiempo tiene peligro y dificultad, por la irritacion de los animos, que lleua aqui, y alli el amor de los suyos, el odio de los enemigos, de quien nacen las perturbaciones, que son ciegas, y se fingen para impedir el juizio recto, y no ver lo que conuiene, y lo que es honesto, por mas que guarde igualdad, y neutralidad" (To write about the events of one's own time is dangerous and difficult on account both of the irritation of minds here and of the love of one's own there, as well as the hatred of enemies, from

which disturbances are born. These disturbances are blind, and they deceive in order to impede right judgment, and obscure what is needed and honest, rather than guard equality and neutrality).

12. Ibid., f. 45r. Cabrera de Córdoba cites the Italian mathematician and historian Girolamo Cardano, who disagreed with Pausanias: "Quicum viro Principe familiariter viuis, neceβe est ad fauorem eius scripta accommodare" (Whoever is intimate with the prince finds it necessary to accommodate his writing to his favor).

13. Kagan, *Clio and the Crown*, 1–15. On Hurtado de Mendoza's critical approach, see Márquez Villanueva, "El problema historiográfico," 120; Varo Zafra, *Don Diego Hurtado de Mendoza*, 69–126.

14. Hurtado de Mendoza, *Guerra de Granada*, 95–96: "Mi propósito es escribir la guerra que el rey católico de España don Filipe el Segundo, hijo del nunca vencido emperador don Cárlos, tuvo en el reino de Granada contra los rebeldes nuevamente convertidos . . . Bien sé que muchas cosas de las que escribiere parecerán a algunos livianas y menudas para historia, comparadas a las grandes que de España se hallan escritas: guerras largas de varios sucesos, tomas y desolaciones de ciudades populosas, reyes vencidos y presos, discordias entre padres y hijos, hermanos y hermanas, suegros y yernos, desposeídos, restituidos, y otra vez desposeídos, muertos a hierro; acabados linajes, mudadas sucesiones de reinos: libre y extendido campo, y ancha salida para los escriptores. Yo escogí camino más estrecho, trabajoso, estéril y sin gloria, pero provechoso y de fructo para los que adelante vinieren: comienzos bajos, rebelión de salteadores, junta de esclavos, tumulto de villanos, competencias, odios, ambiciones y pretensiones; dilación de provisiones, falta de dinero, inconvenientes o no creídos o tenidos en poco; remisión y flojedad en ánimos acostumbrados a entender, proveer y disimular mayores cosas; y así, no será cuidado perdido considerar de cuán livianos principios y causas particulares se viene a colmo de grandes trabajos dificultades y daños públicos y cuasi fuera de remedio." See also Darst, "El pensamiento histórico," 288; Williams, "Beyond the Limits of Genre," 81–82.

15. Fox Morcillo, *De historiae institutione dialogus*, recently translated as *Diálogo sobre enseñanza de la historia*; Páez de Castro, *De las cosas*; Cuart Moner, "La larga marcha."

16. Though the friend in this case is anonymous, Hurtado de Mendoza apparently did not shy away from directly exchanging his text with the eminent scholars of his day, such as the Aragonese historian and author of *Anales de la Corona de Aragón*, Jerónimo Zurita. See Darst, "El pensamiento histórico," 262.

17. Seneca, *Epistulae morales*, 210–11 (letter 79 to Lucius): "Nulla virtus latet, et latuisse non ipsius est damnum: veniet qui conditam et saeculi sui malignitate conpressam dies publicet. Paucis natus est qui populum aetatis suae cogitat. Multa annorum milia, multa populorum supervenient: ad illa respice" (Virtue is never lost to view; and yet to have been lost to view is no loss. There will come a day which will reveal her, though hidden away or suppressed by the spite of her contemporaries. That man is born merely for a few, who thinks only of the people of his own generation. Many thousands of years and many thousands of peoples will come after you; it is to these that you should have regard).

18. González Palencia and Mele, *Vida y obras*, vol. 3, 362–84.

19. Kagan, *Clio and the Crown*, 63–68, 94–123; Ostenfeld-Suske, "Writing Official History," 439–41.

20. Ditchfield, "What Was Sacred History?"; Liere, "Renaissance Chroniclers."

21. Cirot, *Mariana historien*.

22. Páez de Castro, *De las cosas*: "Escribir historia no es cosa tan fácil y ligera como la gente piensa." See also Ostenfeld-Suske, "Writing Official History," 442.

23. Hurtado de Mendoza, *Guerra de Granada*, 96: "Victoria dudosa y de sucesos tan peligrosos, que alguna vez se tuvo duda si éramos nosotros o los enemigos los a quien Dios quería castigar; hasta que el fin della descubrió que nosotros éramos los amenazados, y ellos los castigados."

24. Hurtado de Mendoza, "Carta al capitán Salazar." Hurtado de Mendozo's name for such first-person narration was "little see-everything devil" (*diablillo Obsérvalo-todo*).

25. Grafton and Marchand, "Proof and Persuasion," 4.

26. Hurtado de Mendoza, *Guerra de Granada*, 96: "que no sea conforme a la opinión de muchos."

27. Ibid., 97: "Los alárabes y asianos hablan de los sitios como escriben; al contrario y revés que las gentes de Europa."

28. Mármol Carvajal, *Historia del rebelión*, bk. 1, chap. 3: "'Iliberia' (aunque otros leen Eliberia, porque como en la gramática árabe son las vocales puntos, fácilmente se toma la *e* por la *i*, y la *o* por la *u*, porque diferencian poco en los lugares de los caracteres donde se ponen . . .)." For a later summary of these debates about Granada's name, see Bermúdez de Pedraza, *Antigvedad y excelencias de Granada*, f. 48r.

29. Guadix, *Diccionario de arabismos*.

30. Mármol Carvajal, *Historia del rebelión*, bk. 1, chaps. 4, 7.

31. Ibid. bk. 3, chap. 9: "una talega de lienzo, en que llevaba un libro grande de letra arábiga, y dentro dél se hallaron una carta y una lamentación, que del tenor de lo uno y de lo otro pareció ser cosa ordenada por el mesmo Daud."

32. For more on this issue and its role in the Alpujarras conflict, see Garrad, "La industria sedera granadina."

33. Mármol Carvajal, *Historia del rebelión*, bk. 3, chap. 9: "cosa muy ordinaria entre los moros."

34. Ibid., bk. 3, chap. 9: "Habéis de saber, señores nuestros, que los cristianos nos han mandado quitar la lengua arábiga, y quien pierde la lengua arábiga pierde su ley."

35. For recent takes on "maurophilia," see Fuchs, *Exotic Nation*, 1–30; Kimmel, "Local Turks," 21–24.

36. Pérez de Hita, *Guerras civiles de Granada*, vol. 2, 30–31: "Estas coplas se cantaron en arábigo al son de un añafil, y por sacarlas á su medida del arábigo, que es cosa muy dificultosa, no van tan buenas como pudieran."

37. Carrasco Urgoiti, *Moorish Novel*, 85; Márquez Villanueva, *El problema morisco*, 35–38.

38. Luna, *La verdadera historia*, 16: "por ser entre si tan repugnantes." See also Fuchs, *Mimesis and Empire*, 59–60.

39. Momigliano, "Rhetoric of History," 51, 58. On this tension, see also Ginzburg, *History, Rhetoric, and Proof*, 49; LaCapra, *History and Criticism*, 15–44.

40. Grethlein, "Experientiality and 'Narrative Reference,'" 324–29.

41. Hurtado de Mendoza, *Guerra de Granada*, 118: "españoles contra españoles."

42. Ibid., 120: "Tal fue la habla que don Fernando el Zaguer les hizo; con que quedaron animados, indignados y resueltos en general de rebelarse presto."

43. Rufo, *La Austriada*, 8: "Crecían sus haciendas y linajes / Y nuestras guerras y peregrinajes."

44. Ibid., 8.

45. Pérez de Hita, *Guerras civiles de Granada*, vol. 2, 9: "y estuvo bien acordado y mandado, porque el corazón del rey está en la mano de Dios . . . es verdad también que dello resultó gran pérdida y derramiento de cristiana sangre, grande menoscabo en las rentas de S. M. y ruina de muchos pueblos del Reino de Granada, que han caído y sa han perdido para siempre."

46. Mármol Carvajal, *Historia del rebelión*, bk. 2, chap. 8: "fue tanta su turbación, que ninguna persona de buen juicio dejara de entender sus dañadas voluntades."

47. Ibid., bk. 2, chap. 8.

48. Ibid., bk. 3, chap. 2: "disimulando unos, otros más atrevidos, que tenían menos que perder, comenzaron a convocar rebelión." On these and related prophecies, see García-Arenal and Rodríguez Mediano, *Un Oriente español*, 127–32; Green-Mercado, "Mahdī in Valencia," 201–2, 218; Kagan, *Lucrecia's Dreams*, 86–113.

49. See Mármol Carvajal's letter in Cabanelas Rodríguez, *El morisco granadino*, 251: "causa principal de su levantamiento, por la confianza que allí tenían puesta."

50. Rubenstein, *Armies of Heaven*, xi–xiv, 263–73.

51. Mármol Carvajal, *Historia del rebelión*, bk. 3, chap. 3: "Tenían los moriscos de Granada ciertos

jofores o pronósticos, o por mejor decir, unas ficciones, que debieron hacer algunos gramáticos árabes para consuelo de los espectantes cuando nuestros cristianos hubieron acabado de conquistar aquel reino."

52. Ibid., bk. 3, chap. 3: "La lengua árabe es tan equívoca, que muchas veces una mesma cosa, escrita con acento, agudo o luengo, significa dos cosas contrarias." On the reading of these and similar prophecies aloud, see Green-Mercado, "Mahdī in Valencia," 99.

53. Ibid., bk. 3, chap. 3. "parecía estar torcidos a voluntad de los desconsolados y afligidos moros."

54. Ibid., bk. 3, chap. 3. "no es de maravillar que los moriscos . . . entendiesen una cosa por otra."

55. El Alaoui, *Jésuites, morisques et indiens*, 545: "Algo destos inconvenientes tiene el libro que sacó Luis de Mármol de la rebelión de Granada y mayor en los pronósticos que pone suyos porque los tienen por ciertos como diré. Compran ellos estos libros en saliendo y, causándoles el resfriarse del todo en la fe, los encienden e inflaman en sus cosas." Green-Mercado also refers to this passage in "Morisco Apocalypticism," 99.

56. Hurtado de Mendoza, *Guerra de Granada*, 119: "No dejó de acordarles a este propósito, cuantos años atrás por boxa de grandes sabios en movimiento y lumbre de estrellas, y profetas en su ley, estaba declarado, que se levantarían a tornar por si; cobrarían la tierra y reinos que sus pasados perdieron . . . y venía justo con esta rebelión."

57. Cabanelas Rodríguez, *El morisco granadino*, 252, 258.

58. Ibid., 254: "bien se entiende que tratan de una misma materia."

59. Hess, "Moriscos"; Márquez Villanueva, "El mito," 277–78. On Rufo's Virgilian allusions, particularly in the context of Lepanto, see Quint, *Epic and Empire*, 49.

60. Hurtado de Mendoza, *Guerra de Granada*, 222–23: "Su comisión fue sin limitación ninguna; mas su libertad tan atada, que de cosa grande ni pequeña podía disponer sin comunicación y parecer de los consejeros y mandado del Rey, salvo deshacer y estorbar."

61. Ibid., 223.

62. Ibid., 224: "Habían pocos oficiales de pluma, perdían los soldados el respeto, hacíase costumbre el vicio, envilacíase el buen nombre y reputación milicia . . . parecía remediarse."

63. Mármol Carvajal, *Historia del rebelión*, bk. 5, chap. 37. For a discussion of Granada Venegas and his circle, see García-Arenal and Rodríguez Mediano, *Un Oriente español*, 87–105; Spivakovsky, "Some Notes on the Relations."

64. Mármol Carvajal, *Historia del rebelión*, bk. 5, chap. 37: "Mas aun esto, que les pudiera ser de algún provecho en lo de adelante, no lo merecieron las culpas de aquellos malaventurados, pareciendo al Consejo que ni era conveniente a la autoridad de un príncipe tan poderoso, ni daban lugar a ello las grandes ocupaciones de negocios que ocurrían de otras partes."

65. Ibid., bk. 5, chap. 37: "y lo que peor es, que los mesmos que iban con orden eran los que hacían las mayores desórdenes."

66. Ibid., bk. 6, chap. 5: "espectáculo piadoso y digno de compasión, aunque industriosamente hecho para provocarle a ira contra los moriscos . . . De allí entró en la ciudad, donde vio menos lástimas y más galas y regocijos; porque estaban las ventanas de las calles por donde había de pasar entoldadas de paños de oro y de seda, y mucho número de damas y doncellas nobles en ellas, ricamente ataviadas, que habían acudido de toda la ciudad por verle."

67. Hurtado de Mendoza, *Guerra de Granada*, 402: "Los moros que quedaban, unos se dieron de paz, y otros se pasaron a Berbería; y los demás las cuadrillas, y la frialdad de la sierra, y mal pasar los acabó; feneció la guerra y levantamiento."

68. Ibid., 402: "Quedó la tierra despoblada y destruida."

69. Spivakovsky, *Son of the Alhambra*, 3–27.

70. Cabrera de Córdoba, *Felipe II, Rey de España*, bk. 9, chap. 19.

71. Mármol Carvajal, *Historia del rebelión*, bk. 10, chap. 8: "¡Oh cuán felice hora fue para ti, insigne ciudad de Granada, cuando los católicos reyes don Hernando y doña Isabel te sacaron

de la sujeción del demonio! Ellos te ennoblecieron con suntuosos edificios, aumentáronte y adelantáronte en religión divina y estado temporal haciendo tus ceremoniosas mezquitas, en que se veneraba el falso Mahoma, templos sagrados."

72. Pérez de Hita, *Guerras civiles de Granada*, vol. 2, 466: "'¡Ay Dios mío! ¡Ay tierras mías, que no esperamos veros más!' Muchos pronunciaban aquellas mismas palabras que dijo Eneas al salir de Troya: '¡Oh tres y cuatro fortunados aquellos que peleando murieron al pie de sus muros, pues al fin quedaron en sus tierras, aunque muertos!' Así se lamentaban los moriscos piadosamente llorando."

CHAPTER SIX

1. Cited in Escrivà, *Vida del illvstrissimo y excellentissimo Señor*, 357: "Reuoquese a la memoria lo que ayer vimos en lo de Granada."

2. El Alaoui, *Jésuites, morisques et indiens*, 420–21: "La conversion de todos los descendientes de moros que ay oy en España pende a mi juizio (y no me engaño) de solo el convertirse los del reyno de Valencia y es la razón porque entienden los demás que éstos eschuchan y ven todos los ritos y ceremonias de su secta y saben todo su Alcorán exactamente . . . pero como los dividieron y se an ydo acabando los que sabían leer y escrevir en su lengua y se la prohibieron y años antes el leer y escrevir, a faltado esta honrra y crédito en los del reyno de Valencia."

3. Bunes Ibarra, *Los moriscos*, 31–54; Gutiérrez Nieto, "El pensamiento," 248–58; Vincent and Sánchez-Blanco, "Estudio preliminar," 19–24; Sánchez-Blanco and Ciscar Pallarés, "La Iglesia ante la conversión y expulsión"; Pastore, "La posición del Vaticano."

4. For the text of the expulsion decree, see a recent reprint of Janer, *Condición social de los moriscos*, 371–72: "mandé hacer en esa ciudad la junta . . . para ver si se podia excusar el sacallos destos reinos." See also Domínguez Ortiz and Vincent, *Historia de los moriscos*, 172. On the reservations of the Valencian theologian Jaime Benet, see Vincent, *El río morisco*, 111; Feros, "Retóricas de la expulsión."

5. Janer, *Condición social de los moriscos*, 371: "el peligro y irreparables daños que en disimular con ellos podia suceder."

6. Aznar Cardona, *Expvlsion ivstificada*, part 2, ff. 9v–10r: "Maravilla es, que dos pares de hombres leales, sin otras armas algunas, mas de ser el vno dellos Comissario Real, sacassen y guiassen por donde dicho es mil y tres mil dellos, sin suceder escandalo, sedicion, alboroto, ni muerte de algun Christiano. Quien lo creyera?" On the Denia episode, see Janer, *Condición social de los moriscos*, 337; Bernabé Pons, *Los moriscos*, 109–47.

7. González de Cellorigo, *Memorial de la politica necesaria*, f. 30v: "no se puede dar monarchia perfecta en nuestra España, como la de entonces . . . que despues començò à declinar hasta estos." Nineteenth-century Spanish authors concerned with North Africa, such as Pedro Antonio de Alarcón, instead looked for the origins of imperial decline in the expulsion of the Moriscos, "of whom it could be said that they took the talisman of our fortune" (quienes pudiera decirse que se llevaron el talisman de nuestra fortuna). See Antonio de Alarcón, *Diario*, iii. Thanks to Ryan Calderwood for the reference.

8. Aguilar, *Expulsión de los moros*, 353: "Pues del mal que han tenido en esta feria / se saca el bien universal."

9. Vincent, *El río morisco*, 132: "el problema morisco es ante todo un problema histórico."

10. Valencia, *Tratado acerca de los moriscos*, 118.

11. Ibid., 91, 118.

12. Gómez Canseco, *El humanismo*, 234–41; Magnier, *Pedro de Valencia*, 199, 245–89; Márquez Villanueva, *Moros, moriscos y turcos*, 178–86.

13. Kamen, *Spanish Inquisition*, 229, 249; Borja de Medina, "La Compañía de Jesús y la minoría morisca."

14. Valencia, *Tratado acerca de los moriscos*, 109.

15. Ibid., 123: "permistión . . . que quiere decir total mezcla, que nos se pueda distinguir ni discerner cuál es de aquesta o aquella nación."

16. Ibid., 80: "diabólica traza."

17. Guevara, *Epistolas familiares*, 544.

18. BNE MS 464, ff. 2r–96r, Pedro de Valencia, *Para declaracion de vna gran parte dela Eystoria Apostolica en los Actos y enla epistola ad Galatas advertencias* (1608): "sin culpa alguna" (76v); "no culpable ensi de ninguna manera" (78v).

19. Valencia, *Tratado acerca de los moriscos*, 99: "los Santos Apóstoles, por divina dispensación y economía de Espíritu Santo, disimuló mucho tiempo en la Iglesia con los flacos convertidos del judaísmo, que juntamente con la luz querían entretener y conservar las sombras de la ley y guardaban todavía las ceremonias de ella después del bautismo."

20. Ibid., 126: "aunque sea con mentira . . . ciudadanos de una república que todos son hermanos de una sangre y linaje, y naturales de aquella misma tierra."

21. Ibid., 125: "así quiere y ha de acabar a los judíos y a los moros, juntándolos en un nuevo cuerpo y nombre de república."

22. González de Cellorigo, *Memorial al Rey*, ff. 3v–6r. In a bit of underhanded marketing to a xenophobic audience, the hostile title of the pamphlet belies its more measured content.

23. Valencia, *Tratado acerca de los moriscos*, 78: "todas las toleraron como no siguiesen opiniones que impidiesen la paz pública."

24. W. Brown, *Regulating Aversion*, 1–24. For early modernists grappling with the similar issues of "charitable hatred" and "rough tolerance," see Walsham, *Charitable Hatred*, and MacEvitt, *Crusades and the Christian World*.

25. See, for example, Valencia's account of Quito in *Relaciones de Indias: Nueva Granada y Virreinato de Peru*, 115–26, and his account of Mexico in *Relaciones de Indias: México*, 144–325.

26. El Alaoui, *Jésuites, morisques et indiens*, 40: "dudas y no errores ciertos y asentados . . . están de suerte que ni son absolutamente moros ni christianos sino como atheos, confiando salvarse con sola la ley natural sin creer a nada de la ley escrita ni de gracia."

27. González de Cellorigo, *Memorial al Rey*, f. 2v: "su entendimiento natural los vuiera sacado de la ceguedad de su falsa secta."

28. Previous scholarship has tended to focus only on the importance of the peninsular example in the New World, and not the other way around. See, for instance, two works by Garrido Aranda: *Moriscos e indios* and *Organización de la iglesia*.

29. Loyola, *Spiritual Exercises*, 12.

30. Fonseca, *Del givsto scacciamento*, 179.

31. Escrivà, *Vida del illvstrissimo y excellentissimo Señor*, 410: "Para tratar desto, me ha parecido ponderar las palabras del Apostol S. Pablo, escritas a los de Galacia: Vtinam abscindantur qui vos conturbant. Auia el sagrado Apostol procurado de reduzir a los Griego gentiles de aquella ciudad a la Fe del Euangelio, y muchos de ellos auian dado muestras de su conuersion; pero con la mala compañia de los Gentiles que estauan entre ellos, se auian inquietado, de manera que era mucha la turbacion que auia en la Ciudad. Escriueles el Apostol, desseando euitar estos inconuenientes, y el primer remedio que pone para que se conserue la paz y cesse la pertubacion, e inquietud, es suplicar a nuestro Señor que sean cortados (no desmochados, sino cortados) los Infieles y perturbadores."

32. The Latin Vulgate reads, "nam in Christo Iesu neque circumcisio aliquid valet neque praeputium sed fides quae per caritatem operatur." See *Bibliorum sacrorum iuxta vulgatam clementinam*, 1092. The English is the New Revised Standard Version.

33. Cited in Vincent and Sánchez-Blanco, "Estudio preliminar," 12: "único cuchillo de la nación morisca."

34. Escrivà, *Vida del illvstrissimo y excellentissimo Señor*, 441: "sobre la expulsion y materias de Estado."

35. *Bibliorium sacrorum cum Glossa ordinaria*, vol. 6, col. 512: "Utinam abscindantur. Ipsi vos conturbant, sed utinam abscindantur, non carnaliter, sed vim generandi perdant in vobis, vel in aliis."

36. Ibid., vol. 5, cols. 111–12, 301–302 (Matthew 5:30, 18:8).

37. Escrivà, *Vida del illvstrissimo y excellentissimo Señor*, 366: "arrancarlos de raiz, porque no puedan dañar ellos, ni sus raizes echar nueuos pimpollos que en breue tiempo crezcan en arboles." On the extent to which this root removal became a shorthand for the expulsion advocates' argument, see Domínguez Ortíz and Vincent, *Historia de los moriscos*, 247.

38. Escrivà, *Vida del illvstrissimo y excellentissimo Señor*, 366: "Dixo Dios a los de su pueblo por vn Propheta (para enseñarles como auian de gouernar sus cosas) No sembreys en campos que tengan malas yeruas, sino arrancaldas primero y despues sembrad."

39. Ibid., 366–67: "Estas mismas letras sagradas nos muestran . . . que de tener entre nosotros gente mala, e infiel; y nos aconsejan y mandan, que la arranquemos de quajo de nuestra compañia."

40. Ibid., 368: "mouido de los desseos que tenia el Apostol San Pablo quando dezia: Oxala se arrancassen de entre vosotros los que os conturban."

41. Pastore, *Un herejía española*, 98–111; Bainton, "The Parable of the Tares."

42. *Bibliorum sacrorum iuxta vulgatam clementinam*, 939–94: "Non: ne forte colligentes zizania, eradicetis simul cum eis et triticum. Sinite utraque crescere usque ad messem, et in tempore messis dicam messoribus: Colligite primum zizania, et alligate ea in fasciculos ad comburendum: triticum autem congregate in horreum meum."

43. The question for Augustine was how to answer the Donatist claim that they were the wheat. See Bainton, "Parable of the Tares," 69–70; Leclerc, *Histoire de la tolérance*, 53–54, 83–88; Prosperi, "Il grano e la zizzania," 213–14.

44. Escrivà, *Vida del illvstrissimo y excellentissimo Señor*, 483: "Dizen que estos son plantas nueuas. No son Catholica Magestad, plantas nueuas, sino arboles reuegidos, llenos de ñudos de heregias, y traycion."

45. Ibid., 384: "Mas ha de ochenta años que nacieron estas plantas, y llamaremoslas nueuas; los de Auila, Valladolid, y otras ciudades, deuieron quedar desde que se perdio España, y diremos que son plantas nueuas?"

46. Ibid., 351: "hablando con propriedad, deuemos llamarlos no Moriscos, sino Moros." See also Valencia, *Tratado acerca de los moriscos*, 79: "Y para que prudencia y recato se deba presuponer que los moriscos de España, por la mayor parte y en general, son moros."

47. Fonseca, *Del givsto scacciamento*, 196.

48. Escrivà, *Vida del illvstrissimo y excellentissimo Señor*, 441: "Esta sermon de ninguna suerte queria el señor Patriarca que se imprimiesse, aunque parecia que conuenia; en fin vino bien en ello vencido de los ruegos y razones de muchos: pero no permitio que se pusiesse en el su nombre, ni que se imprimiessen mas que ciento, y que estos se repartiessen y embiassen a diuersas partes, a personas señaladas."

49. Ehlers, *Between Christians and Moriscos*, 151–57.

50. Guadalajara y Xavier, *Memorable expvlsion*, unnumbered prologue to the reader: "plumas agenas."

51. Ibid., 75–93. One minor difference between this sequence and the one established by Escrivà was the inversion of Gaspar de Córdoba's and the duke of Lerma's texts.

52. It was through this editorial process that the opinions of Ribera and other expulsion advocates became "singular events" (*événements singuliers*), to borrow a term from Michel Foucault's discussion of archives and archeological method. See Foucault, *L'archéologie du savoir*, 170.

53. Guadalajara y Xavier, *Memorable expvlsion*, unnumbered prologue to the reader: "cito con proprio nombre los autores, y pongo sus mismos originales, y razones; entresacando de sus compendiosas obras, lo que a mi proposito conuenia, de vnos mas, y de otros menos; formando vn panal a la manera de industriosas auejas; y todo esto para beneficio de los pobres, que no tienen possibilidad para comprar sus grandes y costosos libros"; "poner en orden esta Expulsión."

54. Serrano Morales, *Reseña histórica*, 45–46.

55. For an example of such binding, see the edition of Guadalajara y Xavier's *Memorable expvlsion* held at the New York Public Library; Usanáriz, "Entre dos expulsiones."

56. As Jacques Derrida put it in another context, "Archivable meaning . . . begins with the printer." See Derrida, "Archive Fever," 18.

57. Aguilar, *Expulsión de los moros*, 117: "Es fiel traslado al castellano del original en valenciano." On Aguilar's hagiographic play about Ribera, see Magnier, *Pedro de Valencia*, 137.

58. Serrano Morales, *Reseña histórica*, 285–327; Delgado Casado, *Diccionario de impresores españoles*, 451–57.

59. Bleda, *Corónica de los moros*, 895.

60. Domínguez Ortiz and Vincent, *Historia de los moriscos*, 160.

61. Ripol, *Dialogo de consvelo*, 17: "Y si antes era España tenida por esteril, por la poca gente, que sera agora?"

62. Moncada, *Restauración política*, discourse 1, chap. 2: "España corre riesgo." See also Elliott, *History in the Making*, 124–25.

63. Moncada, *Restauración política*, discourse 1, chap. 2: "A muchos parece eternal la Monarquía de España por su grandeza. Pero mucho se habla de su peligro en todas partes, y estos días se ha advertido a V. Majestad en varios libros, y memoriales." For more on this crisis, its origins, and scholarly debate about its history, see Vilches, *New World Gold*, 210–70; Kamen, "Decline of Spain."

64. Gutiérrez Nieto, "El pensamiento," 335–36; Elliot, "Self-Perception and Decline," 51–52. See also *La junta de reformación*, 12.

65. Fernández de Navarrete, *Conservación de monarquías*, 71: "La primera causa de la despoblacion de España ha sido las muchas y numerosas expulsiones de Moros y Judíos, enemigos de nuestra santa fe católica."

66. Ibid., 74–75: "Y así vuelvo á decir, que tengo por cierto, que si á los principios se hubiera tomado algun modo de no tener señalados con nota de infamia á los Moriscos, hubieran procurado todos reducirse á la Religion católica: que si la tomáron ódio y horror, fué por verse en ella abatidos y despreciados, y sin esperanza de poder con el tiempo borrar la nota de su baxo nacimiento."

67. González de Cellorigo, *Memorial al Rey*, 21r: "Pero estando estos convertidos, y en disposicion de que siendo intruydos en la fè, pueden ser perfectos: nuestro Rey Catholico como Christianissimo, ha de procurar conseruar su gente, y inchir sus Reynos: atrayendo à todos al verdadero conocimiento de la Fè."

68. Moncada, *Restauración política*, discourse 2, chap. 2: "Y es indicio claro, porque en muchas ciudades en estas pestes y expulsions se moraban todas las casas, y de dos o tres años acá están cerradas muchas . . . Lo tercero, porque como enemigos de España, eran causa de muchas muertes (como dijo V. M. en el Real Bando de la expulsión) y así antes fue aumentar la nación española."

69. Valencia, *Discurso sobre el acrecentamiento*, 156–157: "No se les debe permitir que sean labradores. Esto hará el oficio más honrado, y a los moriscos no los hará ejercitados y valientes; antes, ni se les habían de consentier otros oficios semejantes que crían buenos soldados, sino que solamente fuesen tenderos y tratantes en las ciudades y plazas. Si con esto se hiciesen ricos, no sería inconveniente; pagarían más imposiciones y serían más afeminados y temerosos y cobardes, porque, como dice Eurípides, las riquezas hacen este efecto."

70. González de Cellorigo, *Memorial al Rey*, 5r–v. See also Gutiérrez Nieto, "El pensamiento," 326–28.

71. Valencia, *Discurso contra la ociosidad*; Pérez de Herrera, *Discvrsos del amparo*: "la grande ociosidad de vida." For more on the stereotype of Spanish laziness as it appeared in the authors examined here, see MacKay, *"Lazy Improvident People,"* 89–98.

72. Pulido Serrano, *Injurias a Cristo*, 26–70; Israel, *European Jewry*, 46–50; Meyerson, *Muslims of Valencia*, 183.

CONCLUSION

1. Tueller, "Los moriscos que se quedaron," 196–208; Domínguez Ortíz and Vincent, *Historia de los moriscos*, 247–66. The return of the Moriscos was shaped in part by their experiences elsewhere. See the introduction to a recent series of articles on the Morisco diaspora in *Quaderni storici*: Fiume and Pastore, "Premessa."

2. Matar, *Europe through Arab Eyes*, 29–117.

3. I borrow the word "multiconfessional" from the art historian Cynthia Robinson. See her *Imagining the Passion in a Multiconfessional Castile.*

4. Villaverde Amieva, "Los manuscritos aljamiado-moriscos"; López Morillas, "Los manuscritos aljamiados."

5. In an account of purchasing such found manuscripts, the Arabist Francisco Codera humorously recalled how in Almonacid de la Sierra the local discoverers, "for whom such books were not even worthy of conservation, came to believe that they were worth the mines of Potosí, and want to relinquish them only for exorbitant prices" (para quienes tales libros no merecían la pena de ser conservados, creyeron entonces que valian un Potosí, y no quieren cederlos sino por precios exorbitantes). See Codera, "Almacén de un librero morisco," 270. On the role of Asín Palacios and Conde, among other Spanish and Italian philologists, in the construction of new national philologies, see Mallette, *European Modernity*, 34–64.

6. Monroe, *Islam and the Arabs*, 49–11, 151–73; López Baralt, *Huellas del Islam*, 119.

7. Martin-Márquez, *Disorientations*, 14–16, 30–31.

8. See the Ministry of Culture's unnumbered introductory note to the exhibit catalogue, *Memoria de los moriscos*: "una recuperación del pasado islámico."

9. Bamford, "Manuscript and Philology," 210.

10. Valencia, *Tratado acerca de los moriscos*, 105: "nos hallaremos en peligro y perplejidad grande, muy semejante a la del proverbio antiguo auribus lupum teneo: El que tiene asido al lobo por las orejas ni tiene presa firme y segura ni le está bien tenerlo ni soltarlo."

Bibliography

ARCHIVES

AASG	Archivo de la Abadía de Sacromonte de Granada (Granada)
ABFZ	Archivo y Biblioteca de la Fundación Zabálburu (Madrid)
AFG	Archivo de la Fundación Galdiano (Madrid)
AHN	Archivo Histórico Nacional (Madrid)
APR	Archivo del Palacio Real (Madrid)
BL	British Library (London)
BNE	Biblioteca Nacional de España (Madrid)
BUS	Biblioteca Universitaria de Salamanca (Salamanca)
RAH	Real Academia de la Historia (Madrid)

PUBLISHED SOURCES

Acosta, José de. *De procuranda indorum salute.* Edited by Luciano Pereña. 2 vols. Corpus Hispanorum de Pace. Madrid: Centro Superior de Investigaciones Científicas, 1984–87.

———. *Natural and Moral History of the Indies.* Edited by Jane E. Mangan. Introduction by Walter D. Mignolo. Translated by Francis López-Morillas. Durham: Duke University Press, 2002.

———. *Obras.* Biblioteca de Autores Españoles 73. Madrid: Ediciones Atlas, 1954.

Adorno, Rolena. *The Polemics of Possession in Spanish American Narrative.* New Haven: Yale University Press, 2007.

Agamben, Giorgio. *The Time That Remains: A Commentary on the Letter to the Romans.* Translated by Patricia Daily. Stanford: Stanford University Press, 2005.

Aguilar, Gaspar de. *Expulsión de los moros de España.* Edited by Manuel Ruiz Lagos. Seville: Editorial Guadalmena, 1999.

Alcalá, Pedro de. *Arte para ligeramente saber la lengua arauiga.* New York: Hispanic Society of America, 1928.

Aldrete, Bernardo de. *Del origen y principio de la lengua castellana ò Romance que hoy se usa en España.* Rome: Carlo Vulliet, 1606.

———. *Varias antiguedades de España, Africa, y otras provincias.* Antwerp: Iuan Hafrey, 1614.

Alfonso X. *Las siete partidas.* Edited by Samuel Parsons Scott and Robert Ignatius Burns. Philadelphia: University of Pennsylvania Press, 2001.

———. *Las siete partidas del sabio rey Don Alonso el nono, glosadas por el licenciado Gregorio López . . . Con su reportorio muy copioso assi testo como de glosa.* Salamanca: A. de Portonaris, 1555.

Alonso, Carlos. *Los apócrifos del Sacromonte*. Valladolid: Estudio Agustiniano, 1979.

Álvar, Manuel. *Nebrija y estudios sobre la edad de oro*. Madrid: Centro Superior de Investigaciones Científicas, 1997.

Amelang, James S. *Historias paralelas: Judeoconversos y moriscos en la España moderna*. Translated by Jaime Blasco Castiñeyra. Madrid: Ediciones Akal, 2011.

Ames, Christine Caldwell. *Righteous Persecution: Inquisition, Dominicans, and Christianity in the Middle Ages*. Philadelphia: University of Pennsylvania Press, 2009.

Antonio de Alarcón, Pedro. *Diario de un testigo de la guerra de África*. Madrid: Imprenta y Librería de Gaspar y Roig, 1859. http://books.google.com/.

Aquinas, Thomas. *Scriptum super libros Sententiarum Magistri Petri Lombardi Episcopi Parisiensis*. Edited by Enrique Alarcón. Fundación Tomás de Aquino, University of Navarre, 2000–2009. www.corpusthomisticum.org.

———. *Summa theologica*. Edited by Enrique Alarcón. Fundación Tomás de Aquino, University of Navarre, 2000–2009. www.corpusthomisticum.org.

———. *The Summa Theologica of St. Thomas Aquinas*. Translated by Fathers of the English Dominican Province. 2nd ed. London: Burns, Oates and Washbourne, 1920. www.newadvent.org.

Aristotle. *Nicomachean Ethics*. Translated by Terence Irwin. Indianapolis: Hackett, 1985.

Asad, Talal. *Formations of the Secular: Christianity, Islam, Modernity*. Stanford: Stanford University Press, 2003.

———. *Genealogies of Religion: Disciplines and Reasons of Power in Christianity and Islam*. Baltimore: Johns Hopkins University Press, 1993.

———. "The Idea of an Anthropology of Islam." Occasional Papers. Washington, DC: Georgetown University Center for Contemporary Arabic Studies, 1986.

———. "Medieval Heresy: An Anthropological View." *Social History* 2, no. 3 (1986): 345–62.

Asensio, Eugenio. *El erasmismo y las corrientes espirituales afines*. Salamanca: Sociedad Espanola de Historia del Libro, 2000.

———. *La España imaginada de Américo Castro*. Barcelona: Ediciones El Albir, 1976.

———. "Exégesis bíblica en España: Encuentro de Fray Cipriano de la Huerga con Juan de Valdés en Alcalá." In *Actas del coloquio interdisciplinar: Doce consideraciones sobre el mundo hispano-italiano en tiempos de Alfonso y Juan de Valdés*. Rome: Instituto Español de Lengua y Literatura de Roma, 1979.

Augustine, Aurelius. *De baptismo libri VII*. In *Patrologia Latina*, vol. 43.

———. *De correctione donatistarum*. In *Patrologia Latina*, vol. 33.

———. *De mendacio*. In *Patrologia Latina*, vol. 40.

———. *Epistola XXVIII*. In *Patrologia Latina*, vol. 33.

———. *Letters*. In *The Fathers of the Church*, vol. 1. Translated by Wilfrid Parsons. Washington, DC: Catholic University of America Press, 1951.

———. "Scripta contra donatistas." In *Corpus scriptorum ecclesiasticorum latinorum*, edited by M. Petschenig. Vienna: F. Tempsky, 1908–10.

———. *The Works of Aurelius Augustine: A New Translation*. Vol. 3. Edited by Marcus Dods. Translated by Rev. J. R. King. Edinburgh: T. & T. Clark, 1892.

Aveling, J. C. H. *The Jesuits*. London: Blond and Briggs, 1981.

Azevedo Alves, André, and José Manuel Moreira. *The Salamanca School*. New York: Continuum, 2010.

Aznar Cardona, Pedro. *Expvlsion ivstificada de los moriscos españoles*. Huesca: Pedro Cabarte, 1612.

Badiou, Alain. *Saint Paul: The Foundation of Universalism*. Stanford: Stanford University Press, 2003.

Bahner, Werner. *La linguística española del siglo de oro: Aportaciones a la conciencia linguística en la España de los siglos XVI y XVII*. Madrid: Ciencia Nueva, 1966.

Bainton, Roland H. "The Parable of the Tares as the Proof Text for Religious Liberty to the End of the Sixteenth Century." *Church History* 1, no. 2 (June 1932): 85–96.

Bamford, Heather M. "Manuscript and Philology as Curatorial Practice in 'Memoria de los Moriscos.'" *La corónica* 41, no. 2 (Spring 2013): 201–24.

Barletta, Vincent. *Covert Gestures: Crypto-Islamic Literature as Cultural Practice in Early Modern Spain.* Minneapolis: University of Minnesota Press, 2005.

Barreda, Jesús A. "*La Apología* en su contexto teológico." In Bartolomé de Las Casas, *Apología, o declaración y defensa universal de los derechos del hombre y de los pueblos*, edited by Vidal Abril Castelló, lix–lxviii. Salamanca: Junta de Castilla y León, 2000.

Barrios Aguilera, Manuel, and Mercedes García-Arenal, eds. *Los plomos del Sacromonte: Invención y tesoro.* Zaragoza: Universidad de Zaragoza, 2006.

Bataillon, Marcel. "L'Arabe à Salamanque au temps de la Renaissance." *Hespéris* 21 (1935): 1–17.

———. *Erasmo y España: Estudios sobre la historia espiritual del siglo XVI.* Translated by Antonio Alatorre. Mexico City: Fondo de Cultura Económica, 1950.

———. *Études sur Bartolomé de Las Casas.* Paris: Centre de Recherches de l'Institut d'Etudes Hispaniques, 1965.

Beaver, Adam. "From Jerusalem to Toledo: Replica, Landscape, and the Nation in Renaissance Iberia." *Past and Present* 218 (February 2013): 55–90.

Becerra Hiraldo, José María. Introduction to Luis de León, *El Cantar de los Cantares de Salomón.* Madrid: Cátedra, 2003.

Beltrán de Heredía, Vicente. *Los manuscritos de Fray Francisco de Vitoria.* Madrid: Santo Domingo el Real, 1928.

Bermúdez de Pedraza, Francisco. *Antigvedad y excelencias de Granada.* Madrid: Luis Sanchez, 1608. http://books.google.com/.

Bernabé Pons, Luis F. "Los libros plúmbeos de Granada desde el pensamiento islámico." In García-Arenal and Barrios Aguilera, *¿La historia inventada?*, 57–81.

———. "Los mecanismos de una resistencia: Los libros plúmbeos del Sacromonte y el *Evangelio de Bernabé*." In Barrios Aguilera and García-Arenal, *Los plomos del Sacromonte*, 385–402.

———. *Los moriscos: Conflicto, expulsión y diáspora.* Madrid: Catarata, 2009.

Beuchot, Mauricio. *Los fundamentos de los derechos humanos en Bartolomé de Las Casas.* Barcelona: Anthropos, 1994.

The Bible. Douay-Rheims Version, Challoner Revision. http://www.gutenberg.org/.

Bibliorum sacrorum cum Glossa ordinaria. 6 vols. Venice: Iuntas, 1603. www.lollardsociety.org.

Bibliorum sacrorum iuxta vulgatam clementinam. Milan: U. Hoepli, 1914. http://www.hathitrust.org/.

Binotti, Lucia. *La teoría del "Castellano Primitivo": Nacionalismo y reflexión lingüística en el Renacimiento español.* Münster: Nodus Publikationem, 1995.

Bisaha, Nancy. *Creating East and West: Renaissance Humanists and the Ottoman Turks.* Philadelphia: University of Pennsylvania Press, 2004.

Bleda, Jaime. *Corónica de los moros de España.* Valencia: Felipe Mey, 1619. Facsimile edition, Valencia: Universitat de València, 2001.

Borja de Medina, Francisco de. "La Compañía de Jesús y la minoría morisca (1545–1614)." *Archivum historicum Societatis Iesu* 57 (1988): 3–136.

Bossy, John. *Christianity in the West, 1400–1700.* Oxford: Oxford University Press, 1988.

Bourdieu, Pierre. *The Field of Cultural Production: Essays on Art and Literature.* New York: Columbia University Press, 1993.

Boureau, Alain. *L'empire du livre: Pour une histoire du savoir scolastique (1200–1380).* Paris: Les Belles Lettres, 2003.

Bouza Álvarez, Fernando J. *Corre manuscrito: Una historia cultural del siglo de oro.* Madrid: Marcial Pons, 2001.

Boyarin, Daniel. *A Radical Jew: Paul and the Politics of Identity.* Berkeley: University of California Press, 1997.

Brann, Ross. "Andalusi 'Exceptionalism.'" In *A Sea of Languages: Rethinking the Arabic Role in Medieval Literary History*, edited by Suzanne Conklin Akbari and Karla Mallette. Toronto: University of Toronto Press, 2013.

Breva-Claramonte, Manuel. *Sanctius's Theory of Language: A Contribution to the History of Renaissance Linguistics*. Amsterdam: J. Benjamins, 1983.

Brown, Catherine. *Contrary Things: Exegesis, Dialectic and the Poetics of Didacticism*. Stanford: Stanford University Press, 1998.

Brown, James Scott. *The Spanish Origins of International Law: Francisco de Vitoria and His Law of Nations*. Oxford: Clarendon Press, 1934.

Brown, Peter. *Augustine of Hippo: A Biography*. Berkeley: University of California Press, 1970.

———. "St. Augustine's Attitude to Religious Coercion." *Journal of Roman Studies* 54 (1964): 107–16.

Brown, Wendy. *Regulating Aversion: Tolerance in the Age of Identity and Empire*. Princeton: Princeton University Press, 2006.

Buc, Philippe. *The Dangers of Ritual: Between Early Medieval Texts and Social Scientific Theory*. Princeton: Princeton University Press, 2001.

Bunes Ibarra, Miguel Ángel de. *Los moriscos en el pensamiento histórico: Historiografía de un grupo marginado*. Madrid: Cátedra, 1983.

Burgaleta, Claudio M. *José de Acosta, S.J. (1540–1600): His Life and Thought*. Chicago: Loyola University Press, 1999.

Burman, Thomas E. *Reading the Qur'ān in Latin Christendom, 1140–1560*. Philadelphia: University of Pennsylvania Press, 2007.

Bynum, Caroline Walker. *Christian Materiality: An Essay on Religion in Late Medieval Europe*. New York: Zone Books, 2011.

Cabanelas Rodríguez, Darío. "Intento de supervivencia en el ocaso de una cultura: Los libros plúmbeos de Granada." *Nueva Revista de Filología Hispánica* 30, no. 2 (1981): 334–58.

———. *El morisco granadino Alonso de Castillo*. Granada: Patronato de la Alhambra y Generalife, 1991.

Cabrera de Córdoba, Luis. *De historia para entenderla y escriverla*. Madrid: Luis Sanchez, 1611. http://books.google.com/.

———. *Felipe II, Rey de España*. Madrid: Luis Sanchez, 1619.

Cano, Melchor. *Relectio de Sacramentis in genere*. In *Opera omnia*, vol. 2. Madrid, 1770.

Cantineau, J. "Lettre du moufti d'Oran aux musulmans d'andalousie." *Journal Asiatique* (January–March 1927): 1–17.

Cantor, Pierre. *Verbum abbreviatum*. In *Patrologia Latina*, vol. 205.

Caro Baroja, Julio. *Las falsificaciones de la historia (en relación con la de España)*. Barcelona: Seix Barral, 1992.

———. *Los moriscos del Reino de Granada*. Madrid: Ediciones Istmo, 2000.

Carrasco Urgoiti, María Soledad. *The Moorish Novel: "El Abencerraje" and Pérez de Hita*. Boston: Twayne, 1976.

Carro, Venancio D. *Teología y los teólogos juristas españoles ante la conquista de América*. 2nd ed. Salamanca: Biblioteca de Autores Españoles, 1951.

Cascardi, Anthony J. *Ideologies of History in the Spanish Golden Age*. University Park: Pennsylvania State University Press, 1997.

———. *The Subject of Modernity*. Cambridge: Cambridge University Press, 1992.

Castillo Fernández, Javier. "Las estructuras sociales." In *Historia del Reino de Granada*, edited by Manuel Barrios Aguilera, vol. 2, 179–230. Granada: Universidad de Granada, 2000.

Castro, Américo. "Disputa entre un cristiano y un judío." *Revista de Filología Española* 1 (1914): 173–80.

———. *España en su historia: Ensayos sobre historia y literatura*. In *Obra reunida*, vol. 3. Madrid: Trotta, 2004.

Castro, Daniel. *Another Face of Empire: Bartolomé de Las Casas, Indigenous Rights, and Ecclesiastical Imperialism*. Durham, NC: Duke University Press, 2007.

Catholic Encyclopedia. Washington, DC: Catholic University of America, 2003.

Catlos, Brian. *The Muslims of Medieval Latin Christendom, c. 1050–1614*. Cambridge: Cambridge University Press, 2014.

Centurión, Adán. *Informacion para la historia del Sacro Monte, llamado Valparaiso y antiguamente Illipulitano junto à Granada*. Granada: B. Borenzana, 1632.

Cepeda Adán, José. "El barroco español y el cultivo de la historia." In *Historia de España: El siglo del Quijote (1580–1680)*, edited by Rámon Menéndez Pidal, vol. 1, 525–39. Madrid: Espasa-Calpe, 1986.

Certeau, Michel de. *The Practice of Everyday Life*. Translated by Steven Rendall. Berkeley: University of California Press, 1984.

Cervantes Augustiniano, Fr. Gonçalo. *Parecer de S. Augustin en favor de la concepcion purissima de la Virgen Maria Madre de Dios, sin pecado original*. Seville: Gabriel Ramos Bejarano, 1618.

Chadwick, Henry. *The Early Church*. Harmondsworth, Middlesex: Penguin, 1967.

Charland, T. M. *Ars praedicandi: Contribution à l'histoire de la rhétorique au moyen âge*. Paris: J. Vrin, 1936.

Chartier, Roger. *Inscrire et effacer: Culture écrite et littérature (XIe–XVIIIe siècle)*. Paris: Gallimard, 2005.

Childers, William. "Hispanic Casuistry Studies: Room to Grow." *Hispanic Review* 79, no. 2 (Spring 2011): 317–26.

Chomsky, Noam. *Cartesian Linguistics: A Chapter in the History of Rationalist Thought*. Edited by James McGilvray. Cambridge: Cambridge University Press, 2009.

———. *Language and Mind*. New York: Harcourt, Brace and World, 1968.

Christodouleas, Tina P., and Nabil Matar. "The Mary of Sacromonte." *Muslim World* 95 (2005): 199–215.

Cirot, George. *Mariana historien*. Bordeaux, 1904. www.archive.org.

Clénard, Nicolas. *Correspondance*. Vol. 1. Edited by Alphonse Roersch. Brussels: Palais des Academies, 1940.

Codera, Francisco. "Almacén de un librero morisco descubierto en Almonacid de la Sierra." *Boletín de la Real Academia de la Historia* 5 (1884): 269–76. www.cervantesvirtual.com.

Coelle de la Rosa, Alexandre. "Más allá del Incario: Imperialismo e historia en José de Acosta, SJ (1540–1600)." *Colonial Latin American Review* 14, no. 1 (June 2005): 55–81.

Coleman, David. *Creating Christian Granada: Society and Religious Culture in an Old-World Frontier City, 1492–1600*. Ithaca, NY: Cornell University Press, 2003.

Concilium Toletatum quartum. www.benedictus.mgh.de/quellen/chga/chga_046t.htm.

Contreras, Rafael. "Nuevos datos sobre la guerra y expulsión de los moriscos." *Revista de España* 69 (1879): 185–209.

Corriente, Federico. *A Dictionary of Andalusi Arabic*. Leiden: Brill, 1997.

Creppell, Ingred. *Toleration and Identity: Foundations in Early Modern Political Thought*. New York: Routledge, 2003.

Cuart Moner, Baltasar. "La larga marcha hacia las historias de España en el siglo XVI." In *La construcción de las Historias de España*, edited by Ricardo García Cárcel, 45–126. Madrid: Marcial Pons, 2004.

Cueva, Luis de la. *Dialagos de las cosas notables de Granada, y lengua española, y algunas cosas curiosas*. Seville: Fernando de Lara, 1603. http://books.google.com/.

Dahan, Gilbert. *L'exégèse chrétienne de la Bible en Occident médiéval*. Paris: Cerf, 2008.

Dannenfeldt, Karl H. "The Renaissance Humanists and the Knowledge of Arabic." *Studies in the Renaissance* 2 (1955): 96–117.

Darst, David H. "El pensamiento histórico del granadino Diego Hurtado de Mendoza." *Hispania: Revista española de historia* 43, no. 154 (1983): 281–94.

Dawkins, Richard. *The God Delusion.* Boston: Houghton Mifflin, 2006.

Delgado Casado, Juan. *Diccionario de impresores españoles (Siglos XV–XVII).* Madrid: Arco/Libros, 1996.

Del Valle, Ivonne. "Jesuit Baroque." *Journal of Spanish Cultural Studies* 3, no. 2 (2002): 141–63.

Derrida, Jacques. "Archive Fever: A Freudian Impression." Translated by Eric Prenowitz. *Diacritics* 25, no. 2 (Summer 1995): 9–63.

De Soto, Domingo. *Quartum Sententiarum.* Vol. 1. Salamanca: Ioannes à Canoua, 1557.

Diccionario histórico de la Companía de Jesús. Edited by Charles Edwards O'Neill and Joaquín María Domínguez. 3 vols. Madrid: Universidad Pontificia Comillas, 2001.

Ditchfield, Simon. "What Was Sacred History? (Mostly Roman) Catholic Uses of the Christian Past after Trent." In *Sacred History: Uses of the Christian Past in the Renaissance World,* edited by Katherine Van Liere, Simon Ditchfield, and Howard Louthan, 72–100. Cambridge: Cambridge University Press, 2012.

Dodds, Jerrilynn D., María Rosa Menocal, and Abigail Krasner Balbale. *The Arts of Intimacy: Christians, Jews, and Muslims in the Making of Castilian Culture.* New Haven: Yale University Press, 2008.

Domínguez Ortíz, Antonio, and Bernard Vincent. *Historia de los moriscos: Vida y tragedia de una minoría.* Madrid: Allianza Editorial, 1978.

Droixhe, Daniel. *La linguistique et l'appel de l'histoire (1600–1800): Rationalisme et revolutions positivistes.* Geneva: Droz, 1978.

Drost, Gerrit. "El Arte de Pedro de Alcalá y su Vocabulista: De tolerancia a represión." In *Las prácticas musulmanas de los moriscos andaluces (1492–1609),* edited by Abdeljelil Temimi, 57–69. Zaghouan: Centre d'Etudes et de Recherches Ottomanes, Morisques, de Documentation et d'Information, 1989.

Dubois, Claude-Gilbert. *Mythe et langage au seizième siècle.* Bordeaux: Éditions Ducros, 1970.

Dunkelgrün, Theodor William. *"The Multiplicity of Scripture: The Confluence of Textual Traditions in the Making of the Antwerp Polyglot Bible (1568–1573)."* PhD Diss., University of Chicago, 2012.

Dussel, Enrique. "Núcleo simbólico lascasiano como profética crítica al imperialismo europeo." In *Bartolomé de Las Casas (1474–1974) e historia de la iglesia en América latina,* 11–17. Barcelona: Editorial Nova Rerra, 1976.

Eagleton, Terry. *Reason, Faith, and Revolution: Reflections on the God Debate.* New Haven: Yale University Press, 2009.

Eden, Kathy. *Poetic and Legal Fiction in the Aristotelian Tradition.* Princeton: Princeton University Press, 1986.

Ehlers, Benjamin. *Between Christians and Moriscos: Juan de Ribera and Religious Reform in Valencia, 1568–1614.* Baltimore: Johns Hopkins University Press, 2006.

Eimeric, Nicolas. *Directorivm inqvisitorvm.* Edited by Francisco Peña. Venice: Marcum Antonium Zalterium, 1595.

———. *El manual de los inquisidores.* Translated by Francisco Martín. Barcelona: Muchnick Editores, 1983.

El Alaoui, Youssef. "Ignacio de Las Casas, jesuita y morisco." *Sharq al-Andalus* 14–15 (1997–98): 317–39.

———. *Jésuites, morisques et indiens: Étude comparative des méthodes d'évangélisation de la Compagnie de Jésus d'après les traités de José de Acosta (1588) et d'Ignacio de las Casas, (1605–1607).* Paris: Honoré Champion, 2006.

Elliott, J. H. *History in the Making.* New Haven: Yale University Press.

———. "Self-Perception and Decline in Early Seventeenth-Century Spain." *Past and Present* 74 (February 1977): 41–61.

The Encyclopaedia of Islam. Leyden: E. J. Brill, 2005.

Escrivà, Francisco de. *Vida del illvstrissimo y excellentissimo Señor Don Ivan de Ribera, Patriarca del Antiochia y Arçobispo de Valencia*. Valencia: Pedro Patricio Mey, 1612.

Farrell, Allan P. *The Jesuit Code of Liberal Education*. Milwaukee: Bruce, 1938.

Ferguson, Margaret W. *Trials of Desire: Renaissance Defenses of Poetry*. New Haven: Yale University Press, 1983.

Fernández, Gil. *Panorama social del humanismo español (1500–1800)*. Madrid: Alhambra, 1981.

Fernández de Navarrete, Pedro. *Conservación de monarquías y discursos políticos*. Madrid: Don Benito Cano, 1792.

Fernández Marcos, Natalio. *Filología bíblica y humanismo*. Madrid: Centro Superior de Investigaciones Científicas, 2012.

Feros, Antonio. "Retóricas de la expulsión." In García-Arenal and Wiegers, *Los moriscos*, 67–102.

Firpo, Massimo. *Entre alumbrados y "espirituales": Estudios sobre Juan de Valdés y el valdesianismo en la crisis religiosa del '500 italiano*. Madrid: Fundación Universitaria Española and Universidad Pontificia de Salamanca, 2000.

Fiume, Giovanna, and Stefania Pastore. "Premessa." Diaspora Morisca. *Quaderni storici* 3 (December 2013): 663–88.

Fonseca, Damiano. *Del givsto scacciamento de moreschi da Spagna*. Translated by Cosimo Gaci. Rome: Bartholomea Zannetti, 1611.

Foucault, Michel. *L'archéologie du savoir*. Paris: Gallimard, 2002.

———. *Discipline and Punish: The Birth of the Prison*. New York: Vintage Books, 1995. www.ebrary.com.

Foulché-Delbosc, R. "Étude sur la Guerra de Granada de Don Diego Hurtado de Mendoza." *Revue Hispanique* (1894): 83–165.

Fox Morcillo, Sebastián. *De historiae institutione dialogus*. Paris: Martinum Iuuenem, 1557. http://www.proyectos.cchs.csic.es/humanismoyhumanistas/.

———. *Diálogo sobre enseñanza de la historia*. Translated and edited for the web by Antonio Cortijo Ocaña. Madrid: Centro Superior de Investigaciones Científicas, 2011. http://www.proyectos.cchs.csic.es/humanismoyhumanistas/.

Frazee, Charles A. *Catholics and Sultans: The Church and the Ottoman Empire, 1453–1923*. Cambridge: Cambridge University Press, 2006.

Fuchs, Barbara. "1492 and the Cleaving of Hispanism." *Journal of Medieval and Early Modern Studies* 37, no. 3 (Fall 2007): 493–510.

———. "Don Quijote 1 and the Forging of National History." *MLQ* 68, no. 3 (September 2007): 395–416.

———. *Exotic Nation: Maurophilia and the Construction of Early Modern Spain*. Philadelphia: University of Pennsylvania Press, 2009.

———. *Mimesis and Empire: The New World, Islam, and European Identities*. Cambridge: Cambridge University Press, 2001.

———. "Virtual Spaniards: The Moriscos and the Fictions of Spanish Identity." *Journal of Spanish Cultural Studies* 2, no. 1 (2001): 13–26.

Gaddis, Michael. *There Is No Crime for Those Who Have Christ: Religious Violence in the Christian Roman Empire*. Berkeley: University of California Press, 2005.

Galmés de Fuentes, Álvaro. *Los manuscritos aljamiado-moriscos de la biblioteca de la Real Academia de la Historia*. Madrid: Real Academia de la Historia, 1998.

———. *Los Moriscos (desde su misma orilla)*. Madrid: Instituto Egipcio de Estudios Islámicos en Madrid, 1993.

García-Arenal, Mercedes. "El entorno de los plomos: Hagiografía y linaje." In Barrios Aguilera and García-Arenal, *Los plomos del Sacromonte*, 51–78.

———. *Los Moriscos*. Madrid: Editora Nacional, 1975.

———. "Moriscos e indios: Para un estudio comparado de métodos de conquista y evangelización." *Chronica Nova* 20 (1992): 153–76.

———. "Religious Dissent and Minorities: The Morisco Age." *Journal of Modern History* 81, no. 4 (December 2009): 888–920.

———. "The Religious Identity of the Arabic Language and the Affair of the Lead Books of Sacromonte." *Arabica* 56 (2009): 495–528.

García-Arenal, Mercedes, and Manuel Barrios Aguilera, eds. *¿La historia inventada? Los libros plúmbeos y el legado sacromontano*. Granada: Universidad de Granada, 2008.

———. *Los plomos de Sacromonte: Invención y tesoro*. Valencia: Universitat de València, 2006.

García-Arenal, Mercedes, and Felipe Pereda. "A propósito de los alumbrados: Confesionalidad y disidencia religiosa en el mundo ibérico." *La corónica* 41, no. 1 (Fall 2012): 109–48.

García-Arenal, Mercedes, and Fernando Rodríguez Mediano. *Un Oriente español: Los moriscos y el Sacromonte en tiempos de Contrarreforma*. Madrid: Marcial Pons Historia, 2010.

García-Arenal, Mercedes, and Gerard Wiegers, eds. *Los moriscos: Expulsión y diáspora*. Valencia: Universitat de València, 2012.

García Cárcel, Ricardo. "Estudio crítico del catecismo Ribera-Ayala." In *Les morisques et leur temps*, 161–68. Paris: Éditions du Centre National de la Recherche Scientifique, 1983.

García de Oro, José. *El Cardenal Cisneros: Vida y empresas*. Vol. 2. Madrid: Biblioteca de Autores Cristianos, 1992.

Garrad, Keith. "La industria sedera granadina en el siglo XVI y su conexión con el levantamiento de las Alpujarras (1568–71)." In *Miscelánea de estudios árabes y hebraicos*, 73–98. Granada: University of Granada, 1956.

———. "The Original Memorial of Don Francisco Núñez Muley." *Atlante* 2 (1954): 199–226.

Garrido Aranda, Antonio. *Moriscos e indios: Precedentes hispánicos de la evangelización en México*. Mexico City: Universidad Nacional Autonoma de Mexico, 1980.

———. *Organización de la iglesia en el reino de Granada y su proyección en Indias, siglo XVI*. Seville: Escuela de Estudios Hispano-Americanos, 1979.

Gilman, Stephen. "An Introduction to the Ideology of the Baroque in Spain." *Symposium* 1, no. 1 (November 1946): 82–107.

Giménez-Eguibar, Patricia, and Daniel I. Wasserman Soler. "La Mala Algaraba: Church, Monarchy and the Arabic Language in Sixteenth-Century Spain." *Medieval History Journal* 14, no. 2 (2011): 229–58.

Ginzburg, Carlo. *History, Rhetoric, and Proof*. Hanover, NH: University Press of New England, 1999.

Godoy Alcántara, José. *Historia crítica de los falsos cronicones*. Madrid: Alcatar, 1981. http://www.archive.org/.

Gómez Canseco, Luis María. *El humanismo después de 1600: Pedro de Valencia*. Seville: Secretariado de Publicaciones de la Universidad de Sevilla, 1993.

González de Cellorigo, Martín. *Memorial al Rey sobre asesinatos, atropellos, e irrevencias contra la religion cristiana cometidos por los moriscos*. Valladolid, 1597.

———. *Memorial de la politica necesaria, y vtil restauracion à la Republica de España*. Valladolid: Juan de Bostillo, 1600.

González Palencia, Angel, and Eugenio Mele. *Vida y obras de Don Diego Hurtado de Mendoza*. 3 vols. Madrid: Instituto de Valencia de Don Juan, 1943.

Grafton, Anthony. *Forgers and Critics: Creativity and Duplicity in Western Scholarship*. Princeton: Princeton University Press, 1990.

Grafton, Anthony, and Lisa Jardine. *From Humanism to the Humanities: Education and the Liberal Arts in Fifteenth- and Sixteenth-Century Europe*. Cambridge: Harvard University Press, 1986.

Grafton, Anthony, and Suzanne Marchand. "Proof and Persuasion in History: A Preface." *History and Theory* 33, no. 4 (December 1994): 3–4.

Grafton, Anthony, and Joanna Weinberg. *"I have always loved the holy tongue": Isaac Casaubon, the Jews, and a Forgotten Chapter in Renaissance Scholarship*. Cambridge: Harvard University Press, 2011.

Grazia, Margreta de. "The Modern Divide: From Either Side." *Journal of Medieval and Early Modern Studies* 37, no. 3 (Fall 2007): 453–67.

Green-Mercado, Marya T. "The Mahdī in Valencia: Messianism, Apocalypticism and Morisco Rebellions in Late Sixteenth-Century Spain." *Medieval Encounters* 19 (2013): 193–220.

———. "Morisco Apocalypticism: Politics of Prophecy in the Early Modern Mediterranean." PhD Diss., University of Chicago, 2012.

Gregory IX. *Liber Extra* (1234). "De baptismo & eius effectu." In *Corpus juris canonici*. Rome: Aedibus Populi Romani, 1582. http://digital.library.ucla.edu/canonlaw/.

Gregory the Great. *Moralium libri, sive expositio in librum B. Job*. In *Patrologia Latina*, vol. 76. http://pld.chadwyck.com/.

Grethlein, Jonas. "Experientiality and 'Narrative Reference,' with Thanks to Thucydides." *History and Theory* 49 (October 2010): 315–35.

Grévin, Benoît. *Le parchemin des cieux: Essai sur le Moyen Âge du langage*. Paris: Éditions du Seuil, 2012.

Griffin, Nigel. "'Un muro invisible': Moriscos and Cristianos Viejos in Granada." In *Mediaeval and Renaissance Studies on Spain and Portugal in Honour of P. E. Russell*, edited by F. W. Hodcroft, D. G. Pattison, R. D. F. Pring-Mill, and R. W. Truman, 133–54. Oxford: Society for the Study of Mediaeval Languages and Literatures, 1981.

Guadalajara y Xavier, Marco de. *Memorable expvlsion y ivstissimo destierro de los moriscos de España*. Pamplona: Nicolas Assiayn, 1613.

Guadix, Diego de. *Diccionario de arabismos: Recopilación de algunos nombres arábigos*. Edited by María Águeda Moreno Moreno and Ignacio Ahumada. Jaén: University of Jaén, 2007.

Guevara, Antonio de. *Epistolas familiares*. Madrid: La Biuda de Pedro Madrigal, 1595.

Gumbrecht, Hans Ulrich. *The Powers of Philology: Dynamics of Textual Scholarship*. Urbana: University of Illinois Press, 2003.

Gutiérrez, Gustavo. *En busca de los pobres de Jesucristo: El pensamiento de Bartolomé de Las Casas*. Lima: Instituto Bartolomé de Las Casas, 1992.

Gutiérrez Nieto, Juan Ignacio. "El pensamiento económico político y social de los arbitristas." In *Historia de España: El Siglo del Quijote (1580–1680)*, edited by José María Jover Zamora, vol. 1, 233–351. Madrid: Espasa-Calpe, 1986.

Hagerty, Miguel José. "Los apócrifos granadinos, ¿sincretismo o simbiosis?" In García-Arenal and Barrios Aguilera, *¿La historia inventada?*, 45–56.

———. *Los libros plúmbeos del Sacromonte*. 2nd ed. Madrid: Editorial Comares, 2007.

Hamilton, Alastair. "The Long Apprenticeship: Casaubon and Arabic." Appendix to Grafton and Weinberg, *"I have always loved the holy tongue,"* 293–306.

Hamilton, Bernice. *Political Thought in Sixteenth-Century Spain: A Study of the Political Ideas of Vitoria, De Soto, Suárez and Molina*. Oxford: Clarendon Press, 1963.

Hanke, Lewis. *All Mankind Is One: A Study of the Disputation between Bartolomé de Las Casas and Juan Ginés de Sepúlveda in 1550 on the Intellectual and Religious Capacity of the American Indians*. DeKalb: Northern Illinois University Press, 1974.

Harris, A. Katie. "Forging History: The *Plomos* of the Sacromonte of Granada in Francisco Bermúdez de Pedraza's *Historia Eclesiástica*." *Sixteenth Century Journal* 30, no. 4 (Winter 1999): 945–66.

———. *From Muslim to Christian Granada: Inventing a City's Past in Early Modern Spain*. Baltimore: Johns Hopkins University Press, 2007.

Harris, Randy. *Linguistics Wars*. New York: Oxford University Press, 1993.

Harvey, L. P. *Muslims in Spain, 1500–1614*. Chicago: University of Chicago Press, 2005.

Harvey, L. P., and Gerard A. Wiegers. "The Translation from Arabic of the Sacromonte Tablets and the Archbishop of Granada: An Illuminating Correspondence." *Qurtuba: Estudios Andalucíes* 1 (1996): 59–78.

Hava, J. F. *Al-farā'id al-durīyya*. Beirut: Dar el-Mashreq, 1982.

Hendrickson, Jocelyn. "The Islamic Obligation to Emigrate: Al-Wansharīsī's Ansā al-matājir Reconsidered." PhD Diss., Emory University, 2010.

Hess, Andrew. "The Moriscos: An Ottoman Fifth Column in Sixteenth-Century Spain." *American Historical Review* 74, no. 1 (1968): 1–25.

Homza, Lu Anne. *Religious Authority in the Spanish Renaissance*. Baltimore: Johns Hopkins University Press, 2000.

———. *The Spanish Inquisition, 1478–1614: An Anthology of Sources*. Indianapolis: Hackett, 2006.

Horozco y Covarrubias, Juan de. *Tratado de la verdadera y falsa profecía*. Segovia: Juan de la Cuesta, 1588.

Hurtado de Mendoza, Diego. "Carta al capitán Salazar." In *Curiosidades bibliográficas*, edited by Adolfo de Castro, 548–50. Bibioteca de Autores Españoles, vol. 36. Madrid: M. Rivadeneyra, 1855. www.cervantesvirtual.com.

———. *Guerra de Granada*. Edited by Bernardo Blanco-González. Madrid: Castalia, 1970.

Ibn Ezra, Moshe. *Maḥberet mi-shire*. Edited by Heinrich Brody and Solomon Solis-Cohen. Philadelphia: Ha-Ḥevrah ha-yehudit le-hotsa'at sefarim asher be-Amerikah, 1945.

Ibn Qāsim al-Ḥajarī, Aḥmad. *Kitāb nāṣir al-dīn 'alā'l-qawm al-kāfirīn* (The Supporter of Religion against the Infidel). Edited and translated by P. S. Van Koningsveld, Q. Al-Samarrai, and G. A. Wiegers. Madrid: Centro Superior de Investigaciones Científicas, 1997.

Ife, Barry W. *Reading and Fiction in Golden-Age Spain: A Platonist Critique and Some Picaresque Replies*. Cambridge: Cambridge University Press, 1985.

Illich, Ivan. *In the Vineyard of the Text: A Commentary to Hugh's Didascalicon*. Chicago: University of Chicago Press, 1993.

Innocent III. *De missarum mysteriis*. In *Patrologia Latina*, vol. 217.

Israel, Jonathan I. *European Jewry in the Age of Mercantilism*, 1550–1570. 3rd ed. London: Littman Library of Jewish Civilization, 1998.

Janer, Florencio. *Condición social de los moriscos en España*. Spain: Espuela de Plata, 2006.

Jay, Martin. *The Virtues of Mendacity: On Lying in Politics*. Charlottesville: University of Virginia Press, 2010.

Jiménez Monteserín, Miguel. *Introducción a la inquisición española: Documentos básicos para el estudio del Santo Oficio*. Madrid: Editora Nacional, 1980.

Jonsen, Albert R., and Stephen Toulmin. *The Abuse of Casuistry: A History of Moral Reasoning*. Berkeley: University of California Press, 1988.

La junta de reformación. Edited by D. Ángel González Palencia. Valladolid: Academia de Estudios Históricos-Sociales de Valladolid, 1932.

Kagan, Richard L. *Clio and the Crown: The Politics of History in Medieval and Early Modern Spain*. Baltimore: Johns Hopkins University Press, 2009.

———. *Lawsuits and Litigants in Castile, 1500–1700*. Chapel Hill: University of North Carolina Press, 1981.

———. *Lucrecia's Dreams: Politics and Prophecy in Sixteenth-Century Spain*. Berkeley: University of California Press, 1990.

———. *Students and Society in Early Modern Spain*. Baltimore: Johns Hopkins University Press, 1974.

Kallendorf, Craig, trans. and ed. *Humanist Educational Treatises*. I Tatti Renaissance Library. Cambridge: Harvard University Press, 2002.

Kamen, Henry. "The Decline of Spain: A Historical Myth?" *Past and Present* 81 (November 1978): 24–50.

———. *The Rise of Toleration*. New York: McGraw-Hill, 1967.

———. *The Spanish Inquisition: A Historical Revision*. New Haven: Yale University Press, 1997.

———. "Strategies of Survival: Minority Cultures in the Western Mediterranean." In *Early Modern History and the Social Sciences: Testing the Limits of Braudel's Mediterranean*, edited by John Marino, 205–24. Kirksville, MO: Truman State University Press, 2002.

———. "Toleration and Dissent in Sixteenth-Century Spain: The Alternative Tradition." *Sixteenth Century Journal* 19, no. 1 (Spring 1988): 3–23.

Kaplan, Benjamin J. *Divided by Faith: Religious Conflict and the Practice of Toleration in Early Modern Europe*. Cambridge: Harvard University Press, 2007.

Keane, Webb. *Christian Moderns: Freedom and Fetish in the Mission Encounter*. Berkeley: University of California Press, 2007.

Kelley, Donald R. "Humanism and History." In *Renaissance Humanism: Foundations, Forms, and Legacy*, edited by Albert Rabil Jr., vol. 3. Philadelphia: University of Pennsylvania Press, 1988.

Kendrick, T. D. *St. James in Spain*. London: Methuen, 1960.

Kennedy, Daniel. "Sacraments." In *The Catholic Encyclopedia*, vol. 13. New York: Robert Appleton Co., 1912.

Kimmel, Seth. "'In the Choir with the Clerics': Secularism in the Age of Inquisition." *Comparative Literature* 65, no. 3 (2013): 285–305.

———. "Local Turks: Print Culture and Maurophilia in Early Modern Spain." *Journal of Spanish Cultural Studies* 13, no. 1 (2012): 21–38.

———. "Writing Religion: Sacromonte and the Literary Conventions of Orthodoxy." In *Poiesis and Modernity in the Old and New Worlds*, edited by Anthony J. Cascardi and Leah Middlebrook, 117–38. *Hispanic Issues* 39. Nashville: Vanderbilt University Press, 2012.

Klor de Alva, J. Jorge. "Colonizing Souls: The Failure of the Indian Inquisition and the Rise of Penitential Discipline." In *Cultural Encounters: The Impact of the Inquisition in Spain and the New World*, edited by Mary Elizabeth Perry and Anne J. Cruz, 3–23. Berkeley: University of California Press, 1991.

Koningsveld, P. S. Van, and G. A. Wiegers. "The Parchment of the 'Torre Turpiana': The Original Document and Its Early Interpreters." *Al-Qanṭara: Revista de Estudios Árabes* 24, no. 2 (2003): 327–58.

LaCapra, Dominick. *History and Criticism*. Ithaca: Cornell University Press, 1985.

Lancelot, Claude, and Antoine Arnauld. *Grammaire générale et raisonnée*. Stuttgart-Bad Cannstatt: Frommann, 1966.

Las Casas, Bartolomé de. *Apología, o declaración y defensa universal de los derechos del hombre y de los pueblos*. Edited by Vidal Abril Castelló. Salamanca: Junta de Castilla y León, 2000.

———. *Aquí se contiene una disputa o controversía, entre el Obispo don fray Bartholomé de las Casas o Casaus y el doctor Ginés de Sepúlveda*. In *Obras Completas*, edited by Ramón Hernández and Lorenzo Galmés, vol. 10, 101–93. Madrid: Alianza Editorial, 1992.

———. *Del único modo de atraer a todos los pueblos a la verdadera religión*. Edited by Agustín Millares Carlos. Introduction by Lewis Hanke. Translated by Atenógenes Santamaría. Mexico City: Fondo de Cultura Económica, 1942.

———. *Historia de las Indias*. Edited by Agustín Millares Carlos. Mexico City: Fondo de Cultura Económica, 1986.

———. "Memorial de los remedios." In *Obras escogidas*, edited by Juan Pérez de Tudela y Bueso, vol. 5, 5–27. Madrid: Biblioteca de Autores Españoles, 1957–58.

Laursen, John Christian, and Cary J. Nederman, eds. *Beyond the Persecuting Society: Religious Toleration before the Enlightenment*. Philadelphia: University of Pennsylvania Press, 1998.

Lea, Henry Charles. *History of the Inquisition of Spain*. New York: Macmillan, 1906–7.

———. *Los moriscos españoles: Su conversión y expulsión*. Alicante: Editorial Aguaclara, 1990.

Leclerc, Joseph. *Histoire de la tolérance au siècle de la réforme*. Vol. 1. Paris: Éditions Montaigne, 1954.

Le Goff, Jacques. *Les intellectuels au moyen âge*. Paris: Seuil, 1985.

León, Luis de. *Et Diuinorum librorum primi apud Salmanticenses interpretis explanationum in eosdem*. Salamanca: Guillelmum Foquel, 1589.

Lerer, Seth. *Error and the Academic Self: The Scholarly Imagination, Medieval to Modern*. New York: Columbia University Press, 2002.

Liere, Katherine Elliot Van. "After Nebrija: Academic Reformers and the Teaching of Latin in the Sixteenth-Century." *Sixteenth Century Journal* 34, no. 4 (Winter 2003): 1065–1105.

———. "Renaissance Chroniclers and the Apostolic Origins of Spanish Christianity." In *Sacred History: Uses of the Christian Past in the Renaissance World*, edited by Katherine Van Liere, Simon Ditchfield, and Howard Louthan, 121–44. Oxford: Oxford University Press, 2012.

Liu, Yu. "The Intricacies of Accommodation: The Proselytizing Strategy of Matteo Ricci." *Journal of World History* 19, no. 4 (2008): 465–87.

Lombard, Peter. *Sentences*. Translated by Giulio Silano. 3 vols. Pontifical Institute of Mediaeval Studies, 2008.

———. *Sententiarum libri IV*. In *Patrologia Latina*, vol. 192.

Lopetegui, León. "Notas sobre la actividad teológica del P. José de Acosta S.I." *Gregorianum* 21 (1940): 527–63.

López Baralt, Luce. *Huellas del Islam en la literatura española: De Juan Ruiz al Juan Goytisolo*. Madrid: Hiperión 1985.

López Baralt, Luce, and Reem F. Iversen. *A zaga de tu huella: La enseñanza de las lenguas semíticas en Salamanca en tiempos de San Juan de la Cruz*. Madrid: Editorial Trotta, 2006.

López de Madera, Gregorio. *Historia y discvrsos dela certidvmbre de las reliqvias, laminas, y prophecia descubiertas en el MonteSanto y Yglesia de Granada, desde el año mil y quinientos y ochenta y ocho, hasta el de mil y quinientos y nouenta y ocho*. Granada: Sebastian de Mena, 1601.

López Morillas, Consuelo. "Los manuscritos aljamiados." *Al-Qanṭara: Revista de Estudios Árabes* 19 (1998): 425–44.

Lotz-Heumann, Ute. "Confessionalization." In *The Ashgate Research Companion to the Counter-Reformation*, edited by Alexandra Bamji, Geert H. Janssen, and Mary Laven, 33–53. Farnham, UK: Ashgate, 2013.

Loyola, Ignatius of. *The Spiritual Exercises of St. Ignatius*. Translated by Louis J. Puhl. New York: Vintage Books, 2000.

Luna, Miguel de. *La verdadera historia del Rey Don Rodrigo*. Granada: Pedro Patricio Mey junto a S. Martin, 1606. Facsimile edition, Valladolid: Ed. Maxtor, 2003.

Lynn, Kimberly. *Between Court and Confessional: The Politics of the Spanish Inquisitors*. Cambridge: Cambridge University Press, 2013. http://ebooks.cambridge.org/.

MacEvitt, Christopher. *The Crusades and the Christian World of the East: Rough Tolerance*. Philadelphia: University of Pennsylvania Press, 2007.

Macías Rosendo, Baldomero. *La Correspondencia de Benito Arias Montano con el Presidente de Indias Juan de Ovando*. Huelva: Universidad de Huelva, 2008.

MacKay, Ruth. *"Lazy Improvident People": Myth and Reality in the Writing of Spanish History*. Ithaca, NY: Cornell University Press, 2006.

Magnier, Grace. "The Dating of Pedro de Valencia's *Sobre el pergamino y láminas de Granada*." *Sharq Al-Andalus* 14 (1997–98): 353–73.

———. *Pedro de Valencia and the Catholic Apologists of the Expulsion of the Moriscos: Visions of Christianity and Kingship*. Leiden: Brill, 2010.

Mahmood, Saba. *Politics of Piety: The Islamic Revival and the Feminist Subject*. Princeton: Princeton University Press, 2005.

Mahn-Lot, Marianne. *Bartolomé de Las Casas et le droit des Indiens*. Paris: Payot, 1982.

Mallette, Karla. *European Modernity and the Arab Mediterranean: Toward a New Philology and a Counter-Orientalism*. Philadelphia: University of Pennsylvania Press, 2010.

Maman, Aharon. *Comparative Semitic Philology in the Middle Ages: From Sa'adiah Gaon to Ibn Barūn (10th–12th C.)*. Translated by David Lyons. Leiden: Brill, 2004.

Mandosio, Quintiliano, and Vendramenus Petrus. *Le dictionnaire des inquisiteurs*. Translated by Luis Sala-Moulins. Paris: Galilée, 1981.

———. *Repertorivm inqvisitorvm pravitatis haereticae, in qvo omnia, qvae ad haeresum cognitionem ac S. Inquisitionis forum pertinent, continentur*. Venice: D. Zenarum, 1575. http://books.google.com/.

Mann, Vivian, Thomas Glick, and Jerrilynn Dodds, eds. *Convivencia: Jews, Muslims, and Christians in Medieval Spain*. New York: G. Braziler and The Jewish Museum, 1992.

Maravall, José Antonio. *La cultura del Barroco*. 9th ed. Barcelona: Editorial Ariel, 2002.

Marcuse, Herbert. "Repressive Tolerance." In *A Critique of Pure Tolerance*, edited by Robert Paul Wolff, Barrington Moore Jr., and Herbert Marcuse, 95–137. Boston: Beacon Press, 1969.

Mariscal, George. "Bartolomé de las Casas on Imperial Ethics and the Use of Force." In *Reason and Its Others: Italy, Spain, and the New World*, edited by David Castillo and Massimo Lollini, 259–78. Nashville: Vanderbilt University Press, 2006.

Mármol Carvajal, Luis de. *Historia del rebelión y castigo de los moriscos del Reino de Granada*. Biblioteca de Autores Españoles. Madrid: M. Rivadeneyra, 1852. www.cervantesvirtual.com.

Márquez Villanueva, Francisco. "El mito de la gran conspiración morisca." In *Religion, identité et sources documentaires sur les Morisques andalous*, edited by Abdeljelil Temimi, vol. 2, 267–84. Tunis: Institut Supérieur de Documentation, 1984.

———. *Moros, moriscos y turcos de Cervantes: Ensayos críticos*. Barcelona: Ediciones Bellatera, 2010.

———. "El problema historiográfico de los moriscos." *Bulletin Hispanique* 86, nos. 1–2 (1984): 61–69.

———. *El problema morisco: Desde otras laderas*. Madrid: Ediciones Libertarias, 1998.

Martin-Márquez, Susan. *Disorientations: Spanish Colonialism in Africa and the Performance of Identity*. New Haven: Yale University Press, 2008.

Maryks, Robert Aleksander. *The Jesuit Order as a Synagogue of the Jews: Jesuits of Jewish Ancestry and Purity-of-Blood Laws in the Early Society of Jesus*. Leiden: Brill, 2010. http://www.ebrary.com/corp/.

Masuzawa, Tomoko. *The Invention of World Religions*. Chicago: University of Chicago Press, 2005.

Matar, Nabil. *Europe through Arab Eyes, 1578–1727*. New York: Columbia University Press, 2009.

Mateos, Francisco. "Personalidad y escritos del P. José de Acosta." In José de Acosta, *Obras*. Biblioteca de Autores Españoles 73. Madrid: Ediciones Atlas, 1954.

McKenzie, D. F. *Bibliography and the Sociology of Texts*. Cambridge: Cambridge University Press, 1999.

Memoria de los moriscos: Escritos y relatos de una diáspora cultural, en la Biblioteca Nacional de España. Bilbao: Sociedad Estatal de Conmemoraciones Culturales, 2010.

Menéndez y Pelayo, Marcelino. *Historia de los heterodoxos españoles*. Madrid: Librería católica de San José, 1880–81. http://www.hathitrust.org/.

Menocal, María Rosa. *The Ornament of the World: How Muslims, Jews and Christians Created a Culture of Tolerance in Medieval Spain*. Boston: Little, Brown, 2002.

Meserve, Margaret. *Empires of Islam in Renaissance Historical Thought*. Cambridge: Harvard University Press, 2008.

Meyerson, Mark D. *The Muslims of Valencia in the Age of Fernando and Isabel: Between Coexistence and Crusade*. Berkeley: University of California Press, 1991.

Mignolo, Walter D. *The Darker Side of the Renaissance: Literacy, Territoriality, and Colonization*. Ann Arbor: University of Michigan Press, 2003.

———."El metatexto historiográfico y la historiografía indiana." *MLN* 96, no. 2 (Hispanic Issue, March 1981): 358–402.

Momigliano, Arnaldo. "The Rhetoric of History and the History of Rhetoric: On Hayden White's Tropes." In *Settimo contributo alla storia degli studi classici e del mondo antico*, 49–59. Rome: Edizione di storia e letteratura, 1984.

Moncada, Sancho de. *Restauración política de España*. Alicante: Biblioteca Virtual Miguel de Cervantes, 1999. www.cervantesvirtual.com.

Monroe, James. "A Curious Morisco Appeal to the Ottoman Empire." *Al-Andalus* 31 (1966): 281–303.

———. *Islam and the Arabs in Spanish Scholarship (Sixteenth Century to the Present)*. Leiden: Brill, 1970.

Montero Díaz, Santiago. "La doctrina de la historia en los tratadistas españoles del siglo de oro." *Hispania* (July 1941): 3–39.

Moore, Robert I. *The Formation of a Persecuting Society: Power and Deviance in Western Europe, 950–1250*. Oxford: Blackwell, 1987.

Moreno, Doris. *La invención de la inquisición*. Madrid: Marcial Pons, 2004.

Mungello, David E. *Curious Land: Jesuit Accommodation and the Origins of Sinology*. Honolulu: University of Hawaii Press, 2005.

Nebrija, Antonio de. *Gramática de la lengua castellana*. Salamanca, 1492. www.bne.es.

———. *Introductiones latinae*. Salamanca, 1481.

Nederman, Cary J. "Introduction: Discourses and Contexts of Tolerance in Medieval Europe." In *Beyond the Persecuting Society: Religious Toleration before the Enlightenment*, edited by John Christian Laursen and Cary J. Nederman, 13–24. Philadelphia: University of Pennsylvania Press, 1998.

———. *Worlds of Difference: European Discourses of Toleration, c. 1100–c. 1550*. University Park: Pennsylvania State University Press, 2000.

Nelson, Eric. *The Hebrew Republic: Jewish Sources and the Transformation of European Political Thought*. Cambridge: Harvard University Press, 2010.

Nelson, William. *Fact or Fiction: The Dilemma of the Renaissance Storyteller*. Cambridge: Harvard University Press, 1973.

Nichols, Stephen J. "Introduction: Philology in a Manuscript Culture." *Speculum* 65, no. 1 (January 1990): 1–10.

Nieto Jiménez, Lidio. "La lengua primitiva." In Bernardo de Aldrete, *Del origen y principio de la lengva castellana, ò romance, que oi se usa en España*, edited by Lidio Nieto Jiménez, vol. 2, 139–70. Madrid: Centro Superior de Investigaciones Científicas, 1975.

Nightingale, Andrea. *Once Out of Nature: Augustine on Time and the Body*. Chicago: University of Chicago Press, 2011.

Nirenberg, David. *Anti-Judaism: The Western Tradition*. New York: Norton, 2013.

———. *Communities of Violence: Persecution of Minorities in the Middle Ages*. Princeton: Princeton University Press, 1996.

No, Song. "Teaching De unico vocationis modo: The Maternal Discourse of Bartolomé de Las Casas." In *Approaches to Teaching the Writings of Bartolomé de Las Casas*, edited by Santa Arias and Eyda M. Merediz, 124–31. New York: Modern Language Association of America, 2008.

Novikoff, Alex. "Between Tolerance and Intolerance in Medieval Spain: An Historiographic Enigma." *Medieval Encounters* 11, nos. 1–2 (2005): 7–36.

Núñez Muley, Francisco. *Memorandum for the President of the Royal Audiencia and Chancery Court of the City and Kingdom of Granada*. Edited and translated by Vincent Barletta. Chicago: University of Chicago Press, 2007.

O'Banion, Patrick J. *The Sacrament of Penance and Religious Life in Golden Age Spain*. University Park: Pennsylvania State University Press, 2012.

Olds, Katrina. "The 'False Chronicles,' Cardinal Baronio, and Sacred History in Counter-Reformation Spain." *Catholic Historical Review* 100, no. 1 (Winter 2014): 1–26.

Olender, Maurice. *The Languages of Paradise: Race, Religion, and Philology in the Nineteenth Century*. Translated by Arthur Goldhammer. Cambridge: Harvard University Press, 1992.

O'Malley, John W. *The First Jesuits*. Cambridge: Harvard University Press, 1993.

———. *Trent: What Happened at the Council*. Cambridge: Belknap Press of Harvard University Press, 2012.

Ostenfeld-Suske, Kira von. "Writing Official History in Spain: History and Politics, c. 1474–1600." In *The Oxford History of Historical Writing*, edited by José Rabasa, Masayuki Sato, Edoardo Tartarolo, and Daniel Woolf, vol. 3, 428–48. Oxford: Oxford University Press, 2012.

Páez de Castro, Juan. *De las cosas necesarias para escribir historia*. Edited by Esteban Eustasio. *La ciudad de dios* 28 (1892): 604–10.

Pagden, Anthony. *The Fall of Natural Man: The American Indian and the Origins of Comparative Ethnology*. Cambridge: Cambridge University Press, 1982.

———. "Ius et Factum: Text and Experience in the Writing of Bartolomé de Las Casas." In *New World Encounters*, edited by Stephen Greenblatt, 85–100. Berkeley: University of California Press, 1993.

Palencia, Pedro de. *Glosas rabínicas y sagrada escritura: Tratado de Pedro de Palencia, O. P., sobre la utilidad de las glosas rabínicas*. Edited by Elvira Pérez Ferreiro. Salamanca: Editorial San Esteban, 2004.

Pascal, Blaise. *Les lettres provinciales*. Edited by H. F. Stewart. Manchester: University Press, 1920.

Pastore, Stefania. *Una herejía española: Conversos, alumbrados e Inquisición (1449–1559)*. Madrid: Marcial Pons, 2010.

———. "La posición del Vaticano frente a la Expulsión." In García-Arenal and Wiegers, *Los moriscos*, 127–48.

———. *Il vangelo e la spada: L'inquisizione di castiglia e i suoi critici (1450–1598)*. Rome: Edizioni di storia e letteratura, 2003.

Patrologia Latina. Edited by J. P. Migne. 1844–65. Ann Arbor: ProQuest Information and Learning Company, 1996. http://pld.chadwyck.com/.

Pereda, Felipe. *Las imágenes de la discordia: Política y poética de la imagen sagrada en la España del 400*. Madrid: Marcial Pons, 2007.

Pérez de Ayala, Martín. *Catechismo para instrvccion de los nveuamente conuertidos de moros*. Valencia: Pedro Patricio Mey, 1599.

———. "Discurso de la vida." In *Autobiografías y memorias*, edited by Manuel Serrano y Sanz, 211–38. Madrid: Bailly, Baillière, 1905.

———. *Doctrina Christiana en lengua Arauiga y Castellana . . . para instruccion de los nueuamente conuertidos deste Reyno*. Valencia: Ian Mey, 1566.

———. *Sínodo de la diócesis de Guadix y Beza*. Edited by Carlos Asenjo Sedano. Granada: University of Granada, 1994.

Pérez de Herrera, Cristóbal. *Discvrsos del amparo de los legitimos pobres y redvccion de los fingidos*. Madrid: Luis Sánchez, 1598. www.cervantesvirtual.com.

Pérez de Hita, Ginés. *Guerras civiles de Granada: Novela histórica*. 2 vols. Madrid: Manuel Minuesa de los Ríos, 1891–92.

———. *Historia de los bandos de Zegríes y Abencerrajes (Primera parte de Las guerras civiles de Granada)*. Introduction by Paula Blanchard-Demouge. Madrid: E. Bailly-Baillière, 1913.

Perry, Mary Elizabeth. *The Handless Maiden: Moriscos and the Politics of Religion in Early Modern Spain*. Princeton: Princeton University Press, 2005.

Pezzi Martínez, Elena. "El problema de la confesión de moriscos en Pedro de Alcalá." In *Homenaje al Prof. Darío Cabanelas, O.F.M., con motivo de su LXX aniversario*, vol. 1, 433–44. Granada: University of Granada, 1987.

El proceso inquisitorial de Fray Luis de León. Edited by Ángel Alcalá. Salamanca: Junta de Castilla y León, 1991.

Prosperi, Adriano. "Confessione e dissimulazione." *Les dossiers du Grihl*, no. 2 (2009). http://dossiersgrihl.revues.org/3671.

———. "Il grano e la zizzania: L'eresia nella cittadella cristiana." In *America e apocalisse e altri saggi*, 211–32. Pisa: Istituti editoriale e poligrafici internazionali, 1999.

———. "'Otras indias': Missionari della controriforma tra contadini e selvaggi." In *Scienze, credenze occulte, livelli di cultura: Convegno internazionale*, 205–34. Florence: L. S. Olschki, 1982.

———. *Tribunali della coscienza: Inquisitori, confessori, missionari*. Turin: G. Einaudi, 1996.

Pulgar, Hernando de. *Crónica de los señores Reyes Católicos Don Fernando y Doña Isabel de Castilla y de Aragón*. Edited by Juan de Mata Carriazo. Madrid: Espasa-Colpe, 1943.

Pulido Serrano, Juan Ignacio. *Injurias a Cristo: Religión, política, y antijudaísmo en el siglo XVII (Análisis de las corrientes antijudías durante la Edad Moderna).* Alcalá de Henares: Instituto Internacional de Estudios Sefardíes y Andalusíes and the Universidad de Alcalá, 2002.

Quevedo, Francisco de. *Obras completas en prosa,* edited by Alfonso Rey, vol. 1, no. 1. Madrid: Castalia, 2003.

Quint, David. *Epic and Empire.* Princeton: Princeton University Press, 1993.

Rabasa, José. "Utopian Ethnology in Las Casas's Apologética." *1492–1992: Re/Discovering Colonial Writing,* edited by René Jara and Nicholas Spadaccini, 263–90. *Hispanic Issues* 4. Minneapolis: Prisma Institute, 1989.

Rabil, Albert. *Renaissance Humanism: Foundations, Forms, and Legacy.* Philadelphia: University of Pennsylvania Press, 1988.

Ratio Studiorum: The Official Plan for Jesuit Education (Ratio atque Institutio Studiorum Societatis Iesu). Translated by Claude Pavur. St. Louis: Institute of Jesuit Sources, 2005.

Raz-Krakotzkin, Amnon. *The Censor, the Editor, and the Text: The Catholic Church and the Shaping of the Jewish Canon in the Sixteenth Century.* Translated by Jackie Feldman. Philadelphia: University of Pennsylvania Press, 2007.

Redondo, Augustín. *Antonio de Guevara et l'Espagne de son temps.* Geneva: Librairie Droz, 1976.

Reinhard, Wolfgang. "Reformation, Counter-Reformation and the Early Modern State: A Reassessment. " *Catholic Historical Review* 75, no. 3 (July 1989): 385–403.

Rekers, B. *Benito Arias Montano (1527–1598).* London: Warburg Institute and Brill, 1972.

Ricard, Robert. "Remarques sur l'*Arte* et le *Vocabulista* de Fr. Pedro de Alcalá." In *Études et documents pour l'histoire missionnaire de l'Espagne et du Portugal,* 220–28. Paris: J. M. Peigues, 1930.

———. *The Spiritual Conquest of Mexico.* Translated by Lesley Byrd Simpson. Berkeley: University of California Press, 1966.

Rico, Francisco. *Nebrija frente a los bárbaros: El canon de gramáticos nefastos en las polémicas del humanismo.* Salamanca: Universidad de Salamanca, 1978.

Ripol, Juan. *Dialogo de consvelo por la expvlsion de los moriscos de España.* Pamplona: Nicolas de Assiayn, 1613.

Robinson, Cynthia. *Imagining the Passion in a Multiconfessional Castile: The Virgin, Christ, Devotions, and Images in the Fourteenth and Fifteenth Centuries.* University Park: Pennsylvania State University Press, 2013.

Rodríguez Mediano, Fernando, and Mercedes García-Arenal. "De Diego de Urrea a Marcos Dobelio, intérpretes y traductores de los plomos." In Barrios Aguilera and García-Arenal, *Los plomos del Sacromonte,* 297–334.

Roisse, Philippe. "La historia del sello de Salomón: Estudio, edición crítica y traducción comparada." In Barrios Aguilera and García-Arenal, *Los plomos del Sacromonte,* 141–72.

Rojinksy, David. *Companion to Empire: A Genealogy of the Written Word in Spain and New Spain, c. 550–1550.* Amsterdam: Rodopi, 2010.

Root, Debora. "Speaking Christian: Orthodoxy and Difference in Sixteenth-Century Spain." *Representations* 23 (1988): 118–34.

Rosemann, Philipp W. *Peter Lombard.* New York: Oxford University Press, 2004.

Rosier-Catach, Irène. *La parole efficace: Signe, rituel, sacré.* Paris: Seuil, 2004.

Rubenstein, Jay. *Armies of Heaven: The First Crusade and the Quest for Apocalypse.* New York: Basic Books, 2011.

Rufo, Juan. *La Austriada.* In *Biblioteca de Autores Españoles: Poemas épicos,* vol. 2, edited by Don Cayetano Rosell. Madrid: M. Rivadeneyra, 1864.

Rummel, Erika. *Jiménez de Cisneros: On the Threshold of Spain's Golden Age.* Tempe: Arizona Center for Medieval and Renaissance Studies, 1999.

Said, Edward. *Orientalism.* 25th Anniversary Edition. New York: Vintage Book, 1994.

Sánchez-Blanco, Rafael Benítez. "De Pablo a Saulo: Traducción, crítica y denuncia de los libros plúmbeos por el P. Ignacio de las Casas, S. J." In Barrios Aguilera and García-Arenal, *Los plomos del Sacromonte*, 173–200.

Sánchez-Blanco, Rafael Benítez, and Eugenio Ciscar Pallarés. "La Iglesia ante la conversión y expulsión de los moriscos." In *Historia de la Iglesia de España*, vol. 4, 253–307. Madrid: BAC, 1979.

Sánchez de las Brozas, Francisco. *Minerva, seu de causis linguae latinae*. Amsterdam: P. den Hengst, 1809. http://www.hathitrust.org/.

———. *Minerva o de causis linguae latinae*. Edited and translated by E. Sánchez Salor and C. Chaparro Gómez. Cáceres: Institución Cultural El Brocense, 1995. http://iessapostol.juntaextremadura.net/latin/minerva/I_2es.html.

Sánchez Ocaña, Juan. *El Sacro Monte de Granada: Imaginación y realidad*. Granada: Ayuntamiento de Granada, 2007.

Sánchez Ramos, Valeriano. "El mejor cronista de la guerra de los moriscos." *Sharq al-Andalus* 13 (1996): 235–55.

Sandoval, Prudencio de. *Historia de la vida y hechos del emperador Carlos V*. Part 1. Pamplona: Bartholome Paris, 1618.

Santa Cruz, Alonso de. *Crónica del Emperador Carlos V*. Edited by Ricardo Beltrán y Rózpide and Antonio Blázquez y Delgado-Aguilera. 5 vols. Madrid: Real Academia de la Historia, 1920.

Schilling, Heinz. "Confessional Europe." In *Handbook of European History, 1400–1600: Late Middle Ages, Renaissance, and Reformation*, edited by Thomas A. Brady Jr., Heiko A. Obermans, and James D. Tracy, vol. 2, 641–81. Leiden: Brill, 1995.

Schmitt, Carl. *The Nomos of the Earth in the International Law of the Jus Publicum Europaeum*. Translated by G. L. Ulmen. New York: Telos Press, 2003.

Schwartz, Stuart B. *All Can Be Saved: Religious Tolerance and Salvation in the Iberian Atlantic World*. New Haven: Yale University Press, 2008.

Schwickerath, Robert. *Jesuit Education: Its History and Principles Viewed in the Light of Modern Educational Problems*. Saint Louis: Herder, 1904. www.archive.org.

Seneca. *Epistulae morales*. Translated by Richard M. Gummere. Vol. 2. Loeb Classical Library. Cambridge: Harvard University Press, 1970.

Sepúlveda, Juan Ginés de. *Apologia pro libro de iustis belli causis*. Edited by Antonio Moreno Hernández. Translated by Ángel Losada. In Juan Ginés de Sepúlveda, *Obras completas*, vol. 3, 191–222. Salamanca: Excmo. Ayuntamiento de Pozoblanco, 1997.

———. *Demócrates segundo, o de las justas causas de la guerra contra los indios*. Edited by Ángel Losada. Madrid: Consejo Superior de Investigaciones Científicas, Instituto Francisco de Vitoria, 1951.

Serrano Morales, José Enrique. *Reseña histórica en forma de diccionario de las imprentas que han existido en Valencia*. Valencia: F. Domonech, 1899. www.archive.org.

Shaw, Brent. *Sacred Violence: African Christians and Sectarian Hatred in the Age of Augustine*. Cambridge: Cambridge University Press, 2011.

Shuger, Deborah K. *The Renaissance Bible: Scholarship, Sacrifice, and Subjectivity*. Berkeley: University of California Press, 1994.

Sigüenza, José de. *Historia de la Orden de San Jerónimo*. Vol. 12. Madrid: Bailly, 1907.

Silverblatt, Irene. *Modern Inquisitions: Peru and the Colonial Origins of the Civilized World*. Durham: Duke University Press, 2004.

Simpson, James. *Burning to Read: English Fundamentalism and Its Reformation Opponents*. Cambridge: Harvard University Press, 2007.

Snyder, Jon R. *Dissimulation and the Culture of Secrecy in Early Modern Europe*. Berkeley: University of California Press, 2009.

Soifer Irish, Maya. "Beyond Convivencia: Critical Reflections on the Historiography of Interfaith Relations in Christian Spain." *Journal of Medieval Iberian Studies* 1, no. 1 (January 2009): 19–35.

Spivakovsky, Erika. "Some Notes on the Relations between D. Diego Hurtado de Mendoza and D. Alonso de Granada Venegas." *Archivum* 14 (1964): 212–32.

———. *Son of the Alhambra: Diego Hurtado de Mendoza, 1504–1575*. Austin: University of Texas Press, 1970.

Standert, Nicolas. "Jesuits in China." In *The Cambridge Companion to the Jesuits*, edited by Thomas Worcester, 169–85. Cambridge: Cambridge University Press, 2008.

Stevens-Arroyo, Anthony M. "The Evolution of Marian Devotionalism within Christianity and the Ibero-Mediterranean Polity." *Journal for the Scientific Study of Religion* 37, no. 1 (March 1998): 50–73.

Stock, Brian. *The Implications of Literacy: Written Language and Models of Interpretation in the Eleventh and Twelfth Centuries*. Princeton: Princeton University Press, 1983.

Strabus. *Glossa ordinaria*. In *Patrologia Latina*, vol. 114.

Stratton, Suzanne L. *The Immaculate Conception in Spanish Art*. Cambridge: Cambridge University Press, 1994.

Stroumsa, Guy G. *A New Science: The Discovery of Religion in the Age of Reason*. Cambridge: Harvard University Press, 2010.

Suberbiola Martínez, Jesús. *Real Patronato de Granada. El arzobispo Talavera, la Iglesia y el estado moderno, 1486–1516: estudios y documentos*. Granada: Caja General de Ahorros y Monte Piedad de Granada, 1985.

Sullivan, Karen. *The Inner Lives of Medieval Inquisitors*. Chicago: University of Chicago Press, 2011.

Sullivan, Winnifred Fallers. *The Impossibility of Religious Freedom*. Princeton: Princeton University Press, 2005.

Szpiech, Ryan. "Preaching Paul to the Moriscos: The *Confusión o confutación de la secta mahomética y del Alcorán* (1515) of 'Juan Andrés.'" *La corónica* 41, no. 1 (Fall 2012): 317–43.

Talmage, Frank Ephraim. *David Kimhi: The Man and the Commentaries*. Cambridge: Harvard University Press, 1975.

Targoff, Ramie. *Common Prayer: The Language of Public Devotion in Early Modern England*. Chicago: University of Chicago Press, 2005.

Taylor, Charles. *A Secular Age*. Cambridge: Belknap Press of Harvard University Press, 2007.

Taylor, William B. "The Virgin of Guadalupe in New Spain: An Inquiry into the Social History of Marian Devotion." *American Ethnologist* 14, no. 1 (February 1987): 9–33.

Thompson, E. A. *The Goths in Spain*. Oxford: Clarendon Press, 1969.

Todorov, Tzvetan. *The Conquest of America: The Question of the Other.* Oklahoma: University of Oklahoma Press, 1999.

Torre, Esteban. *Ideas linguísticas y literarias del doctor Huarte de San Juan*. Seville: Universidad de Sevilla, 1977.

Tsiapera, Maria, and Garon Wheeler. *The Port-Royal Grammar: Sources and Influence*. Münster: Nodus, 1993.

Tueller, James B. "Los moriscos que se quedaron o que regresaron." In García-Arenal and Wiegers, *Los moriscos*, 191–209.

Urdáñoz, Teófilo. "Las Casas y Francisco de Vitoria." In *Las Casas et la politique des droits de l'homme*, 235–304. Paris: Centre National de la Recherche Scientifique, 1976.

———. "La necesidad de la fe explícita para salvarse según los teólogos de la Escuela de Salamanca." *Ciencia Tomista* 59 (1940): 398–414.

Usanáriz, Jesús M. "Entre dos expulsiones: Musulmanes y moriscos en Navarra (1516–1610)." *Al-Qanṭara: Revista de Estudios Árabes* 33, no. 1 (January–June 2012): 45–81.

Valdés, Juan de. *Diálogo de la lengua*. Edited by Juan M. Lope Blanch. Madrid: Castalia, 1985.

Valencia, Pedro de. *Discurso contra la ociosidad*. In *Obras completas*, vol. 4, edited by Rafael González Cañal, pt. 1, 159–73. Introduction by Jesús Luis Paradinas Fuentes. León: Universidad de León, 1994.

———. *Discurso sobre el acrecentamiento de la labor de la tierra*. In *Obras completas*, vol. 4, Edited by Rafael González Cañal, pt. 1, 137–58. Introduction by Jesús Luis Paradinas Fuentes. León: Universidad de León, 1994.

———. *Relaciones de Indias: México*. In *Obras completas*, vol. 5, edited by Rafael González Cañal, pt. 2. León: Universidad de León, 1995.

———. *Relaciones de Indias: Nueva Granada y Virreinato de Peru*. In *Obras completas*, vol. 5, edited by Francisco Javier and Jesús Fuente Fernández, pt. 1. León: Universidad de León, 1993.

———. *Sobre el pergamino y láminas de Granada*. Edited by Grace Magnier. Bern: Peter Lang, 2006.

———. *Tratado acerca de los moriscos de España*. In *Obras completas*, vol. 4, edited by Rafael González Cañal, pt. 2, 67–139. Introduction by Rafael Carrasco. León: Universidad de León, 1999.

Varo Zafra, Juan. *Don Diego Hurtado de Mendoza y la* Guerra de Granada *en su contexto histórico*. Valladolid: University of Valladolid, 2012.

Vilches, Elvira. *New World Gold: Cultural Anxiety and Monetary Disorder in Early Modern Spain*. Chicago: University of Chicago Press, 2010.

Villaverde Amieva, Juan Carlos. "Los manuscritos aljamiado-moriscos: Hallazgos, colecciones, inventarios y otras noticias." In *Memoria de los moriscos*, 91–128.

Vincent, Bernard. "Les Jésuites et les Indes." In *Structures et cultures des sociétés ibéro-américaines*, 273–78. Paris: Éditions du Centre National de la Recherche Scientifique, 1990.

———. *El río morisco*. Valencia: Universitat de València, 2006.

Vincent, Bernard, and Rafael Benítez Sánchez-Blanco. "Estudio preliminar." In Jaime Bleda, *Corónica de los moriscos de España*, 9–47. Valencia: Universitat de València, 2001.

Vitoria, Francisco de. *Comentarios a la Secunda secundae de Santo Tomás*. Edited by Vicente Beltrán de Heredia. Salamanca: Biblioteca de teólogos españoles, 1932.

———. *Political Writings*. Edited by Anthony Pagden and Jeremy Lawrance. Cambridge: Cambridge University Press, 1991.

———. *Relecciones*. Edited by Luis G. Alonso Getino. Madrid: Asociación Francisco de Vitoria, 1933.

Vitto, Cindy L. "The Virtuous Pagan in Middle English Literature." *Transactions of the American Philosophical Society*, new series 79, no. 5 (1989): 1–100.

Vives, Juan Luis. *De disciplinis*. Leyden, 1612. http://eebo.chadwyck.com/home.

———. *On Education: A Translation of the* De tradendis disciplinis *of Juan Luis Vives*. Cambridge: Cambridge University Press, 1913.

Voet, Leon. *The Golden Compass: The History of the House of Plantin-Moretus*. 2 vols. Amsterdam: Vangendt, 1969–72.

Wallerstein, Immanuel. *European Universalism: The Rhetoric of Power*. New York: New Press, 2006.

Walsham, Alexandra. *Charitable Hatred: Tolerance and Intolerance in England, 1500–1700*. Manchester: Manchester University Press, 2006.

Wechter, Pinchas. *Ibn Barūn's Arabic Works on Hebrew Grammar and Lexicography*. Philadelphia: Dropsie College for Hebrew and Cognate Learning, 1965.

Wehr, Hans. *Dictionary of Modern Written Arabic*. 4th ed. Urbana, IL: Spoken Language Services, 1994.

Wilkinson, Robert J. *The Kabbalistic Scholars of the Antwerp Polyglot Bible*. Leiden: Brill, 2007.

Williams, Diane S. "Beyond the Limits of Genre: The Rhetoric of History in the *Guerras civiles de Granada*." PhD Diss., Princeton University, 1993.

Woolard, Kathryn A. "Bernardo de Aldrete, Humanist and Laminario." *Al-Qanṭara: Revista de Estudios Árabes* 24, no. 2 (2003): 449–76.

Zagorin, Perez. "The Historical Significance of Lying and Dissimulation." *Social Research* 63, no. 3 (Fall 1996): 863–912.

———. *How the Idea of Religious Toleration Came to the West*. Princeton: Princeton University Press, 2003.

———. *Ways of Lying: Dissimulation, Persecution and Conformity in Early Modern Europe*. Cambridge: Harvard University Press, 1990.

Index